The Sexual I

GREG THOMAS

The Sexual Demon of Colonial Power

Pan-African Embodiment and Erotic Schemes of Empire

INDIANA UNIVERSITY PRESS
Bloomington and Indianapolis

This book is a publication of

Indiana University Press
601 North Morton Street
Bloomington, IN 47404-3797 USA

http://iupress.indiana.edu

Telephone orders   800-842-6796
Fax orders   812-855-7931
Orders by e-mail   iuporder@indiana.edu

© 2007 by Greg Thomas

The paper used in this publication meets the minimum requirements of American National Standard for Information Sciences—Permanence of Paper for Printed Library Materials, ANSI Z39.48-1984.

Manufactured in the United States of America

Library of Congress Cataloging-in-Publication Data

Thomas, Greg, date
   The sexual demon of colonial power : Pan-African embodiment and erotic schemes of empire /
Greg Thomas.
      p.   cm.
   Includes bibliographical references and index.
   ISBN 978-0-253-34841-8 (cloth : alk. paper) — ISBN 978-0-253-21894-0 (pbk. : alk. paper)
   1. Blacks—Social conditions. 2. Sex role. 3. African Americans—Social conditions. 4. Sex role—United States.
5. Race relations. 6. United States—Race relations. 7. White supremacy movements. 8. Imperialism. I. Title.
   HT1581.T46 2007
   305.896—dc22

                                                                                          2007000629

1 2 3 4 5   12 11 10 09 08 07

For
Doris Brown
and
All my *Auntees*:
Elizabeth Blowe, Ernestine Reid,
Rebecca Campbell, and Frances Summers

Listening to Hoop, one would think that he was amused by the eroticism of white people. But Tomsson Black didn't think it was funny. . . . This eroticism had made the whites into liars, cheats, thieves, and hypocrites, and had proved to be more dangerous than their hatred.

Chester Himes, *Plan B*

Contents

Preface

The appearance of the late Kwame Ture's autobiographical *Ready for Revolution* (Carmichael 2003) might have been a pivotal moment for Black Studies, Black intellectualism, Black politics, Black activism—and that other Black formulation at the bottom of it all:

> Who could have thought it? I mean, two simple, clear, very commonly used English words. One an adjective, the other a noun. Basic. Nothing the least obscure or academically pretentious about them. Nothing mysterious or even slightly ambiguous either. Just two ordinary, unthreatening, everyday words in common usage. . . . But in combination? He'p us Jesus! (Carmichael 2003, 523–24)

The combination was explosive. The words, of course, were "Black Power." Today may represent a low point for this dream, its nadir for now, its destabilization and disappointment. But this is no cause for pessimism as far as Ture is concerned: "That is why I say, despite its apparent power, and precisely because of its excesses, American capitalism is weaker today than it has ever been. As sure as Africa is my mother, and she is my mother, revolution will come to America" (781). So concluded this student of history from Harlem, New York, and Conakry, Guinea, via Port of Spain, Trinidad.

The last reflections on Black Power by this All-African People's Revolutionary Party organizer should not be overlooked: "Suddenly rendered menacing, sinister, and subversive of public order and stability, the two words would, in short order, have me denied entry into France and Britain, declared persona non grata, and banned in thirty territories of the former British Empire, including the country of my birth" (524). They reveal the depth and ferocity of something even bigger. For if this concept was and is "beyond the cognitive reach of the white national [and international] media and public" (524), it must be because "white power" continues to rule with an iron (if largely unnamed) fist. This is the power of white colonial rule, politically, economically, culturally, etc., past and present. Yet, as neo-colonialism and imperialism are replaced by the language of post-coloniality and multi-culturalism (not to mention post-modernism), for example, this other power dynamic goes largely unchecked, especially in U.S. academia. And, certainly, the critical rhetoric of "race, gender, class, and sexuality" has done virtually no damage to Western empire in its North American–dominated phase.

This is not because there is anything necessarily tame about the topics named "gender" and "sexuality" themselves, not at all. It is because the framework in which they have been addressed has been inadequate, increasingly so since the emergence of Black Studies as a project and paradigm. Indeed, many articulations of race, gender, class, and sexuality take no account of a global historical context of domination or hegemony; and, what's more, Black radical traditions are ironically seen as anathema, even pathological, as if they were a social menace or scourge. This view is clearly in keeping with the logic of white colonial power itself. But there can and must be a sexual analysis of the colonial and neo-colonial power complex of white racist imperialism. The contemporary scholarship of Occidentalism makes this kind of analysis appear unthinkable for the academic and non-academic status quo as well as many of those who claim to challenge it, whether in Western or non-Western fashion.

This study is undertaken in the spirit of Pan-African traditions out of vogue in a conservative, counter-revolutionary age; and it seeks to improve upon those studies to which it is seriously indebted. Chapter 1 examines the concept and categories of a history of sexuality current in Europe and North America from the vantage point of Africa and African Diaspora. It outlines the serious limitations of Michel Foucault's historicization by interrogating the cultural politics of its notion of history and juxtaposing it with that of Martin Bernal, Cheikh Anta Diop, and Ifi Amadiume. No modern category of sexual identity or manner of thinking escapes the consequences of this treatment of Aryan models of historiography. Chapter 2 continues this line of inquiry with regard to gender. It analyzes the racial politics of the Victorian cult of domesticity in the context of U.S. chattel slavery, along with recent writings on the social construction of identity. It illustrates how white colonial womanhood is strangely reinscribed by even the most challenging academic work on slavery (e.g., that of Hazel V. Carby, Deborah Gray White, and Angela Y. Davis), and how current theories of social construction steer clear of this space of gender's racial construction, so to speak.

Chapter 3 stresses the centrality of class conflict in the reproduction of Western ideologies of gender and sexuality in colonized Black communities. It recovers the erotic dynamic of classic profiles of the Black elite (or "bourgeoisie") with a focus on the sociology of E. Franklin Frazier. Chapter 4 articulates these same insights vis-à-vis four volumes of Frantz Fanon. It notes the extreme similarities and differences between Fanon and Frazier, giving particular attention to the revolutionary transformation of the former, and all the conventional critical confusion concerning the latter.

Chapter 5 provides a case study of sorts in the sphere of literature. It interprets the autobiographical fiction of Jamaica Kincaid as emblematic of the systematic production of erotic desire and identification for colonial or neo-colonial purposes. It also notes that the failure to recognize this process in the canonical reading of these texts is itself a sign of its general success, until alternative readings and writings are advanced. Chapter 6 dissects the contemporary academic commercialization of gender and sexuality discourse in the West. It observes a problematic shift in the general orientation of prevailing sexual politics and epistemologies, contrasting Cheryl Clarke and Joseph Beam, on the one hand, with Isaac Julien and Marlon Riggs, on the other hand. Ultimately, considering Walter Rodney on neo-colonialism and Dhoruba Bin Wahad on FBI counter-intelligence (i.e., COINTELPRO), it ends by charting a dialectic of revolution and counter-revolution that frames many of these discussions, which fail to truly address the problems at hand.

In short, the book aims to counter this school of thought, and hopefully even reverse it. It concentrates on the settler-colonial context of what becomes the United States of America, without effacing its colonial character or treating this social context in isolation from the rest of the world. Unlike most studies of race, it does not seal the subject into one national unit or confine it to some narrow periodization, making important socio-historical connections impossible. Unlike most studies of gender or sexuality, it connects sex and eroticism to geopolitics both politically and epistemologically. It does all of the above with an awareness of the significance of class conflicts and capitalism for considerations of these equally material and symbolic concerns. It works to radically reformulate the discussion of "race, gender, class, and sexuality" in addition to sexism, homophobia, misogyny, and heterosexism; political economy and social stratification; racism and white supremacy; colonialism and anti-colonialism; and an assortment of intellectual disciplines along with a range of historical, intellectual, and political figures central to Black Studies, African Studies, Diaspora Studies, etc., beyond Women's Studies and Gay and Lesbian Studies. The point is not to demonstrate conformity or "literacy" with respect to institutionalized ideas about sex, gender, and sexuality. The point is most certainly not to disdain or discipline Black or non-white people, culture, or politics by virtue of this particular brand of conformism, as popular as this activity has become. This would defeat the purpose of Black political and intellectual resistance to white supremacism, historically and internationally. The point is to counter conceptual frameworks and categories simply taken for granted by Western intellectual studies of all kinds; to do so in the interests of Black people, culture, and politics (not to mention non-conformity, anti-discipline, other "literacies," and the like).

Counter-disciplinary or anti-disciplinary in character, such coverage is equally central in terms of time and space. This project begins with reference to the period before enslavement and colonization in continental Africa. It then changes hemispheres to confront "America" in its northern location. It travels forward to trace the social biography of comprador elites, colonized in English and French, on both sides of the Atlantic Ocean. The place between colonialism and neo-colonialism, even British and U.S. imperialism, is then captured through a literature of West Indian or Caribbean migration. This project closes with a focus on the neo-colonial dynamic of North American or U.S. Occidentalism, a global and local project itself. It therefore paradigmatically spans the last five-hundred-plus years. Grounded in the past, these words are offered for a Pan-Africanism of the future—in theory and practice—so that the end of the present politics of sex and empire will come, surely, like the All-African revolution of Kwame Ture.

Acknowledgments

For producing me, sustaining me, and empowering me to think critically and passionately, I thank my family and community at large. I recognize them first of all. I struggle to achieve a piece of the wisdom and intelligence of my aunts, to whom I have dedicated this first book. My peace of mind and body has always been indebted to the support provided by my sisterly and brotherly cousins, who number in the millions, such as Christine Branom, John and Karen Ramey, and Doris Brown, who gave me her old laptop computer before she passed on, and to whom this book is also dedicated. I thank my sister, Deidre Dunnington Davis, for my three little nephews, Quinton, Nicolas, and Isaac, who make me happy! They bring me joy, which inspires me further to do what needs to be done in this world. I am thankful to my whole family and my people everywhere, at all times.

I found righteous intellectual kinship (in academia, of all places) when I met Carole Boyce Davies, who makes sure I come through. She is a model scholar, comrade, and friend. She is also my ideal audience, always. I am sure we will never leave the context we were a part of at SUNY-Binghamton behind. Our critical mass of students and faculty there when I was a graduate student were a vital part of my development. I shout them out, wherever they may be today, in the spirit of what we stood for then and, I hope, now.

The influence of Sylvia Wynter on my thinking and writing has been profound and enabling. She makes joining what she often calls the intellectual struggle irresistible. I benefited from the academic and institutional support of Judith P. Butler, Felipe Gutteriez, and Saidiya V. Hartman at UC-Berkeley, where Eliza Noh became my partner in crime. I thank them along with kindred spirits Janis A. Mayes and Babacar M'Bow, who push and spark and support me in the best of ways, against colonial-national limitations of all kinds. On that note, I must acknowledge my fellow travelers in the Coloniality Working Group (CWG), which was international in composition but based in Binghamton. It created a serious space for my work to be read and heard around the same time that I took great advantage of a fellowship awarded by the Carolina Postdoctoral Program at UNC-Chapel Hill. A sample of CWG scholarship is joined by a portion of the opening chapter of this book in "Coloniality's Persistence," a special issue of *CR: The New Centennial Review* 3:3 (Fall 2003).

A mélange of portions of the third and fourth chapters here first appeared in *Présence africaine* 159 (1999). This "Cultural Review of the Black World" impressed me so much in all phases of my research: I was truly honored by this publication. My best wishes to Mme. Christiane Yandé Diop. Thanks to my students, past, present, and future, who touch me and make me appreciate all that is possible in our work together. Thanks to Africa Resource Center, especially for giving me the opportunity to publish the e-journal I founded and edit, *Proud Flesh: New Afrikan Journal of Culture, Politics & Consciousness*. Much love to Véronique Tadjo, for art. Thanks to Pan-Africa, and Black radical traditions. Thanks to our Ancestors. Thanks to our Ancestors. Thanks to our Ancestors.

The Sexual Demon of Colonial Power

1   Pan-Africanism or Sexual Imperialism

WHITE SUPREMACY, HELLENOMANIA, AND DISCOURSES OF SEXUALITY

Before somebody else dies, literally, I want to begin with an illustration; to make my ultimate point about white sexual violence, historically, and Black people. I want to begin with a powerfully illustrative reference, or set of references. Yet as soon as I get specific, to make this case poignant and current, current events manage to date my examples, make them look old, manufacturing new cases overnight which insist upon our attention despite all filtering by the popular as well as academic media. I could recall the public strip-searching of Black Power activists, deployed nationwide to at once humiliate and titillate; the new gang plunger rapes of Black males in police departments (or prisons) on one U.S. coast, for example, before a carnival of bullets was fired on an unwitting Black male by a special police squad in search of its own serial rapist; the town shower-hanging and draggings to death of Black men in the South and the Rocky Mountains; or the state murder of a young Black female, on the other U.S. coast, whose person was seen as so dangerous that she was said to pose a lethal threat even after she had fallen asleep, afraid, in her stalled car. From coast to coast, and beyond, I want to begin with *one* current illustration, but . . .

The entire history of our African presence in American captivity lays bare a raw sexual terror that defines the cult of white supremacy here and elsewhere. Whether we think of the ceaseless assault on Black family existence, the obscene hysterics of apartheid lynching, the physical violations of direct and indirect colonization, or the sadomasochistic torture of formal enslavement and its trans-oceanic trade in flesh, we see that the rule of Europe has assumed a notably erotic form. Even so, despite a certain common sense rooted in Africana resistance to the ravages of empire, the carnal dynamics of white domination rarely receive sustained critical attention.

An eruption of "sexual [intellectual] discourse" in the 1980s and '90s changed this situation very little, if at all. In certain quarters of the United States of America, not to mention the West at large, the professed social construction of gender and sexuality has acquired the status of a cliché, however controversial a theory it may remain for some. The biological naturalization of erotic life is refuted, in principle, by the facts of cultural formation. Still, only certain forces of culture are acknowledged by such accounts. The really nasty fact that sexual personas and practices are ritually constructed as well as theorized in the service of colonial imperial structures of "race," or white supremacy, has not been the subject of academic commerce under Occidentalism.[1] The much-celebrated de-naturalization of sex is not concerned with this program. The even trendier refrain of "race, gender, class, and sexuality" actually obscures key aspects of social life insofar as it reifies these contingent Western analytic categories as dis-crete empirical phenomena that can be ideologically negotiated at will. As a rule, therefore, the erotic brutality of what is termed race is cleanly repressed by the very language of sex in "First World" orientations, and quite consequentially for so-called "Third World" peoples.

Historicity and Sexuality or Aryanism and Hellenomania

We can see how this is done in the now-canonical deliberation on ho-mosexuality conducted by John Boswell ("Revolutions, Universals, and Sexual Categories") and David Halperin ("Sex before Sexuality") in *Hidden from History: Reclaiming the Gay and Lesbian Past,* the prominent anthology edited by Martin Duberman, Martha Vicinus, and George Chauncey, Jr. (1989). They frame a spurious debate between "genetic essentialism" and "social construc-tionism" (17) in which all parties involved restate the basic dogma of Occiden-talist historiography. Boswell, author of *Christianity, Social Tolerance, and Homo-sexuality* (1980), posits a timeless gay subject across a symbolic order that includes ancient Greece, the Roman empire, the Christian feudal period, and industrial Europe. Halperin counters this bold embrace of biological determinism in the spirit of his own claim to fame, *One Hundred Years of Homosexuality and Other Essays on Greek Love* (1989a). The position he promotes, that human sexuality itself is contingent, presumes the same ideological time-space of his theoretical opposition. Halperin reviews classical Athens and modern Europe alone, with nothing in between, while drawing conclusions about all of human civilization. This foundational discussion considers no other culture or history beyond the "rise of the West," which is an "Eternal West," as Samir Amin notes in *Eurocen-trism* (1989).[2] The geopolitics of empire that enable this generalization receive no treatment whatsoever: *Hidden from History* hides them from history, as it were.

An anti-colonial analysis easily destroys this dichotomy of biological es-sence and social construction, not to mention the other major, unquestioned dichotomy here: that of heterosexuality and homosexuality. By and large, how-ever, a racialized conflation of Occidental specificity and "universal humanity" determines the fashion in which the historicity of erotic identification is recog-nized. Abdul JanMohamed critiques the first volume of Michel Foucault's *The*

History of Sexuality (1978) for its general "ethnic and cultural narcissism" in Domna Stanton's *Discourses of Sexuality: From Aristotle to AIDS* (JanMohamed 1992, 116). This sort of reading should be expanded and applied to the later volumes of Foucault's project, particularly volume 2, *The Use of Pleasure* (1985), in which the modern development of sexuality is reiterated with a difference often ignored by his enthusiasts. Foucault confirms that the term "sexuality" did not appear until the beginning of Europe's nineteenth century, yet he immediately warns that this fact "should be neither underestimated nor overinterpreted." "It does point to something other than a simple recasting of vocabulary, but obviously it does not mark the sudden emergence of that to which 'sexuality' refers" (Foucault 1985, 3). The focus of volume 1 on the "fields of knowledge, types of normativity, and forms of subjectivity" that generate the cultural experience of sexuality is seen as incomplete, in volume 2, without a larger historical lens (4). In other words, the history of sexuality in its strictly modern configuration is transformed into a more comprehensive genealogy of desire of which the contemporary sexual formation is simply one part: "in order to understand how the modern individual could experience himself as a subject of 'sexuality,' it was essential first to determine how, for centuries, Western man had been brought to recognize himself as a subject of desire" (5–6). Foucault's genealogy of desire is nevertheless written as "the history of desiring man" and "the games of truth by which *human beings* came to see themselves as desiring *individuals*" (6–7, emphasis mine). The West is again inscribed as the archaeological essence of humanity and its world historicity, erotic and otherwise. So when Foucault explores a culturally specific thematic complex of sexual problematization that cannot be restricted to a single Occidental epoch, as it is reformulated with a remarkable constancy (22) throughout the core of Greek and Greco-Roman thought, the Christian ethic and the morality of Modern Europe (15), this unfolding of sexual regimes is narrated as a universal history. A chronology of empire dictates a normative genealogy of desire, indeed a colonial *telos* for all individuals or human beings.

The racist appropriation of historicity has a long history itself. Africa and Africans, most of all, have been hurled into the zone of pre-history (if not anti-history) by human sciences well beyond G. W. F. Hegel. Arturo Alfonso Schomburg observed that the invidious representation of Negroes as a people without history was based upon the insidious representation of us as a people without a worthy culture (Schomburg 1925, 237). In his opening remarks at the First International Congress of Black Writers and Artists in Paris, Alioune Diop proclaimed, "History with a capital 'H' is a one-sided interpretation of the life of the World, emanating from the West alone" (A. Diop 1956, 9). Anna Julia Cooper defended her Sorbonne doctoral thesis with a similar charge: "To assume that the ideas inherent in social progress descend by divine favor upon the Nordic people, a Superior Race chosen to dominate the Earth, assuredly pampers the pride of those believing themselves the Elect of God" (A. Cooper 1998, 293). Cedric J. Robinson rehearses these ideas sharply in *Black Marxism: The Making of the Black Radical Tradition,* capturing that rigid depiction of the African "as a different sort of beast: dumb, animal labor, the benighted recipient of the benefits of slavery. Thus the 'Negro' was conceived. . . . From such a creature not even the suspicion of tradition needed to be entertained. In its stead there was the Black slave, a consequence masqueraded as an anthropology and a history" (Robinson 1983, 4). The rewards of history and culture (or history *as* culture, and vice versa) are conventionally reserved for white persons exclusively; and Pan-Africanism resists these racist cultural politics of history as fiercely as Western discourses of sexuality reinscribe them.

A basic anthropological hierarchy cultivates the will to universalize for the benefit of white Western dominance and hegemony. The "master race" of Europe is canonized as the paragon of social and biological development inasmuch as it pretends to embody certain universal laws of human civilization. Still, the claim (or presumption) of universality is far more than a mere *ethnographic* assertion; it reflects a greater *epistemological* assertion which by no means requires cross-cultural historical verification. An immediate, transcendent approximation of objective reality is asserted in a manner that represses the ideological agenda of such a posture. Some supernatural force of reason is supposed to provide access to some truth whose scope is boundless in both space and time. Partiality and relativity are anathema to this perspective, which presumptuously claims to cover all people and all places beyond all conflicts of culture and history. The only earthly intelligence that need be consulted is the hyper-rationalist authority of Europe. A crude particularity is projected as the primordial identity of its colonized subjects. This is how the West is enshrined as the veritable essence of human being, human knowledge, human progress, human civilization. In his critique of Foucault, JanMohamed concludes that the history of Western sexuality can be written as a universal one only "if it averts its gaze" from "its dark other" (JanMohamed 1992, 116). But this insight misses a fundamental point. The West can and does regard itself as universal without averting its gaze at all, for the dark body of the non-West is coded as an eternal sign of the inferior evolutionary development of non-white humanity. The culture and history of Occidentalism can be represented, hence, as at once specific and paradigmatic. Marimba Ani makes this brilliantly plain in "Universalism: The Syntax of Cultural Imperialism," the penultimate chapter of her opus, *Yurugu* (1994).

As a result, the cultural categories of sex and sexuality can function in a way that routinely erases the history of race and empire from their *critical* frame of reference. After Foucault, and in the wake of Duberman, Vicinus, and Chauncey's collection, this unique brand of universalist imperialism was canonized by a range of readers and anthologies, as well as single-authored works, under the commercial rubric of Queer Theory or Gay and Lesbian Studies. By no stretch does all or most of this work concern itself with historicity. Many instead use static Occidental conceptions of sex and seize colonized cultural bodies for the erotic benefit of the colonizer. The anthropology of Will Roscoe (1992) and Gilbert Herdt (1984) is especially noteworthy in this respect.[3] The shift in gender and sexuality paradigms effected by Judith Butler (1989, 1993) was more philosophical (or discursive) than historical, despite her critical engagement with Foucault's *The History of Sexuality: An Introduction*. Lesbian historicizations may be less long historical, given classic Greek phallicism (e.g., Faderman 1981), while, at any rate, the Greek isle of Lesbos remains explicitly central, at least at the level of etymology. On the intellectual whole, then, whether the racist historiography of human civilization is directly or indirectly advanced, the rise of modern Europe from the ground of Hellenic reason is presumed in a neo-colonial politics of racialization which itself constitutes a greater politics of sexuality (or *sexualization*).[4]

A more thorough consideration of this conspicuous yet camouflaged power might begin with attention to another prominent anthology, *Before Sexuality: The Construction of Erotic Experience in the Ancient Greek World*, edited by David Halperin, John J. Winkler, and Froma I. Zeitlin (1990). This example of the "new [erotic] historicism" follows the lead of Foucault, namely his grounding of the singular concept of homosexuality (and, by necessary extension, heterosexuality) in the social history of nineteenth-century Europe. While it claims to denaturalize erotic identity by locating specificities of time and space, this collection too is typical in its reification of white cultural dominance or hegemony. It is equally notable, furthermore, for the way it exposes the Aryanism of empire despite itself, which is to say, the way it exposes what could be termed a Greek fetish in contemporary Western sexual theories.

The central issues at hand are writ large in *Before Sexuality*'s willfully provocative title. Sexuality is casually defined on the opening page of Halperin, Winkler, and Zeitlin's introduction in clearly analytic terms: "the cultural interpretation of the human body's erogenous zones and sexual capacities" (3). Obviously, there can be no "before sexuality" in this sense of the word which would examine human eroticism in the abstract, as an ostensibly organic whole. However, this initial definition is forgotten as other meanings appear and a ritual appropriation of human bodies for white bodies alone becomes evident.

Just pages after an unofficial definition of sexuality, two additional and antagonistic ones are proffered as if they are not in radical conflict with each other. First, under the curious header "Before What Sexuality?" Halperin, Winkler, and Zeitlin translate their book's title to mean "before our sexuality" or "before sexuality as we understand it," which they proceed to name as "our current Western, predominantly middle-class sexualities" (5). It appears that after installing a general framework of sexual-cultural universalism, the editors "come out of the closet," as it were, geographically and economically, if not quite racially, as a relatively anxious afterthought. For this understanding of sexuality would yield a collection called something like *Before Our Sexuality* or *Before Western Middle-Class Sexuality*, surely not *Before Sexuality*, period. Their first official definition thus begs a crucial question. In any case, the fact that the current world order defines this Western bourgeois sexuality, racialized as *white*, as the proper model for all human sexuality is no doubt manifest.

Importantly, the same normative ideal drives the introduction's second official definition of sexuality, which would restrict its scope to those distinct features of modern regimes of erotic discipline (5). This is the understanding most associated with Foucault. The question is no longer a matter of what or whose. It is now a question of when. Halperin, Winkler, and Zeitlin's continued use of other context-specific terminology, such as "desire," "erotic," and "love" (not to mention "sex" and "sexual," without "sexuality") is not thought to pose a problem for the argument. Foucault is invoked as an authority to support this position in a highly problematic fashion. Completely ignored is his rearticulation of his *History of Sexuality*'s first volume in the second, and his move from a modern history of sexuality to a greater genealogy of desire. David Cohen and Richard Saller fault the second volume for "a kind of crypto-Hegelian subjectivity slowly unfolding itself as the centuries progress" (Cohen and Saller 1994, 59). They do not mention the racist Occidentalism at the center of Hegel's infamous philosophy of history. Still, no Hegelian or anti-Hegelian genealogy of desire is conceivable in this second definition, even though it continues to assume an eternal West with ancient Greece posed as modern Europe's unquestionable matrix. There is no rupture in culture, strangely, but there is absolute rupture in sexuality (which is itself supposed to be cultural, of course). What Halperin, Winkler, and Zeitlin do retain from Foucault overall is this ritual construction of the idealized time-space of the West, which is, for them, the sociosexual prototype of human progress or human development. They conclude, accordingly, "In both senses of 'before sexuality,' the study of classical antiquity offers us a special opportunity to test our assumptions about what aspects of our lives might truly be common to all human beings and what aspects are distinctive to the modern world" (6). They draw a conclusion for all humanity while having imagined only *their* historicity, *their* antiquity and modernity, and *theirs* alone.

The gist of this project is shown further by a comment made in support of its "cultural poetics of desire" (Halperin, Winkler, and Zeitlin 1990, 4). In an effort to study the cultural production of desire, while unmindful of the political production of culture itself, the editors summon the names of several "talented nonspecialists" or "stimulating collaborators" in their field of "classicism" (5). Martin Bernal, author of *Black Athena: The Afroasiatic Roots of Classical Civilization* (1987), is listed along with Foucault. Yet *Black Athena*'s basic point is ignored entirely by the whole of *Before Sexuality*. Bernal proposes that there have been two principal paradigms explaining the origins of "classical Greece," "the Ancient Model" and "the Aryan Model." His Ancient model refers to the widespread recognition in Western historiography before the end of the eighteenth century that ancient Egypt was the predominant force in Greek civilization. His Aryan model refers to the subsequent disavowal of this "African origin of civilization," to quote Mercer Cook's "trans-Atlantic translation"[5] of Cheikh Anta Diop (1974), and its replacement by the prevailing myth of an Indo-European or white progenitor of what is now dubbed the Greek miracle. This shift in explanations was effected by socio-political rather than purely epistemic factors. With this exploitation and effacement of Africa, its transformation into an alleged "dark continent," classical Greece becomes the Aryan origin of a rational philosophy and universal culture which will supposedly climax, millennia later, in European modernity. Bernal's notoriety notwithstanding, it is this Hellenomaniacal heritage, according to which Athena could not possibly, logically, be Black, that still structures bodies of work such as *Before Sexuality, The History of Sexuality,* and *Hidden from History.*

The erotics of Plato and the like generate pride in lineage for these "queer" figurations. Duberman, Vicinus, and Chauncey uncritically remark,

> The sexual practices of the classical Greeks, along with the enduring prestige that in modern times has traditionally surrounded their achievements, have long made them a kind of rallying point for lesbians and gay men of the educated classes, to whom they have seemed to offer an ideological weapon in the struggle for dignity and social acceptance. (Duberman, Vicinus, and Chauncey 1989, 37)

Their struggle, for mere acceptance and dignity within the status quo, demands a counter-struggle that rejects the coding of sexuality for empire, resisting colonial imperialist politics in the flesh. What *Before Sexuality*'s ironic reference to Bernal helps reveal is that this classical weapon depends upon the presumption, by intellectual class elites of the West, of the white racial status of the ancient world: upon Aryanism.

The sex of a Black Athena could never serve the same purpose. The embrace of any erotic identified as African would produce an entirely different outcome. Positing scientific reason as the gift of classical Greece to modern Europe has entailed conceptualizing Black people, in particular, as an undisciplined mass of sexual savages. The very notion of Western civilization is therefore founded on a primary opposition between white and non-white persons that is graphically sexualized. Sylvia Wynter maps, in various essays and articles (1987, 1990), a dichotomy between rational and sensory nature which defines humanist imperialism around the sixteenth century. The Man of Reason claims to master the world of sensuality in which primitives are said to dwell. Ani's remarks in *Yurugu* on the Great Chain of Being and the split between reason and emotion in Platonism, to which all of Western culture has been said to be a footnote—

these complement Wynter well (Ani 1994, 35, 323). The early Frantz Fanon observed, writing on racism and anti-Semitism in *Black Skin, White Masks,* "In the case of the Jew, one thinks of money and its cognates. In that of the Negro, one thinks of sex" (F. Fanon 1967a, 160). Though St. Clair Drake insists in "Anthropology and the Black Experience" (1980) that pre-modern racism, unlike modern racism, did not ascribe a cognitive deficit to African peoples (6–7), the centrality of erotic discourse to white-supremacist ideologies of the Occident has a long and lurid history. Indeed, when C. A. Diop wrote on the recent lynching of Emmett Till in his 1955 essay "Alarm in the Tropics," he made a striking comparison: "The complex of the white American reminds one very much of the complex the ancient Greek had towards the Oriental and Black world. In antiquity, apart from economic reasons, wars were often started under the mere pretext that a woman was abducted by a Black or an Oriental" (C. Diop 1996, 102). Without question, these raving erotics of race and racism warrant a central place in any history of sexuality, any genealogy of desire and identity in and under the West.

Yet with the African source of Greek miracles suppressed in favor of Aryanism, there is no cause to interrogate the colonialist tale of the civilized and the uncivilized for its colossal sexual significance. In the theoretical world of social constructionism, this anti-colonial agenda appears unthinkable. Nominal references to the West abound as if they are not actually normative, even though someone like Gayatri Spivak informs the field of Cultural Studies that "to buy into a self-contained version of the West is to ignore its production by the imperialist project" (Spivak 1988, 291). Earlier, Edouard Glissant in *Caribbean Discourse* mocked the notion of "transparent universality" or a "linear and hierarchical History," declaring, "the West is not in the West. It is a project, not a place" (Glissant 1989, 2, 64, 2). More radically, Eric Williams (1944, 1970), C. L. R. James (1938, 1969, 1970), and Walter Rodney (1969, 1972a) worked not only to put the West in its ideological place, but also to reiterate the centrality of African strain and struggle in the cultural, economic, and political production of modern civilization. Fanon would hammer this point home for "Third World" people at large in *The Wretched of the Earth* (1963). This is all to say that the culture which constructs sexuality in the "First World" is itself constructed in and for white racist empire. No variety of social constructionism can be valid unless this social construct of the "great white West" is demystified thoroughly in advance. Only then could a serious *sexual* historical materialism obtain, analyzing cultural articulations of the erotic against the bodily conceits of Aryanism; and only then could the racialization of sexuality across antiquity and modernity become thinkable in anti-imperialist terms.

Interestingly, a certain strain of historicism is critiqued by Eve Kosofsky Sedgwick in *Epistemology of the Closet* (1990). With the writings of Foucault and especially Halperin in mind, she derides the intellectual attempt to locate the precise hour and minute at which modern homosexuality was born (44). This male-biased approach regards a history of sexuality as one long, orderly march from one discrete regime to another; no more than one category of same-sex desire is deemed possible at any given time, and as each new regime or category arises, its precursor apparently dies without a trace. The contemporary field of erotic identity is distorted, homogenized, along with those of previous epochs. Sedgwick hence rebukes Halperin's casual allusion to "sexuality as we understand it," or his "common-sense, present tense conceptualization" of homosexuality "as we know it today" (45). She disclaims what she describes as a "unidirectional narrative of supercession" as a means for repressing the "unrationalized coexistence of different models" (46–47). All the same, the plainly Occidentalist character of these sexual assumptions is never problematized. The cultural-historical specificity of those sitting atop modern civilization (i.e., Europe and North America) goes unnoticed, as do the politics of Hellenomania that uphold it. She is merely interested in the white sexual diversity glossed over when Halperin and others render Foucault's "sexual invert" (the "feminine man," if not the "masculine woman") as the "straight-acting and -appearing gay male" of the Western middle class (46). Even when the teleology of this empire appears to be questioned, these erotics of Aryanism remain firmly intact.

Moreover, Sedgwick rhetorically purifies sexuality of race, ignoring the history of racialization, which is simultaneously a history of sexualization. She objects to the way that the meaning of sexuality, sexual orientation, and sexual theory has been reduced to a matter of the gender of an individual's object of desire. Time and again, the narrow opposition between homosexuality and heterosexuality confines the discussion of sex and sexuality to this one subject area alone. In response, Sedgwick catalogs a range of sexual distinctions which may focus on object choice but not gender (i.e., distinctions like human/animal, adult/child, partnered/unpartnered, one partner/several partners, and bodies-only/manufactured objects), and distinctions which do not focus on object choice at all (i.e., commercial/non-commercial, orgasmic/non-orgasmic, private/public, and spontaneous/scripted) (35). Nevertheless, somehow, the analytics of race and racism make no appearance on this strikingly detailed list—even though the context of critique is a society of slavery and segregation whose laws against miscegenation could co-exist with the institutionalized rape of Black women; even though the symbolics of empire have defined all Black people as sexual beasts of burden, as it were, century after century. It is the super-exploitation of an African laboring force, reproduced in and through sexual violence, which makes modernity possible for Western civilization. Still, this prioritization of sex over race is not undone. Sexual civilization must be exclusively reserved for white elite bodies, normally though not only in terms of its culturally and historically specific binary opposing heterosexuality, on the one hand, and homosexuality on the other hand.

Diop (et al.) or *Black Athena:*
Pan-Africanism or Sexual Imperialism

We get a much better glimpse of this greater sexual divide between so-called civilized and uncivilized, colonizer and colonized in the writings of C. A. Diop (1974, 1987b, 1989, 1996). For those who would forget him, nowadays, Les Nubians (sisters Célia and Hélène Faussart, of Cameroonian parentage in France) climax their second album, *One Step Forward* (2003), with a song specifically for and about him: "Immortel Cheikh Anta Diop." They begin singing in French with Wolof intonation, according to Janis A. Mayes: "Cher, Cher, Cher / Cher, Cher, Cher / Che(r)ikh Anta Diop / Ne dites pas qu'il est mort / Car il demeure immortel / Che(r)ikh Anta Diop / Ne dites pas qu'il est mort / Car les ancêtres il a rejoint. . . . " This popular musical tribute reiterates Diop's earlier recognition at the 1966 First World Festival of Black Arts in Dakar, Senegal, as the most influential Black writer of the twentieth century. Although Cheikh M'Backé Diop has recently published *Cheikh Anta Diop: L'homme et l'oeuvre* (2003) with Présence Africaine, his legacy today is nonetheless repressed by Occidentalism in truly Hellenomaniacal fashion.[6]

Bernal's reception in academia facilitates this repression as of late. For despite the popularity of his work, Bernal was never able to affirm a Black identity for ancient Egypt. Admirers of *Black Athena* have wrongly inferred from its title that he did. This must explain why the author has even publicly regretted his choice of words—in a journal entitled *Arethusa*—wishing he had named his work "African Athena" instead (Bernal 1989, 31). Such oscillation is certainly true to the text. Bernal studiously avoids the topic of race for almost five hundred pages. Only when his argument is half-finished does he finally pose the question, "What colour were the ancient Egyptians?" (Bernal 1987, 240). Even so, the question is quickly changed to whether or not ancient Egyptian culture was African, not Black. Next, in further avoidance of this central question, Bernal states his suspicion of the category of race, which he continues to view as biological fact rather than socio-historical artifact (241). He doesn't return to the issue until the end of *Black Athena,* where, with bizarre indirection, he writes that he does not "picture all Ancient Egyptians as resembling today's West Africans," but he does "see Egypt as essentially African" (437). The fact of Blackness is averted, again. Bernal begs the question as he opts for a culturalist explanation over an anti-racist one, a concession compromised by his earlier insistence that "the unification and establishment of dynastic Egypt . . . was in some way triggered by developments to the east" (15). More alarming, however, is his binding of "Black" identity to West Africa with recourse to the classic racist anthropological construct of the "True Negro":

> This variant became familiar to the European as the type primarily involved in the slave trade, and the ancestral group to Blacks in the American diaspora. Because of the extreme prejudice against this group, and its role in the U.S. and European colonies, there was a conscientious effort to minimize the influence of this variant (or variants with close affinities) in Nile Valley populations. (Crawford 1994, 56)

Suddenly, for Bernal, the only Africans who are Black are the ones conceptually bound for enslavement in North America. Before now, of course, "Black" and "African" were synonymous for him and his audience. This is why he wrote the following: "If it had been 'scientifically' proved that Blacks were incapable of civilization, how could one explain Ancient Egypt—which had been inconveniently placed on the African continent" (Bernal 1987, 241). Black and African are summarily severed when it's time for cultural capital to accrue, inconveniently, against the interests of empire. How can Aryanism be construed as an exotic academic paradigm of late-eighteenth-century Europe, when white supremacy is the hallmark of the West at large and when its elemental logic constrains Bernal's own analysis in *Black Athena*?

The sexual politics of empire are visible throughout. The underside of romantic Hellenism is the racist conceit of primitive hedonism. After the fall of his Ancient model of historiography, Bernal writes, "the Egyptians were now seen to conform to the contemporary European vision of Africans: gay, pleasure-loving, childishly boastful and essentially materialistic" (30). When ancient Greeks themselves admit overwhelming African cultural influence, they are pronounced guilty of "Negro fetishism" or "Egyptomania," as if admiration of Blacks is a sickness; as if Black people are irrational objects of fetishistic perversion (244). The whole world-view of Aryanism fixates, of course, on racial purity, to be secured by policing sex and sexuality; and this eugenics is behind traditional attempts to imagine an "Aryan Egypt" in the midst of ancient Africa. Where any civilization can be recognized in Egypt at all, it is viewed as the product of a mythical white race later barbarized by sexual contact with "Negro slaves." Sometimes it is seen as the work of Black bodies which become biologically white as a consequence of cultural evolution, before turning Black again, evidently, with cultural degeneration (245).

The African Origin of Civilization had unambiguously decried such an intellectual swindle, wherein "as soon as a race has created a civilization, there can be no more possibility of its being Black" (C. A. Diop 1974, 133). One of the groundings of Walter Rodney might come to mind here as well in the wake of both Diop's committed praxis and Bernal's belated rise to prominence, or celebrity. Rodney's "African History in the Service of Black Revolution" (in Rodney

1969) provides a broad context for the rhetorics of race that Bernal restated in *Arethusa;* and, importantly, it is Ethiopianism[7] that Rodney invokes beyond the limits of Egyptology:

> White propaganda likes to suggest that the achievements of Ethiopia are not the achievements of Africa. Marcus Garvey knew about this lying propaganda and made it look ridiculous. He wrote as follows: Professor George A. Kersnor, after describing the genius of the Ethiopians and their high culture . . . declared that Ethiopians were not African Negroes [but] dark coloured races showing a mixture of black blood. Imagine a dark coloured man in middle Africa being anything else but a Negro. Some white men, whether they be professors or not, certainly have a wide range of imagination. (Rodney 1969, 42)

Rodney's purpose was to transform the terms of this discussion in a fashion that rejects the dictates of imperialism. First, he insists that the study of African history be devoted to "freeing and mobilizing" Black minds as opposed to impressing white colonizers. Any academic distinction between reflection and action is renounced, as this study is itself seen as "directly relevant but secondary to the concrete tactics and strategy which are necessary for our liberation" (52). With a revolutionary agenda set for Africans, at home and abroad (*à la* Garveyism's Universal Negro Improvement Association), the whole concept of culture is redefined. The standard focus on great political states or elite groups and dynasties is criticized for its failure to reject European narcissism (52, 55). Millions of Africans and no small amount of genius are discounted by this approach, in strict conformity with an Aryanist mirage. By contrast, Rodney contends that until the meaning and value of ordinary African life is truly appreciated, Western empire will be able to impose its vision on the past and, consequently, the present, with relative ease (57). This talk is continuous with the Diop invoked throughout his *Groundings with My Brothers* (1969), written decades before *Black Athena* was conceived in Western academia.

Writing after Diop, Rodney can symbolize a whole tradition that is sorely repressed by Bernal and now-standard appropriations of these matters that are no less political than intellectual. John Henrik Clarke, in "The Contribution of Nile Valley Civilization to World Civilization" (1994), describes Egypt as not a "singular civilization . . . in itself" but "a culmination of a number of civilizations, all of them originally coming from the south" (86). His key question is centrally related to Rodney's concerns: "Why are we talking about Egypt outside of context with the rest of Africa?" (85). No longer argumentative about the matter, Clarke maintained, "There is no mystery about Egypt and no mystery about Nile Valley contribution, all of this is documented. If you don't want to read the Black documents, then read the white ones" (93). Of the latter, he cites the work of Gerald Massey, Alvin Boyd, Heeren, Heinrick Barth, Leo Grobenius, William Flinders-Petrie, Count Volney, De Lepsis, Herodotus, Pliny the Elder, and Pliny the Younger (92–93). Likewise, Ivan Van Sertima adds in "Egypt Is in Africa, but Was Ancient Egypt African?" (1994), "Herodotus traveled in Egypt. He speaks of them as being black in color and having wooly hair. He is not alone in this. We can cite Aristotle, Lucian, Appolodorus, Aeschylus, Achilles Tatius of Alexandria, Strabo, Diodorus of Sicily, Diogenes Laertius, [and] Ammianus Marcellinus" (78). But the Black documents are discussed extensively in Asa Hilliard's "Bringing Maat, Destroying Isfet: The African and African Diasporan Presence in the Study of Ancient Kmt" (1994). He gives a certain pride of place to Carter G. Woodson before citing David Walker, Martin Delaney, Frederick Douglass, Drusilla Dunjee Houston, J. C. deGraft-Johnson, and Deidre Wimby. This was just a beginning. Earlier sources include Henry Highland Garnett, Maria W. Stewart, Bishop Henry McNeal Turner, Edward Blyden, A. A. Schomburg, Amy Jacques Garvey, J. A. Rogers, Richard B. Moore, William Leo Hansberry, Charles Seifort, William Huggins, and Pauline Hopkins, as well as W. E. B Du Bois. More contemporary figures include George G. M. James, Chancellor Williams, Anna Melissa Graves, St. Clair Drake, Malcolm X, Yosef Ben-Jochanan, Jacob Carruthers, and Runoko Rashidi, not to mention Joseph Ki-Zerbo, Theophile Obenga, and Ifi Amadiume. The work of Beatrice Lumpkin, Iva Carruthers, and Shirley Graham Dubois fits this category of writing, too. Indeed, Larry Williams has compiled a bibliography, "Black Women in Search of Kemet" (1989), listing contributions by Daima Clark, Irene Diggs, Rosalyn Jeffries, Ife Jogunosimi, Eloise McKinney Johnson, Pauline H. Johnson, Jeanne Noble, Danita Redd, and Virginia Simon, among others. There is scarcely a trace of this history and scholar-activism in the controversy connected to the name of Bernal and *Black Athena*.

In any event, Amadiume writes in *African Matriarchal Foundations* (1987) that it is "indisputable" that the population of ancient Egypt came from the hub of Africa, "some following the Nile route from Uganda and Ethiopia, others following the land route from West Africa." This is her argument: "After the civilization flourished there and was destroyed by Asiatics and Europeans, there was a dispersal and migration back to the hinterland and elsewhere" (1987a, 7). What's more, she adds, "When Egypt was overthrown by the Persians, followed by the Greeks and the Romans, they raped, completely distorted, and misrepresented traditional Egyptian matriarchy" (11). Amadiume's text, like that of Rodney and Clarke—both of whom have also written on matriarchy—and so many others, continues to affirm a profound indebtedness to Diop, an unparalleled pioneer in the study of Africa and matriarchy alike. Nonetheless, he is given precious little space in the contemporary academic world of Bernal.

Indeed, only as *Black Athena* comes to a close does Bernal finally mention the name of Diop. In one truncated paragraph, he describes Diop as a "nuclear physicist" who professed his "faith that the Egyptians were, as Herodotus had specified, black" (Bernal 1987, 435). In this statement, Herodotus functions as an isolated figure devoid of his reputation as the father of history in the West. It was, moreover, not faith to which Bernal himself appealed when he first explained the name of his own project: "it is the conjunction of Neit/Athena's Egypto-Libyan origins, Herodotos' awareness of the connection, and his portrayal of the Egyptians as black, that has inspired the title of this series" (53). The danger of a Diop is deflected by making his argument appear as the pious partiality of a physicist, when it is quite well known that he was knowledgeable in a wide range of disciplines relevant to his wide range of interests (Egyptology, linguistics, anthropology, philosophy, ethnology, history, and archaeology, for example, besides nuclear physics). These disciplines are neatly indexed by Mercer Cook in his preface to the selections from Diop's *Nations nègres et culture* (1955) and *Antériorité des civilizations nègres: Mythe ou vérité historique?* (1967) which he edited and translated as *The African Origin of Civilization: Myth or Reality.* This is the one Diop book referenced in *Black Athena*'s lengthy bibliography. The Pan-Africanist's renown is due, no doubt, to the expansive evidentiary framework he developed to substantiate the thesis of his entire life-work: physical anthropological data, melanin dosage tests on mummies, osteological measurements, blood-type analysis, Biblical historicism, Kemetic self-description, continental cultural comparisons, linguistic studies, etc. (Diop 1974, ix–xi; Obenga 1970). At the "Peopling of Ancient Egypt and the Deciphering of the Meriotic Script" symposium sponsored in Cairo, Egypt, by the United Nations in 1974, these arguments were presented with astounding success. The proceedings were published as *Ancient Civilizations of Africa* (1980), volume 2 of UNESCO's *General History of Africa,* which even declared this debate with the world's most prominent Egyptologists a triumph for the Black opposition. In the conclusion to "Origin of the Ancient Egyptians," his contribution to that volume, Diop was convinced that a new page of African historiography had been written in Cairo (C. A. Diop 1995, 27). Again, none of this is recalled by *Black Athena.*

For Diop, the practice of African historiography was intellectually paramount, whereas Western civilization remains Bernal's essential concern. *Black Athena* sees Aryanism as but a recent error in the history of the West. For Bernal, this error can be corrected in three volumes or fewer, in a fashion that leaves intact a traditional distinction between politics and scholarship, despite an eighteenth-century lapse. Setting things aright, objectively, Bernal writes that the scholarly purpose of his project is "to open up new areas of research to women and men with far better qualifications" than himself; and, additionally, that its political purpose is "to lessen European cultural arrogance" (Bernal 1987, 73). It is always a matter of getting back to what he termed the Ancient model of historical origins, which reigned in a previous epoch. However, several centuries of Western imperialism, scholarly and political, predate this theoretical paradise. A return to the model that prevailed before the eighteenth or nineteenth century would leave Africans literally in chains: Romantic philosophy is not the only problem. The rise of the West (including fifteenth-, sixteenth-, and seventeenth-century imperialism) is strictly safeguarded by this approach. Furthermore, Bernal's second volume, *The Archaeological and Documentary Evidence,* must concede that Greeks and Romans themselves were far from free of racial prejudice (Bernal 1991, 444). The subtitle of this whole series (The Afroasiatic Roots of Classical Civilization, not Classical *Western* Civilization) reveals that "classical civilization" is conceived in Hellenophilic terms, a fact unchanged by its acceptance of African or Afroasiatic roots. Ancient Egypt is not classical civilization here. Ancient *Greece* is by definition classical antiquity. Lessening European cultural arrogance in this way does little to confront past or present Aryanism in theory or practice; and contributing to an intellectual practice of African historiography was never a part of Bernal's agenda, regardless of his work's positive reception in many Black as well as non-Black intellectual circles.

The better qualifications demanded in Bernal had already been mobilized by Diop with a purpose that could not tolerate a separation of politics and scholarship. The title of Diop's preface to *The African Origin of Civilization,* "The Meaning of Our Work," places us solidly in the context of the Rassemblement démocratique africain (RDA), the first inter-territorial movement for total independence in French-colonized Africa. Diop was secretary-general of the student wing of the RDA in Paris and in 1953 he had published a précis of his project in their journal, *Voix de l'Afrique noire,* as "Vers une idéologie politique en Afrique noire" ("Toward a Political Ideology in Black Africa").[8] Thus, *The African Origin of Civilization*'s strategic focus on psychic, historical, and linguistic factors was considered a "point of departure for the cultural revolution properly understood" (C. A. Diop 1974, xiii–xvi). Part of this program Diop would outline in detail in *Les fondements économiques et culturels d'un état fédéral d'Afrique noire* (1974; as *Black Africa: The Economic and Cultural Basis for a Federated State,* 1987), in which he recalls the early days of struggle:

> At that time apart from the Malagasy deputies and the Cameroonian leader Ruben Um Nyobe, there were certainly no French-speaking Black African politicians who dared to voice the concepts of African nations, independence, or, let's face it, culture. Today's after-the-fact statements endorsing such things are almost frauds; at least they are bare-faced misrepresentations. (C. A. Diop 1987a, introduction, n.p.)

The need for psychological and economic as well as actual political autonomy is affirmed once again. This complete liberation effort would land Diop in prison as a leader of opposition in Léopold Sédar Senghor's "post-colonial" Senegal. Diop's prime objective is more than merely lessening European cultural arrogance. Much more than that is at stake. In *Civilisation ou barbarie: Anthropologie sans complaisance* (1981; as *Civilization or Barbarism: An Authentic Anthropology,* 1991), he was emphatic: "The negation of the history and intellectual accomplishments of Black Africa was cultural, mental murder, which preceded and paved the way for their genocide here and there" (C. A. Diop 1991, 1–2). His attack on European Egyptology was an attack on ideologies of imperialism; and the white Western appropriation of classical civilization was at the center of what required this praxis of resistance and revolution.

Erotically speaking, Diop's multi-disciplinary work manifests a positive politics of sexuality with a sustained affirmation of matriarchy, as Amadiume scrupulously reminds us. What is the connection between matriarchy and sexuality, for those who don't recall the Moynihan Report of the 1960s?

> Since the work of [J. J.] Bachofen in 1861, it has been customary to admit universal matriarchy: the human family must have moved up, in spiritual and moral development, from the matriarchal regime associated with the simple materialism of the earth to the patriarchal regime believed to be essential rationality, spirituality and light. (C. A. Diop 1996, 129)

The pride of Western Greco-Roman civilization is purportedly writ large in patriarchal family units. But *L'unité culturelle de l'Afrique noire* (1959; as *The Cultural Unity of Black Africa: The Domains of Matriarchy and of Patriarchy in Classical Antiquity*, 1989) explodes the evolutionary schemes of anthropologist Lewis Henry Morgan and Friedrich Engels as well as those of Bachofen that inform them. All these scholars position matriarchy as an obsolete phase of human existence marked by a "primitive state of promiscuous intercourse" (C. A. Diop 1989, 8, 28). "Man" in Europe is said to have progressed from a matrilineal stage of sexual savagery to a gynocratic one of perverse matriarchal marriage, before ultimately securing the monogamous rule of patriarchy in a third and final stage. Diop maintains that it is merely a "masculine imperialism" which claims superiority for patriarchy while assigning a wild erotic inferiority to matriarchy (5–6). This sexual imperialism is fundamentally racial, for matriarchy is not viewed as a conscious systematic choice by a given society (40); it is pictured as an uncivilized precursor of today's modern, white patriarchal West. The universal transition from matriarchy to patriarchy is always asserted by making aboriginal peoples stand for savage promiscuity (21). Bachofen can locate matriarchy only in Greece and Rome's mythical fiction; Morgan and Engels hold up Indians in North America (12); and many others, such as Mary Douglas (1969), head for the heart of Africa. In a critical approach to civilization extended by Rodney and Amadiume (who will propose a critique that may be even more anti-elite, anti-state), Diop debunks matriarchy's misrepresentation as "the unpitying and systematic vengeance of one sex on another," or a sure sign of savagery or barbarism (C. A. Diop 1989, 108).

A defense of matriarchy defines Diop's overall corpus. This particular form of social organization, "as alive today as it was in Antiquity," supplied ample material for *The African Origin of Civilization* (C. A. Diop 1974, 143). *Black Africa*'s sections on bicameralism and unification made repeated reference to this heritage in their call for "a truly efficacious representation for the feminine element of the nation" (C. A. Diop 1987a, 33–34, 88). Also, Diop's presentation to the 1959 Second International Congress of Black Writers and Artists in Rome, "Africa's Cultural Unity" (in Diop 1996, 129–32), focused on matriarchal family along with the state, philosophy, and ethics as material evidence. This speech cites his thesis on the subject that developed into *L'unité culturelle de l'Afrique noire*. For Diop, on the whole, a militant defense of matriarchy is a militant defense of Africa, and a militant defense of Africa must mean a militant defense of matriarchy. This is a blow against the masculine sexual imperialism that is Western domination. Any value placed on patriarchy in Africa after colonialism is consequently denied the status of an internal evolution: "We cannot emphasize too much the role played by outside factors, such as the religions of Islam and Christianity and the secular presence of Europe" (C. A. Diop 1989, 113).[9]

A similar politics of gender and sexuality surfaces around the vexatious title of Bernal's book. In comments to the American Philosophical Association recorded for a special "Black Athena" issue of *Arethusa,* Bernal concedes that he originally came up with this title himself. However, when he expressed a desire to change it, his publisher is said to have stated, "Blacks no longer sell. Women no longer sell. But black women still sell" (Bernal 1989, 32). So, while Athena is not Black for Bernal after all, Black women can be exploited to sell the product anyway. The body politics of this scheme are left intact. Were Bernal to do otherwise, he might be subject to a very real symbolic contamination. This sociosexual analysis brings clarity to Bernal's colloquial self-identification as the "Elvis of Black Studies," a description tracked and treated by Jacques Berlinerblau in his no less problematic *Heresy in the University: The Black Athena Controversy and the Responsibilities of American Intellectuals* (1999).

Bernal's is a bizarre and belated concession prompted by Pan-African communities critical of *Black Athena* for its non-consideration—or non-citation—of its Black intellectual precursors. Bernal surely never classified himself as a Black Studies scholar at the outset, seriously or not. He would do so later as a joke on the lecture circuit and in some conversation. His book embodies that same cultural politics of appropriation that is supposed to be its object of study: Elvis is himself a sign of sexual contagion, dead or alive: Black bodies threaten white culture by corrupting white youth—body and mind—in this case through the sex of music, song, and dance. Black scholarship is equated with rock 'n' roll (another sexual euphemism) in Bernal's virtually Bill Clintonesque routine. He reserves a serious face for debate with arch-conservatives like Mary Lefkowitz, whose unabashedly anti-Black book, *Not Out of Africa* (1996), pictured a bust of Socrates on its cover defiled by an X cap. This baseball cap was part of Spike Lee's marketing strategy for his Hollywood distortion of the life of Malcolm X, whom none other than John Henrik Clarke deemed "the finest revolutionary theoretician and activist produced by America's Black working class in [the twentieth] century" (Clarke 1992, 146). Is it not mythological Socrates who defiles Malcolm instead? He did not drink hemlock for abstract ethics. He would vomit up colonial values in revolt, as in *The Wretched of the Earth* (F. Fanon 1963, 43). Finally, what real criticisms go unheard as Lefkowitz and other Hellenists command Bernal's attention? The subsequent publication of *Black Athena Writes Back: Martin Bernal Responds to His Critics* (2001) speaks volumes. As Black women continue to sell, or be sold, for white patriarchal profit, Bernal calls to mind a most provocative essay by bell hooks, "Selling Hot Pussy: Representations of Black Female Sexuality in the Cultural Marketplace," in her *Black Looks: Race and Representation* (1992).

V. Y. Mudimbe offers a curious apology for Bernal under the guise of critique in "The Power of the Greek Paradigm," the third chapter of his *The Idea of Africa* (1994). He begins its final section with an epigraph: Bernal's statement on the title of his book and the selling of Black women (Mudimbe 1994, 92–93). But Mudimbe also never supplies any commentary—critical or uncritical—on this specific sexual scandal at all. He is merely concerned that *Black Athena*'s truth might be mobilized by "unscientific" constituencies (104). He is at pains to take issue with Bernal's thesis throughout this piece; and he is equally at pains to rescue Bernal from his own and other criticisms, concluding, "this angle and my critique do not really weaken Bernal's argument" (98). While he freely charges Pan-Africanists with racism (Amadiume 1997, 3), Mudimbe defends European icons of white supremacy as he makes a historically questionable distinction between "racism" and "race-thinking" (Mudimbe 1994, 100). Although the news that Bernal brings is not entirely good, according to Mudimbe's academic values, Bernal represents a lesser evil of sorts. In fact, he is forgiven by Mudimbe for being seduced by "the idea of a 'civilized' African marching in triumph not only across Southwest Asia but also through regions of a 'barbaric' Europe" (101). There are those who are scientific, more or less, and those who are seduced, not to mention those who supposedly do the seducing. This idea continues the Western custom of representing Africa as a seductress who is sexual, as opposed to scientific or rational, and, of course, this explains why Bernal's remark that Black women still sell comes in for no criticism whatsoever in Mudimbe. Mudimbe makes no connection between this line of thought and the material treated at the outset of his chapter, "geographies of monstrosity" (80), or "the 'special place' that *agrioi* (savages), *barbaroi* (barbarians), and *oiorpata* (women killers of men) occupy in the texts of some classical [*sic*] writers (particularly Herodotus, Diodorus Siculus, Strabo and Pliny)" (71). Their classical fear of gynecocracy (rule by women) and doulocracy (rule by slaves) (90) is undoubtedly tied to Mudimbe's own, Bernal-aggravated fear of many other things, like Pan-Africanism, matriarchy, and what he views as Diop's "controverted publications" (102). Both for and against Bernal, ideologically, "The

Power of the Greek Paradigm" upholds "masculine [sexual] imperialism," unequivocally, as a veritable ode to Hellenomania and Occidentalism.

Unlike Mudimbe's work, Amadiume's *African Matriarchal Foundations* did anything but controvert Diop. The case of Igbo societies, it concludes, "will go a long way in supporting Diop's thesis of the cultural unity of Black Africa," adding further that African matriarchal heritage is still vital among Black families in the Caribbean and the United States (Amadiume 1987a, 81–82). Amadiume revises the meaning of the concept as imposed by the West. Diop revindicated matriarchy as a "harmonious dualism" which is accepted and defended by men and women alike (C. A. Diop 1989, 108). Amadiume differs to some extent, noting that the presence of matriarchy does not signify the absence of sexual conflict; it signifies, instead, a collective institutionalization of power and influence. She rejects the anthropological rhetoric of matrilineality in favor of matriarchy, since what is at stake is empowerment—social, economic, and political as well as spiritual—not merely descent. This ability to organize and wield influence in a structurally autonomous manner is ignored by the analytics of patriliny and matriliny in general (Amadiume 1987a, 23). Diop's original articulation of matriarchy may be not so much at odds with Amadiume's rearticulation as it is resolutely opposed to Europeanization as patriarchalization. His description of harmonious dualism was written to counter racist sexual vilifications of "African Amazons" by Aryanists who see white men and white women as blessed by patriarchy, and Black women as hateful, misandrist murderers of men.[10]

Hence, in her introduction to the Karnak House edition of *The Cultural Unity of Black Africa*, Amadiume could look forward to the "legacy of African matriarchy" in a future of struggle which takes Diop as an important guide (Amadiume 1989, xvi). Calling her African motherland "that continent of matriarchy" (xvii), she asks with tongue in cheek why Western matriarchy theorists do not cite his work after more than forty years of publication. She also remarks that "many present-day feminists are unable to handle" the topic because they remain committed to Bachofen's periodization. They dismiss matriarchy as myth since they construe it as "a society totally ruled by women," not as women's social institutions, kinship organizations, popular culture, and spiritual power (xi). Nkiru Nzegwu makes this same observation in "Questions of Identity and Inheritance: A Critical Review of Kwame Anthony Appiah's *In My Father's House*" (Nzegwu 1996, 179, 194) using different terminology; and, among others, Paula Gunn Allen makes it using the very same terminology regarding Native North America throughout *The Sacred Hoop* (P. Allen 1986). When Amadiume recalls a new focus on matriarchy, witchcraft, and women's spirituality in Germany, Britain, Latin America, and North America, along with the worship of nature in the Green movement, she does not hesitate to observe,

"African ethnography serves as a databank, but with little acknowledgment from the users. . . . Is the history of Greek appropriation of African philosophy and science in the nineteenth century repeating itself on this eve of the twenty-first century?" (Amadiume 1989, xvii). She asks further, and most incisively, what scholar will match the sexual militancy of Diop? For he engaged the fundamentals of the matter from a Pan-Africanist perspective "as opposed to a compromised struggle for women's rights in patriarchal systems" (xviii). On the continent, the favored sons and "daughters of the establishment" are faulted for their compromising role in the imposition of "new and borrowed patriarchies," ultimately ruled, from afar, by white capitalist elites (xvii).[11] This is the context for the continued condemnation of Diop by Western self-interest, and the very selective mobilization of him by certain African men, who steer clear of the primary sexual significance of his work (xviii).

If she misses the opportunity to address Bernal and his relationship to Black Africa in general, and Black women in particular, Amadiume revisits the sexual politics of civilization most powerfully in *Re-inventing Africa: Matriarchy, Religion, and Culture* (1997), in which several of Rodney's concerns reappear in a pointed methodological critique of Diop. His emphasis on large political states and dynasties, opposite the West, however strategic, she presents as an ideological trap which fails to eradicate the cultural historical conceits of Aryanism. Rodney's position in *How Europe Underdeveloped Africa* is that "it is preferable to speak of 'cultures' rather than 'civilizations,' " defining or redefining culture simply as "a total way of life" (Rodney 1972a, 34). Amadiume amplifies this approach in her radical reinscription of Diop. She appears to repudiate the very concept of civilization in the name of grassroots revolution (as she put it in her erotically focused collection of poetry entitled *Ecstasy* [Amadiume 1995, 14–18]): "It would be to the point . . . to re-echo the call for the decolonization of the African mind and the dangers of White words and Black people" (Amadiume 1997, 13). Just as *Re-inventing Africa* rejects the terms of anthropology (2), along with the idea that the European slave trade was in actuality a trade, it conscientiously promotes "decentralized anti-state political systems," gender flexibility, and African matriarchal heritage over patriarchy's feudalism, nation-states, and modern civilization. This is, for her, an appropriate *nzagwalu*, or "answering back" (Amadiume 1997, 5), and the most radical Pan-Africanism there is.

Nevertheless, the categorical conceits of the West were resisted only in part by Amadiume's *Male Daughters, Female Husbands: Gender and Sex in an African Society* (1987). In that work, she repudiates the universalizing language of Lesbos or lesbianism, because of its colonial roots and meaning (7), even as she retains the universalizing language of feminism under a generic definition, "a political consciousness by women" (10). Her documentation of ample and militant sexual politics among the Igbo begins by deploring white racist feminism practiced under the guise of sisterhood (with "Third World" women). Why retain this or any other term-concept of Occidentalism, after rejecting "lesbian," if the objective is to move beyond the cultural historical categories of the colonizer, unless colonization by homophobia is at issue? This question is raised again by *Re-inventing Africa*'s citation of Diop's own citation of Kati and Sadi on the introduction of sodomy after the Moroccan invasion in *L'Afrique noire précolonial* (1960; as *Pre-colonial Black Africa*, 1987) (Amadiume 1997, 9). Yet "sodomy" can be traced in Eurocentric discourse as a free-floating term for sexual "perversion" of many, many kinds, most of which are characterized by patently racist norms: "Many regarded sex between Christians and Jews or between Christians and Muslims as sodomy—even potentially procreative sexual acts could be forbidden if improper partners were involved. This argument derived from the belief that these 'infidels' were equivalent to dogs and other animals in the eyes of God; intercourse with them was thus 'unnatural'" (Mondimore 1996, 23). This is not the account of sodomy given to readers of Foucault's *History of Sexuality*, which sees sodomites simply as the pre-history of modern (white bourgeois) homosexuals. This sodomy was construed as bestiality because it construed non-Aryans as sub-human beasts or savages. To accept the terms of sodomization is, accordingly, to accept an entire system of erotic values that undermines any and every Pan-Africanist agenda. The language of heterosexuality, no less than Lesbos or lesbianism, has its ideological roots and meanings squarely in the West and its empire. The dangers of white words and Black people are ferocious, indeed, in the struggle to categorically resist sexual imperialism, to work toward the decolonization of Black minds and bodies—in theory and practice.

Conclusion

Addison Gayle, Jr., assailed what he called the Greek ideal in "Cultural Hegemony: The Southern White Writer and American Letters" (1970). This was the opening essay of an important but ill-fated Black Studies journal, *Amistad*. Gayle argues that the search for a U.S. national literature ultimately chose Platonic idealism over Kantian transcendentalism or realism in its quest (5). The Plantation school, which extends from John C. Calhoun to Williams Faulkner and Styron, found in ancient Greece both a justification for slavery, with its rhetoric of democracy, and a model for an agrarian society (7). There was "a world of superiors and inferiors, each cognizant of his [or her] particular niche in the social, political, and cultural hierarchy" (8). On top of this Great Chain of Being (19) are the masters of the greatest plantations, then the lesser plantation owners, followed by farmers, peasants, and poor whites, and below all of these are the enslaved Africans on whose backs the whole system is grounded (8). This "rebirth of the republic of Athens" on "American soil" (12) supplies

Gayle with much material for literary criticism. He takes it from the strictly Southern to the white nationalist stage. He notes that this Greek ideal reflects an aristocratic ideology against which Black intellectuals and writers wage a perennial struggle. He remarks as well that Black struggle against such ideals has been demonized and dismissed in a highly eroticized fashion. Pan-African resistance, rebellion, and revolution are recast, through miscegenation anxiety, as the desires of "half-men [and half-women]" (22) for "forbidden fruit," not freedom or full and complete liberation.

Highlighted here are this struggle and its eroticization. The study shows how sex, too, is conceived according to a Greek ideal, or fetish, in current studies of sexuality (if not gender, for Queer Theory) which many see as cutting-edge rather than slaveocratic. George L. Mosse's *Nationalism and Sexuality: Respectability and Abnormal Sexuality in Modern Europe* (1985) discusses how hegemonic European nationalisms, of which racism is but a heightened form (Mosse 1985, 41), revamped Greek standards of male beauty while stripping them of explicit homoeroticism (31), and how homosexual Europeans recalled "Ancient Greek battles in which male lovers fought side by side" to assert their own manliness (41)—which is to say, their Europeanism, what Europe's bourgeoisie would consider their "human sexuality." Like Western discourses of sexuality at large, this history cannot see white racist empire at the root of (supra-national) middle-class sex categorization, despite the work of scholars such as Gayle and Fanon and Black Studies globally.

While George Padmore once wrote in *Pan-Africanism or Communism?* (1956) that there was a choice to be made, Pan-Africanism can also be construed as an alternative to sexual imperialism, whether this imperialism is presented in a capitalist or communist mode of production. The possibilities of erotic identity or embodiment are by no means exhausted by what Europe would call heterosexuality and homosexuality. This narrow opposition is neither natural nor universal; it is modern, Western, and bourgeois or ruling-class. It is conventionally white and white supremacist as it upholds a much larger sexual opposition between the "civilized" and the "uncivilized," the colonized and the colonizer. The rather liberal articulation of "race, gender, class, and sexuality" in contemporary academia does not confront but instead consolidates this Occidentalism at the level of politics and epistemology. It leaves intact a concept of civilization that is no less a foundation for past and present debates over economics and society, or capitalism and communism (feudalism, communalism, socialism, etc.). Engaging Cheikh Anta Diop and Ifi Amadiume's writings on matriarchy and patriarchy enables a radical, categorical challenge to sexual imperialism in the name of Pan-Africanism, grassroots Pan-Africanism worldwide.

The shape and substance of sexuality is surely contingent upon time and space, or history and culture. The history of sexuality canonized by Europe and North America claims to make this point in theory. However, the concept of historicity employed normalizes the time-space of Europe as the only imaginable mode of socio-cultural existence. The rise of the West is thought to permit European history to stand as human history. The bourgeois standard for socially constructed sex, whether heterosexual or homosexual, remains basically the same as the standard for biologically essentialized sex. For this reason, sexuality is never truly denaturalized by this historicist discourse of denaturalization. The white world is always renaturalized as a universal standard of human civilization and its erotic practice; and the mechanics of race that inscribe it are erased from the category of sexuality itself. No one else exists; *nor does the sexual violence waged against us, by them.* Such a two-fold erasure cannot be underestimated, for sexuality is academically, analytically coded to mean what colonizers do to themselves for pleasure, not what they do to the colonized for purposes of pain, pleasure, or politics. This is Aryanism, simple and plain. It is not the stuff merely of neo-Nazi skinheads, nor of Adolf Hitler himself. It is not a specious category of anachronistic anthropology, or a distasteful little paradigm in Western historiography. It is the way of white supremacy that structures societies in which all of the above appear, and much more. These are societies in which human sexuality is systematically designated for white bodies and sexual savagery for non-white ones, Black bodies most of all. This is why Sylvia Wynter's anti-imperialist work on humanism is absolutely crucial.[12] Here are histories of empire that are erotics of Aryanism and erotics of Aryanism that are histories of empire.

2 The Madness of Gender in Plantation America

SEX, WOMANHOOD, AND U.S. CHATTEL SLAVERY, REVISITED

Beyond sexuality per se, what is the historical relationship between sex and slavery? What is the relationship between African enslavement (whether it is called chattel slavery, racial slavery, or neo-slavery) and gender categorization? This relationship has not been clarified, despite over five hundred years of white racist imperialism, and our comprehension of this relationship is crucial for contemporary Pan-African struggles, particularly in North America. What resources might be mobilized toward this end, practically and theoretically, to make this a moment of clarity as opposed to continued confusion?

Oyèrónké Oyêwùmí's *The Invention of Women: Making an African Sense of Western Gender Discourses* (1997) begins to write what could legitimately be called a history of sex, or gender. Unlike Michel Foucault, however, Oyêwùmí unearths a politics of race behind the sex and sexuality manufactured by Europe. She argues that "woman" is a culturally specific category of the West which finds no existence in Yorubaland, for example, before the onslaught of empire (ix). The same would be true, by necessary extension, for the category of "man." Still, according to Oyêwùmí, the feminist claim that gender is a social construct manages to obscure these facts, much as do the ideological schools of thought which precede it. For its articulation of gender remains anchored in anatomy in the very Western tradition of biological determinism. Critically, "woman" is seen as the social construction of the anatomical female, or a universal subject constructed, outside of time and space, to be always and everywhere subordinate to her equally monolithic counterpart, "man" (8–11). This doctrine has led to the misleading conception that "native females" are doubly colonized, a notion which Oyêwùmí rejects because it represses the colonial context of gender formation itself, and it suggests that "colonized women" benefit from the process of colonization, the patriarchal project of Europeanization (122, 127). *The Invention of Women* shows how masculinist and feminist naturalizations of sex and gender bind Africa and Africans to the West.

While Oyêwùmí's social history of Yoruba society has garnered some attention among critics, both positive and negative, her sharp critique of social constructionism defies contestation by gender-conservative skeptics. Her strain of thought is shared by *jENdA: A Journal of Culture and African Women Studies,* an electronic journal co-edited by Nkiru Nzegwu, Mojubaolu Okome, and Oyêwùmí for Africa Resource Center. *The Invention of Women* itself pivots around a contrast between past and present relations. There is the world of Africa before colonization by European concepts of gender, and there is a world of body politics experienced in the wake of colonization. But what constructs or categories should be used to address contemporary identities—on and off the continent—without simply accepting European domination after colonialism, conceptually, as if it were only possible to interrogate it with regard to a distant time and place? Importantly, Oyêwùmí's decidedly Yoruba-focused work, whose concept of colonization does not in principle exclude the European slave trade (Oyêwùmí 1997, xi), was not without precedent. It calls to mind a polemic written by Toni Cade Bambara, "On the Issue of Roles" (1970a), which confronted the very same matter long before the rhetoric of social construction became prominent in Western academia.

A militant rejection of "the madness of 'masculinity' and 'femininity'" (Bambara 1970a, 102), Bambara's essay mocks the sexual canons of Western anthropology, biology, and psychiatry, remarking that "human nature" (or the notion of "what a girl's supposed to be like and what a boy's supposed to be like") is an extremely malleable quality (103, 107). She scorns the dogmatic dichotomies of gender as "a hindrance to full development" and "an obstacle to political consciousness," particularly in the movement for Black liberation (101): "Perhaps we need to let go of all notions of manhood and womanhood," Bambara observes, "and concentrate on Blackhood" (103). Every practice of erotic identity should be defined in terms of egalitarian struggle. Existing conventions of sex differentiation are exposed as cultural and historical artifacts of empire. They can never, ever be taken for granted. While Bambara maintains we would do well to reclaim "the old relationships" (105) of Africa before colonialism, she also insists we make a study of "the destructive and corruptive white presence" (104). Invoking Frantz Fanon's *A Dying Colonialism* (1965), his book on sexual transformation in revolutionary Algeria, Bambara concludes,

> We make many false starts because we have been programmed to depend on white models or white interpretations of non-white models, so we don't even ask the correct questions, much less begin to move in a correct direction. Perhaps we need to face the overwhelming and terrifying possibility that there are no models, that we shall have to create from scratch. (Bambara 1970a, 109)

"On the Issue of Roles" closes with a call to forge "revolutionary selves, revolutionary lives, revolutionary relationships" (110), beyond the categorical confines of sex or gender. The white-supremacist "madness of 'masculinity and femininity'" (112), manhood and womanhood, this is all roundly renounced as a part of Pan-African revolt.

Bambara's collection was designed in part to piece together an "overview" of ourselves "too long lost among the bills of sale and letters of transit" (Bambara 1970b, 10). The reference to the West's trade in flesh is anything but coincidental. She was bold enough to interrogate the terminology of *The Black Woman*'s title, even as the editor of this undeniably pioneering effort. Bambara understood that the social logic of a slaveocracy precludes the possibility of there actually being such a person or thing as a "Black man" or a "Black woman." She understood the necessity of interrogating rather than assimilating or accommodating these basic sexual concepts, regarding social formations then as well as now. We might ask, accordingly, what cultural context could denaturalize the concept of gender in the West more fully than the history of Africans in Plantation America?[1] Academic discourse on the subject of sex and slavery ignores this question. We can therefore revisit several foundational texts on gender and slavery with colonialist categorization clearly in mind. For, whatever their professed strengths, the foundational writings of Angela Y. Davis, Deborah Gray White, and Hazel V. Carby all function rhetorically to reinscribe certain sexual conceits of empire where they might have been demystified with ease. It will be made clear that the critical-political perspective laid down by Bambara (and, in some respects, subsequently recast by Oyěwùmí) has no parallel in the prevailing literature on African enslavement in the British settler colony that would become the United States of America.[2]

Angela Y. Davis's "Reflections" (1971) and "Legacy" (1981) and Claudia Jones (1915–1964)

Deciding where to start in this context seems an easy task. Hazel Carby's *Reconstructing Womanhood: The Emergence of the Afro-American Woman Novelist* (1987) states that the "institution of slavery is now widely regarded as the source of stereotypes about the black woman," and that this observation was first made by Angela Davis in her seminal essay "Reflections on the Black Woman's Role in the Community of Slaves" (Carby 1987, 20, 39). Davis wrote this text as a world-famous political prisoner in 1971. It was published twice in *The Black Scholar,* and it was reworked a decade later to become the opening chapter of her book of essays, *Women, Race, and Class,* under the title "The Legacy of Slavery: Standards for a New Womanhood" (1981). Well before Deborah Gray White's *Ar'n't I a Woman? Female Slaves in the Plantation South* (1985), Davis's statements were prominent enough to be the point of departure for standard debates on the subject in North America for years.

Like Bambara's "On the Issue of Roles," Davis's writings appeared in the aftermath of the Moynihan Report. Daniel Patrick Moynihan had declared in *The*

Negro Family: The Case for National Action (U.S. Department of Labor 1965) that what ensured the abject status of Black people in his country was not a colonial imperialist system of white supremacy, but a "tangle of pathology" which was, for him, synonymous with Black culture itself. The Negro family of this propaganda is marred by its matriarchal structure, which, predictably, is said to produce anti-social subjects marked by sexual confusion and chaos.[3] This white racist equation of matriarchy with cultural deprivation (pathology or primitivism) is, in actual fact, a basic element of Western social thought, as the work of Cheikh Anta Diop and Ifi Amadiume has consistently shown. Although apparently unaware of its global historical depth, Davis had to confront this lore in writing "Reflections on the Black Woman's Role in the Community of Slaves," and ultimately concluded, "The image of black women enchaining their men, cultivating relationships with the oppressor, is a cruel fabrication which must be called by its name. It is a dastardly ideological weapon designed to impair our capacity for resistance today by foisting upon us the ideal of male supremacy" (Davis 1971, 14). In "The Legacy of Slavery: Standards for a New Womanhood," she would reiterate this point: "Black women were equal to their men in the oppression they suffered; they were their men's social equals within the slave community; and they resisted slavery with a passion equal to their men's" (Davis 1981, 23). The matriarchy pathologized by the West is not the problem, in other words; and, in the struggle for Black liberation, patriarchy is plainly not a solution.

"Reflections on the Black Woman's Role in the Community of Slaves" (1971)

Yet and still, the profound implications of Davis's discussion of sex and gender have gone almost totally unnoticed. We read in "Reflections" that "the [enslaved] black woman had to be released from the chains of the myth of femininity" and that "in order to function as slave, the black woman had to be annulled as woman" (Davis 1971, 7). When the fact that the majority of them were field workers is then examined in "Legacy," Davis notes that "they might as well have been genderless as far as the slaveholders were concerned. . . . Black women [therefore] were practically anomalies" (Davis 1981, 5). No biologism of sex precludes a violent extraction of their labor by the plantation regime. The oppression of Black females is consequently construed as identical to that of Black males. Moreover, and perhaps in pointed refutation of Moynihan's denial of this whole reality, Davis's account of the qualitative sameness of Black male and female oppression is expanded with a quantitative measure of Black female specificity: "But women suffered in different ways as well, for they were victims of sexual abuse and other barbarous treatment that could only be inflicted on women" (6). This is a common heterosexualist assumption that was articulated in "Reflections" with a notable difference. Given the amplified significance of domestic life for the enslaved, the "custodian of the house of resistance" was said to be targeted by "the most elemental form of terrorism distinctively suited for the female: rape." That is, sexual assault was recognized as an attempt to annihilate her resistance and define her status as a "female *animal*" (Davis 1971, 13), not as a woman. Nevertheless, both "Legacy" and "Reflections" recognize that such violence represents a collective assault as well. The institutionalized rape of the female aims to reinforce the powerlessness of the male (even if sexual violence against males, which would represent an assault against all of the enslaved as well, cannot yet be imagined). By no means, however, was this practice sure to succeed.

The negative equality among the enslaved is solidified by a positive equality found later in "Legacy." For, after "Reflections," Davis confirms a non-hierar-chical and relatively un-rigorous division of labor in the culture of those in bond-age (Davis 1981, 17–18). Thus, when a threefold equality of culture, oppression, and resistance is seen to exist in this anti-slavery realm, the explanation for sexual violence is simple: "they were trying to break this chain of equality through the especially brutal repression they reserved for the women" (23). There is no con-ventional Western construction of sex here in the shorter history of what Bam-bara had called, not uncritically, "the old relationships" (Bambara 1970a, 105).

In any event, Davis ultimately has the cultural life of her slaves conform to the social conceits of colonial slaveocracy. This is how she and Bambara part ways: "Legacy" closes with the curious declaration that "Black women were women indeed," not to mention the claim that "certain personality traits" de-veloped under white domination yield "standards for a new womanhood" (Davis 1981, 29). These traits do not interrogate the concept of womanhood itself. The attachment to this specific rhetoric (and concept) of gender is never questioned. Nor is the necessity of rigid sex differentiation of any kind in any way disputed. Canonical histories by Eugene Genovese and Herbert Gutman are duly chided for their own provincial gender assumptions (4, 19). But a fundamentally Euro-pean sexual framework persists in Davis's "Legacy," even more than in "Reflec-tions." The "madness of 'masculinity' and 'femininity' " (or manhood and woman-hood) is, finally, categorically ensconced via the bodies of enslaved Africans in Plantation America.

"Reflections" did not or could not easily, always, and entirely assume domi-nant concepts of gender. It did mean to rescue them in some fashion for its com-munity of slaves. Of course, the slaveocratic order of settler colonialism con-strues its own as human and its slaves as non-human (or sub-human, if not anti-human). One cannot qualify as human if one is not identified as man or woman, and vice versa, since manhood, womanhood, and humanity are not apolitical notions (as if there were such a thing), but very political notions of empire. History has illustrated as much, repeatedly, and so has Sylvia Wynter

(1982, 1987, 1990, 1995, 2000, 2003). When Western categorizations are taken for granted, however, resistance to domination is often defined as gaining access to such things rather than as rejecting them out of hand for an old, new, or different way of life. Hence, Davis would write of a release from femininity and an annulment of womanhood, as if there were a natural and universal sex or gender experienced by Africans (or Europeans) before colonization and enslavement. After quoting Frederick Douglass as protesting a "manhood . . . lost in chattelhood" (Davis 1971, 5), she herself states, "The community gravitating around the domestic quarters might possibly permit a retrieval of the man and the woman in their fundamental humanity" (6). This is not just expressed as their retrieval of a native sense of self-worth. It is an argument for the likelihood, if not the actuality, of a slave man and slave woman fashioned in the "quarters of resistance," or the counter-hegemonic, oppositional "community they pulled together through sheer force of strength" (6). A human being of womanhood would be achieved, in theory, even where it was at odds with what is referred to as the "historically evolved female role" (8). This is how our foremothers would foil what Davis presented as the oppressor's attempt to define her as a female animal in "Reflections." They could do so through a distinctly Black cultural formation that does bitter battle with the white racist artifacts of gender and sexuality, although Davis presupposes manhood and womanhood as absolute monoliths, to some extent, from the outset.

"The Legacy of Slavery: Standards for a New Womanhood" (1981)

This striking symbolic warfare fades from view in "Legacy." Davis had productively relied in part on a general distinction between sex and gender as she struggled to project a humanism of gender into her community of slaves, a Black community which could never be reduced to beasts of burden in the African Diaspora. While the rhetoric of sex often denotes an anatomical biology that can refer to human beings and non-human animals alike, the rhetoric of gender refers to what has come to be called the social construction of sex as gender among human beings alone—as if its anatomical-biological base were not also itself socially constructed or instituted. The paradigmatic space between sex and gender is, significantly, the place where, even according to this account, gender could be constructed differently by different cultures and different histories at different times and in different places. Yet the fact that gender appears to always, inevitably, get collapsed with sex in Western accounts proves that both sex and gender have been conceived in culturally specific and historically static, Western terms. While "Reflections" went back and forth on this issue, with tremendous insight, "Legacy" makes little or no differentiation between sex and gender, naturalizing both as one, in effect. Tense negotiation of white conceptions of bestiality and humanity through white conceptions of masculinity and femininity is no longer a major part of the analysis, as white conceptions of manhood and womanhood are now taken for granted, if in modified fashion. This time, "women" and "female slaves" are rendered synonymous from beginning to end, like "female" and "woman," on the whole.

The Black cultural formation of Davis's community is no longer what matters most, moreover, when it comes to collective self-definition and sex or gender. *Women, Race, and Class* proceeds if there is, at bottom, a trans-cultural, anatomical-biological distinction underwriting its sexual universalism, guaranteeing its socio-historical relevance for enslaved Africans, when the whole worldview of Western anatomy or biology is grounded in racial distinctions and scientific racism. Now, Black female slaves, "hardly women in the accepted sense" (Davis 1981, 6), can be pronounced "women indeed" regardless of allusions to sexual anomalies, genderlessness (5), and breeding (7). Now, the regulatory practice of rape is one that "could only be inflicted upon women" (6), instead of one "distinctively suited for the female," designed to promote her mythical animality. Indeed, "Legacy" contends, "If Black women had achieved a sense of their own strength and strong urge to resist, then violent sexual assaults—so the slaveholders might have reasoned—would remind the women of their essential and inalterable femaleness" (24). Not only is the ideology of womanhood assumed here, it is assumed to be coextensive with femaleness as the anxiety-producing specter of female animality disappears. The supposed guarantees of biology enable this assumption, again, even though such biologism continues to guard its manhood and womanhood, its humanity, for white Western bodies exclusively.

Certainly, without minimizing Davis's critical contributions, we could continue to raise a series of questions toward further contributions of our own: Why should the legacy of slavery be standards for a new womanhood, one unavoidably grounded in the original, racist standards of gender, for Africa's Diaspora in particular? Why shouldn't slavery's legacy be a critical rejection of all European discourses of sex or gender and the alien tongues in which they have been violently imposed, and are reimposed? Why not repudiate the idea that manhood and womanhood are natural, universal, or necessary features of social existence? Regarding terms like "femininity," "housewife," "mother," and "woman," Davis acknowledges that "among Black female slaves, this vocabulary was nowhere to be found" (Davis 1981, 12). Given this and other historical facts, why should we reproduce that same rhetoric, and in such generic terms—under the guise of freedom or emancipation, no less? In short, why evade the essence of slaveocratic imperialism?

The colonial vocabulary of sex is part and parcel of the modern production of heterosexuality as a defining feature of Occidentalism. The strict division of society into heterosexual and homosexual subjects for a heteronormative agenda shapes the discourse on matriarchal households countered by Davis. She does not counter matriarchy's demonization by patriarchal Europe as Diop had, and as Amadiume would, as Pan-Africanist social historians and activists. Davis rejects it out of hand, and maybe out of state-induced fear, too—for the white patriarchy of Moynihan does seek to intimidate and terrorize any attachment to matriarchy, among the Black masses especially. She makes use of Gutman to uphold certain "marriage taboos, naming practices, and sexual mores as evidence of a thriving and developing [Black] family during slavery" (Davis 1981, 14). Where these relations are distinguished from those of white settler society, they are still made to conform to traditional forms of the West. Davis highlights the participation of male slaves in the domestic sphere of the Black community, but she emphasizes that they were not the mere helpmates of their women, or victims of matriarchal dominance (17); and we are told that their "boys needed strong male models to the very same extent that their girls needed strong female models" (19). The examination of sex, gender, and slavery has almost always been an examination of conjugal or quasi-conjugal dynamics to the exclusion of all other Black family and community dynamics. Where are the studies of relationships between brothers and sisters, parents and children, friends and comrades, etc.: relationships that do not by definition seek to consummate themselves maritally or sexually? Davis's goal is to persuade, like Gutman and in opposition to Moynihan, that "the slaves were not 'not-men' and 'not-women' " (13). The patriarchal West's manhood and womanhood are posed as such natural facts of life (along with its related concepts of family and sexuality) that their social desirability cannot ever be queried. The so-called sexual savagery of African matriarchy is summoned merely to be dismissed, again, by the heterosexualism of empire.

Claudia Jones, Black Woman Communist of West Indian Descent (1915–1964)

Another agenda emerges from the praxis of Claudia Jones, out of the text of Davis itself, as recent work by Carole Boyce Davies will demonstrate.[4] A self-described "Negro Communist woman of West Indian descent" (Jones 1948, 129) who grew up in Harlem during the 1920s and '30s, Jones can be a more fitting point of departure for this discussion of sexual politics and African enslavement. Perhaps her most popular essay, "An End to the Neglect of the Problems of Negro Women!" (1949) maintains that the "traditional stereotype of the Negro slave mother, which to this day appears in commercial advertisements, must be combated and rejected as a device of the imperialists to perpetuate the white chauvinist ideology that Negro women are 'backward,' 'inferior,' and the 'natural slaves' of others." When in "the film, radio, and press, the Negro woman is not pictured in her real role as breadwinner, mother, and protector of the family, but as a traditional 'mammy' who puts the care of children and families of others above her own," we are only seeing the politics of the past being played out in the present (C. Jones 1949, 33). Shortsighted indeed, therefore, is the strict attribution of these ideas to Davis, so baldly restated by Carby. What's more, Jones gives us a more radical, Pan-African, and anti-imperialist interpretation over three decades earlier; and her legacy looms large, if unrecognized, in Davis's "Reflections."

After the Western world's war against the Axis, amid what she dubs the "drive to fascization" in the U.S. (29), Jones writes "Negro Women!" to affirm their position as a matrix of militancy from a Black Marxist-Leninist perspective. She notes that capitalists seem to know better than progressives that when "Negro women take action, the militancy of the whole Negro people, and thus of the anti-imperialist coalition, is greatly enhanced" (28). As a fearless fighter in the genocidal war waged against her, "her sisters, brothers, and children," she is targeted for an intensified oppression which exposes the sexual ideologies of white colonial power and capitalism. The tired boast of big business that American women enjoy the greatest equality in the world ignores the "degradation and super-exploitation [of] Negro and working-class women" (29). It is this super-exploitation of Negro women workers that renders them "the most oppressed stratum" of the population (30). And as the primary breadwinners of their families, which they raise behind the "iron curtain" confines of Jim Crow ghetto existence (29, 30), Black women perform their role as "guardian" and "protector" with fierce determination (28). When they combat the violence of lynching and white supremacy, the "love and reverence [for] mothers of the land" is not extended to them (29). They get swift, systematic injustice instead. This racist sexual scheme leads Jones to scorn the "rotten bourgeois notion [of] the battle of the sexes," a myopic device that represses "the fight of both Negro men and women—the whole Negro people—against their common oppressors, the white ruling class" (36). In strict avoidance of "Social-Democratic bourgeois-liberal thinking" (36), Jones always turned toward the masses, away from the North American bourgeoisie and its opportunistic colored elite (37).

As much as Jones focuses on wage slavery in the post-war period of the late 1940s, a deft analysis of chattel slavery lays the foundation for her argument. She opens with a comprehensive outline of the history of struggle: "From the days of the slave traders down to the present, the Negro woman has had the responsibility of caring for the needs of her family, of militantly shielding it from the blows of Jim-Crow insults, of rearing children in an atmosphere of lynch terror, segregation, and police brutality" (28). She confronts the obscene crimes of slavery as well as the burning hatred for slavery harbored by Black women (32).[5] Regarding the quarters of resistance, she concludes, "The Negro mother was mistress in the slave cabin, and despite the interference of master or overseer, her wishes in regard to mating and in family matters were paramount" (32). While the mother of struggle is rooted in her familial setting, she radiates resistance outward into the larger world. The origins of that resistance are located well beyond the conditions of slavery, to boot, as Jones remarks: "Most of the Negro people brought to these shores by the slave traders came from West Africa where the position of women, based on active participation in property control, was relatively higher in the family than that of European women." This is supplemented by historical tales of East African mothers and their passionate opposition to the European slave trade (32).[6] A pre-colonial, continental circumstance supplies a major source of explanation in Jones's militant work, an absolute rarity in more established historiographies of African enslavement in the U.S.

Her vision is global in geopolitical scope. By contrast, Davis falls prey to a common and very colonial myth of de-Africanization in "Reflections." She writes, "Africans had been uprooted from their natural environment, their social relations, their culture. No legitimate socio-cultural surroundings would be permitted to develop and flourish" (Davis 1971, 5). African Diaspora is no more conceivable in "Legacy," where Black culture is plantation-bound. Davis's account of the super-exploitation (and super-militant resistance) of "the Black woman in the community of slaves" is certainly indebted to Jones, even though Jones is not referenced by name until the biographical survey of Communist women in a separate chapter of *Women, Race, and Class* (Davis 1981, 167–71). However, a crucial part of Jones's work never reappears in Davis, whose own Marxism is more Western than "Third World," as it does not include the Leninist call for national self-determination for oppressed minorities, and this is her Pan-Africanist revalorization of matriarchy. It is the political legacy of the African institution of motherhood that inspires much of the militancy manifested on the colonial plantation. Neither Daniel P. Moynihan nor his predecessors J. M. McLennan, J. J. Bachofen, and Lewis Henry Morgan can stigmatize this tradition for Jones, who is more ideologically in line with Amadiume and Diop. Since this matrix is rendered as extended family, including sisters, brothers, and children, not just conjugal relations, the narrow family ideology of pro-slavery heterosexualism does not go unchallenged in "An End to the Neglect of the Problems of Negro Women!" These are all reasons why Boyce Davies could fittingly describe Jones (who is buried in England's Highgate Cemetery, next to Europe's greatest Communist man) as "left of Marx."

Deborah Gray White: "Female Slaves" (1983) and *Ar'n't I a Woman?* (1985/1999)

The same can by no means be said for academic histories arriving on the heels of Davis, after Jones. *Women, Race, and Class* actually began by marking the "conspicuous" and "disappointing" absence of a book-length study of "slave women," even by the close of the 1970s (Davis 1981, 3). Will any book do here at the center of U.S. imperialism, where Davis's former comrade George Jackson came to theorize neo-slavery in *Soledad Brother* (1970)? Coming to fill the void for many is Deborah Gray White, author of *Ar'n't I a Woman? Female Slaves in the Plantation South*, which was published in 1985 and republished in 1999 with a new introduction, "Revisiting *Ar'n't I a Woman?*" White's short essay "Female Slaves: Sex Roles and Status in the Antebellum Plantation South" (1983) not only precedes her more prominent book, but also paves the way for the ideas that she would eventually elaborate. As is so often the case, the anti-matriarchalism of the West determines the discourse's starting point. Yet, unlike Davis, White will embrace the substance of matriarchy in the language of "matrifocality." Even so, and very much like Davis, White couches this socio-cultural experience in colonial terms. The sex she assigns to matrifocality remains the sex of Occidentalism and the Moynihan Report. The gender of Western heterosexuality is naturalized and universalized, many years after the different militancies of Jones and Davis have passed far out of vogue in North America.

"Female Slaves: Sex Roles and Status in the Antebellum Plantation South" (1983)

"Female Slaves" seeks to counter a certain tendency of histories written in response to Moynihan. The fiery "Reflections" of Davis (not to mention the polemic of Jones) seem too political or radical to merit much mention in White. She takes issue with the historiography of Robert Fogel and Stanley Engerman, Eugene Genovese, Herbert Gutman, and John Blassingame for simply inverting the Moynihan Report. It had perversely exploited E. Franklin Frazier to proclaim that the problem with contemporary Black life was the Black family, and that the problem with the Black family was the "often reversed roles of husband and wife." This "trans-gendered pathology" was to be traced back to slavery (White 1983, 22). After Moynihan, modern historiographers came to save the day by asserting the patriarchal character of Black families on plantations. For them, the sex of slaves is and should be male-dominant and heterosexually discrete. White interrupts this symbolic compensation, maintaining that the pendulum has swung too far from female-dominated families to male-dominated units: "slave women did not play the traditional female role as it was defined in nineteenth-century America, and regardless of how hard we try to cast her in a subordinate or submissive role in relation to slave men, we will have difficulty reconciling that role with plantation realities" (White 1983, 30). White's own conclusions actually mesh well with those of Davis, whom she never engages: "The high degree of female cooperation, the ability of slave women to rank and order themselves, the independence women derived from the absence of property considerations in the conjugal relationship, 'abroad marriages,' and the female slave's ability to provide supplementary foodstuffs are factors which should not be ignored in consideration of the slave family" (28). Unfortunately, these findings are made to assert Black familial normalcy on white-supremacist terms. The cultural and historical specificity of the genders said to be reversed goes entirely unrecognized. The sex roles reinscribed by White end up as matrifocal variations on a Western metaphysical scheme.

Her defense of matrifocality is the culmination of a labor history founded, paradoxically, on the "traditional female role" of European femininity, thanks to a host of unreasoned and undocumented "probabilities." At the outset, White claims that depictions of "female slaves" as full-time field hands virtually identical to male hands are more misleading than not. She is compelled to acknowledge the existence of some female full hands, who were forced to labor like males, but suggests, "It is difficult, however, to say how often they did the same work, and it would be a mistake to say that there was no differentiation of field labor on Southern farms and plantations. The most common form of differentiation was that women hoed while men plowed" (24). White can fathom labor division as always and only gendered, never according to physical capacity, for instance, beyond sexual dictates. She must immediately concede that exceptions to this distinction between hoeing and plowing were "so numerous as to make a mockery of it" (24). Despite the fact that such a sexual division would be not simply rare but ridiculed, this dubious distinction is assumed throughout the rest of White's work. By the close of "Female Slaves," she goes so far as to classify this community as one of many societies where strict sex role differentiation is the norm (30). A ponderous emphasis is placed on "a lot of traditional 'female work'" (24) such as cooking, sewing, and doctoring (25), which contradicts her awkward disclosure that "sex role differentiation in field labor was not absolute but . . . there was differentiation in other kinds of work" (26). The buried confession that "field work occupied the time of most women" (25) confutes the startling yet central presumption that "it is likely that . . . women were more often called to do the heavy labor usually assigned to men after their childbearing years" (24). Likewise, White's categorization of pregnant and nursing slaves as half and three quarter hands (in line with her feminizing incapacitation of all "female slaves") is always presented as a strict difference in kind, not quantity, of production: "at least until thirty-five, slave women probably spent a considerable amount of time doing tasks which men did not do" (24). These probabilities in White are founded more on the fallacies of femininity than on documentation, historical reality, or cogency of argument.

Ar'n't I a Woman? *Female Slaves in the Plantation South (1985)*

This approach is duplicated in *Ar'n't I a Woman?* (the first extended study of the subject anticipated by Davis). In its third chapter, "The Life Cycle of the Female Slave," White speculates in a fashion which is still at odds with all that slips through her previous undertaking: "Although some women of childbearing age plowed and ditched when they were pregnant, in view of the slave owners' concerns about natural increase it is more likely that women who did the same work as men were past their childbearing years. If this was the case, the middle-aged years were the most labor-intensive years of a woman's life" (114). Manifestly, "female slaves" do plow now, and ditch as well, even when pregnant. The point or effect is to downplay the experience of "working like a [slave] man" in favor of more "womanly" pursuits, without interrogating manhood or womanhood. The second chapter, "The Nature of Female Slavery," troubles White's generalization. Until the official abolition of the overseas slave trade, she maintains, a clear priority was given to labor production over labor-force reproduction in "the lower and newer regions of the South (Alabama, Mississippi, Louisiana, and Texas)" (69). This deduction is based on lower fertility rates in those areas and the idea that the slaveholders were slow to realize the profitability of natural increase (69, 67). In any case, the rational solicitude White grants to slaveholders would be logically confined to the period after 1807. All in all, the conditions of possibility for the female laborer White wants to imagine as a prototype shrink considerably with each statement. This prolonged attempt to project femininity into this history of super-exploitation is subverted over and over again.

Such sexual revisionism contradicts conventional academic research, not to mention Black popular consciousness at large. For example, Michael P. Johnson's "Smothered Slave Infants: Were Slave Mothers at Fault?" (1981) considers the matter of Sudden Infant Death Syndrome (SIDS). His cross-regional investigation exhumes a history that *Ar'n't I a Woman?* can only partially efface. Reading the plummeting rates of SIDS after emancipation is proclaimed, Johnson concludes, "The hard physical labor required of pregnant slave women is the most probable explanation for the high incidence of SIDS among slave infants" (518). As for the ruthless program of super-exploitation and the sadistic practice of whipping enslaved mothers, he observes that "the large number of smothered infants and the testimony of the slaves themselves are powerful evidence that many masters found it easier to ignore the risks of hard work for pregnant women than the promise of a cash crop safely harvested [and] they easily blamed slave mothers for smothering their infants" (519–20). The ill effects of rampant abuse are scarcely incompatible with infanticide, so to speak, as an act of anti-slavery resistance—much like suicide on slave ships and elsewhere.[7] At any rate, in spite of this terminology, Johnson confirms another construction of slave women, during pregnancy and beyond it, as "sexually convenient laboring animals" (Grier and Cobbs 1968, 34).[8]

To refuse this history is to renounce a significant source of pride for the ancestors in question. What gets stigmatized as a masculinization of sorts in *Ar'n't I a Woman?* they very often vaunted as power and strength. Many a narrative and interview substantiates what Davis had surmised: "Their awareness of their endless capacity for hard work may have imparted to them a confidence in their ability to struggle for themselves, their families and their people" (Davis 1981, 11). Conversely, White's mission is to uncover an absolute, inviolate sexual division of slaves into men and women as a natural and hierarchical matter of course. Her fourth chapter, "The Female Slave Network," struggles in a manner that makes her ultimate agenda explicit: "It is hardly likely that slave women, especially those on large plantations with sizable female populations, lost their female identity" (20–21). A fear of masculinization prevails even though, properly speaking, female slaves have as little to do with colonial conventions of masculinity proper as do male slaves in the white racist society of slaveocratic imperialism. Their history throws into radical question the dichotomy of male and female identity propagandized from the plantation to the present day.[9]

Nonetheless, it is patriarchy's demonization of matriarchy that produces *Ar'n't I a Woman?*'s curious treatment of motherhood among enslaved Africans. Having made a specious case for strict sexual division in "Female Slaves," White insists that we would be wrong to infer with historiographers after Moynihan that this supposed division was the basis of male dominance. It would be more accurate, or "less culturally biased," to say that women's roles were complementary to those of men (White 1983, 26). Next, a first and simply bibliographical reference to Africa is brought forth and ignored until much later, as White appeals to the colonial anthropological definition of "matrifocality," "a term used to convey the fact that women in their role as mothers are the focus of familial relationships. It does not mean that fathers are absent; indeed, two-parent households can be matrifocal. Nor does it stress a power relationship where women rule men" (28). After Diop, Amadiume embraces the language of matriarchy to reclaim such institutions, while White shies away from both Africa and mother-focus until the very end of her inquiry: "Finally, any consideration of the slaves' attitude about motherhood and the expectations which the slave community had of childbearing women must consider the slave's African heritage. In many West African tribes [*sic*] the mother-child relationship is and has always been the most important of all human relationships" (White 1983, 29–30). This statement appears on the last page of "Female Slaves." Until then, White's subjects have no culture or history that is African. They are merely female slaves in the Plantation South, as the subtitle of *Ar'n't I a Woman?* phrases it. The myth of de-Africanization is disrupted in the most minor way: "While it would seem that the antebellum slave woman had little in common with her African foremother, motherhood was still the black girl's most important rite of passage, and mothers were still the most central figures in the black family" (White 1985, 108). Apart from its isolated appearance in the practice of motherhood, which would save White's slave from Moynihan's "tangle of pathology," African Diaspora is in no way imaginable. The continental source of matrifocality is invoked for the narrowest of purposes in "Female Slaves" and *Ar'n't I a Woman?* It enables a deflection of white Western stigma, by claiming "normal," normative status according to Western doctrines of sex and gender, contemporary and historical.

"*Revisiting* Ar'n't I a Woman?" *(1998)*

These conceptions of sex and gender survive in "Revisiting *Ar'n't I a Woman?*" (White's introduction to a new edition of her book published in 1998, almost a decade and a half after its initial appearance.) She observes that the movement for Black Power was responsible for the rise of African-American Studies (not Black Studies) in U.S. academia; and, in her view, the point of this renaissance was the restoration of masculinity in Black men (White 1998, 3). For White, the related restoration of femininity in Black women had not yet been achieved at the original publication of *Ar'n't I a Woman?* The essential task of her text is explicitly and repeatedly equated with proving womanhood without question. Still unimaginable here is a Black Studies which interrogates or undermines white Western sexual categories, which is to say, male and female, man and woman. In retrospect, White remarks, "some critics allege that I muted slavery's brutality—and the consequent dogged resistance" (9). But this fact is not connected to her sexual-political and ideological agenda. Conceding that she was alarmingly unable to conceptualize the difference between Black and white women, and that she would not currently insist so strongly on their commonalities, she anxiously reasserts, "Black and white women had so little in common because the sexism they both experienced kept them apart" (6). Beyond any prelapsarian commonality of gender, apparently, it is a *white-supremacist* sexism which always disallows in advance the unity she desires. Her wish for it articulates a social as well as biological determinism, not to mention political (and professional) orientations which require that brutalization and resistance be muted as unfeminine, among other things.

So how is White's reassessment to be assessed? The book-length study desired by Davis has yet to be written. "Were I to write *Ar'n't I a Woman?* today," White muses, "I would use the verb 'enslaved' rather than the noun 'slave' to implicate the inhumane actions of white people. The noun 'slave' suggests a state of mind and being that is absolutely unmediated by an enslaver. . . . Enslaved forces us to remember that black men and women were Africans and African-Americans before they were forced into slavery" (8). To whom would "African-Americans" refer, exactly, before the enslavement of Africans by Europeans in the Americas? The rhetorical switch from "slave" to "enslaved" would enable a focus on resistance, and this focus is said to have become possible only recently, now that there is more history than myth available on the topic (5). This is quite a rosy historiographical tale. It recalls the closing lines of "Female Slaves," where White concluded, "Sambo and Sapphire may continue to find refuge in American folklore but they will never again be legitimized by social scientists" (White 1983, 30). Conversely, James Turner and W. Eric Perkins had written "Towards a Critique of Social Science" (1976), and they were clear: "The social sciences were integral to the maintenance of bourgeois rule not only in the United States, but over America's expanding colonial empire in the South Pacific, the Caribbean and Latin America" (4). The discourse and discipline were, in short, built for race and class domination, colonial and imperialist, domestic and global.

Sterling Stuckey, author of the landmark *Slave Culture: Nationalist Theory and the Foundations of Black America* (1987), had already helped display these links between history and sociology and domination in "Twilight of Our Past: Reflections on the Origins of Black History" (1971). Stuckey could explain why "white historians as a group are about as popular among black people as white policemen" (Stuckey 1971, 291). L. D. Reddick concurred with his criticism of hegemonic historians such as Robert Fogel and Stanley Engerman, Eugene Genovese, and Ira Berlin in a foreboding speech entitled "Black History as a Corporate Colony" (1976). Like the whole counter-historical tradition associated with Carter G. Woodson and his *Journal of Negro History,* these anti-imperialist perspectives were available to White and others, as her brief reference to Black Power that opens "Revisiting *Ar'n't I a Woman?*" should very well illustrate. For whom, therefore, is a focus on resistance not possible until the 1990s? This is a question of politics, or perspective, for who focuses more diligently on resistance and revolution than Claudia Jones in 1949; what happened to Angela Davis in 1971 and 1981?[10] Regrettably, the title of White's book represents a simple search for affirmation that is far less probing than Sojourner Truth's radical, boastful, even bicep-flexing oratory—as a militant sexual-political analysis is cast, convolutedly, as a thing impossible in the past.

One very different critique of *Ar'n't I a Woman?* is Evelyn Brooks Higginbotham's "The Problem of Race in Women's History" (1988). Reading White's book as if it were extremely African or Diasporic in character, Higginbotham writes, "Shaped by African traditions and American socio-economic forces, black women are described as perceiving and experiencing womanhood in many ways distinctly different from white women" (126). A "cultural difference" orientation is entertained and, eventually, eschewed for overemphasizing the very differences White admits she repressed in "Revisiting *Ar'n't I a Woman?*" Higginbotham proceeds to explain any cultural difference between Black and white women away as an effect of racial oppression, simply assuming that Blacks and whites are ideally culturally identical: "The acknowledgment of this reality notwithstanding, the singular focus on racial difference misses the bicultural aspects of the black woman's existence. It avoids understanding her as black and American" (127). The condition and situation of Blacks in North America is pictured as biculturalism beyond race and racism. A common culture free of racial conflict is posited as America is reduced to the U.S. imperialist state. The problem with calling Black people both Black and American is revealed immediately when the same formula is applied to whites, who would never be called bicultural ("both white and American") because white racial domination and hegemony is plainly what the nationalist culture of the United States of America means: Black people cannot be described as Black on the one hand and American on the other hand, any more than Native Americans could be described as Native on the one hand and American on the other hand, since this Americanism signifies, ideologically, a white-supremacist appropriation of culture and politics, nationally and internationally. This political, economic, and cultural subjugation is effaced by "The Problem of Race in Women's History," for which race is indeed a problem inasmuch as it signifies an obstacle to the myth of a common culture, of gender, for U.S. colonial nationalism and its version of women's history.

Moreover, when she promotes "biculturation" over "cultural difference," Higginbotham extends this vision to the period after Emancipation, so-called: "The ex-slaves were quick to idealize the role of man as provider and woman as homemaker, even though both were forced to work" (Higginbotham 1988, 129). Not much is offered to substantiate this claim. Nor does Higginbotham explore the implications of idealizing a code of conduct contradicted by social realities of labor, family structure, sex, etc. She is compelled to consider the class dimension of this historical process, but does so only from the vantage point of the privileged: "The visible assimilation or, at least, psychological allegiance to the sexual behavior and attitudes of white middle-class America conveys the class-specific character of gender relations with the black community." Her research on racial "uplift" strategies among Black Baptists is invoked to sanction a movement that "sought to establish a black leadership, a black bourgeoisie that would articulate and advance the cause of the inarticulate masses" (131).[11] This colored middle-class hegemony is never critiqued for its comprador mission. In the work of Claudia Jones, the masses of Negro women know their exploitation and oppression quite intimately and are only rendered inarticulate by the chauvinism of their class enemies (C. Jones 1949, 35) and, even in "The Problem of Race in Women's History" (Higginbotham 1989), Frazier's classic *Black Bourgeoisie* (1957) resounds in muted tones.[12] Still, the culture of the Black majority is disregarded in the pursuit of a monocultural, Western middle-class womanhood.[13] This expropriation of the experience of the masses for the elite occurs repeatedly in academic histories of African peoples in the Americas.

Hazel V. Carby: Slave and Mistress, *Reconstructing Womanhood* (1987)

This same dynamic is reproduced in other, more nuanced work as well. A very engaging text, for instance, Shirley J. Yee's *Black Women Abolitionists: A*

Study in Activism, 1828–1860 (1992), confronts the circumstances of social class glossed over by Higginbotham. At its center are nominally free Black communities before the U.S. Civil War. In the second chapter, "Black Women and the Cult of True Womanhood," Yee observes, "The economic realities underscored the contradictions in 'true' womanhood ideology. But these ideas, no matter how unrealistic, were transmitted so strongly through black institutions that they helped define black women's participation in racial 'uplift' activities" (59). Like their male and female adherents, these ideals and institutions make up the "colored [or Negro] elite" famously profiled by Frazier. Yee suggests as much when she says that she excludes enslaved women from her study of Black women and activism because they require a different analytic framework (159). This much is also suggested when the ideologies of "'true' womanhood and manhood" are defined, explicitly, as the sexual ideologies of "antebellum free black society" (40). The contradictory and illusory promotion of white patriarchal middle-class values (157), values which depend on "notions of male and female natures and separate sex roles as a measure of free status," is criticized by Yee, in hindsight, as trading "one system of oppression for another" (58). She does not celebrate the staging of emancipation as freedom through socio-sexual assimilation. However, she still presumes the Black elite to be paradigmatic for Black people overall. With its lens turned away from the mass struggle on the plantation, Yee's *Black Women Abolitionists* is quick to recast its topic as Black women generically and Black women's activism as a whole, not "free society" Black women specifically.

The sexual ideological confines of women's history simply accepted by both Higginbotham and White were challenged, to some extent, by Carby's *Reconstructing Womanhood: The Emergence of the Afro-American Woman Novelist* and its own exploration of the nineteenth-century cult of true womanhood. Her second chapter, "Slave and Mistress: Ideologies of Womanhood under Slavery," includes a critique of historians of white women who fail to consider the power of this paradigm when they dismiss it as out of sync with the lives of elite planter-class women (Carby 1987, 24). As is customary, feminist historiography defines the plantation system as essentially patriarchal, narrating its control over all women's bodies, evading the racial and racist foundation of patriarchy itself in the process. Carby charts the disparate effects of this system on white and Black women (20) with her literary-historical analysis, which (unlike the Marxian readings of the terrain) examines labor much less than sexuality. This ordinary, artificial split between sex and work has serious consequences, especially for differences or conflicts in class status and identification, in Carby's enormously influential work.

The subtitle of Carby's second chapter, "Ideologies of Womanhood under Slavery," is critically misleading. Since, as she remarks, "woman" meant "white" in the logic of the cult of true womanhood (34), there could be only one reigning idea of woman, and it was embodied by the mistress. The enslaved could certainly have ideas about this womanhood, but she was herself constructed as woman's antithesis. Carby notes that "piety, purity, submissiveness, and domesticity" (21) were the four main features of Victorian femininity and that they were, without question, inaccessible to "the black woman as slave" (21). She goes so far as to recognize that "Black women were not represented as being of the same order of being as their mistresses; they lacked the physical, external evidence of the presence of a pure soul" (26). Needlessly minimizing the economic contours of this embodiment, Carby stresses, "existing outside the definition of true womanhood, Black female sexuality was nevertheless used to define what those boundaries were" (30). Apart from her status as a super-exploited worker in the field, the slaveocracy associates the enslaved with taboo sexual practices and overt sexuality (32). According to this scheme, she is a lascivious animal that breeds, while it is the glorified white woman who mothers. The polar opposition so inscribed is illustrated in the danger she is said to pose to the master's patriarchal home: "the white male, in fact, was represented as being merely prey to the rampant sexuality of his female slaves . . . it was the female slave who was held responsible for being a potential, and direct, threat to the conjugal sanctity of the white mistress" (27). Her healthy resistance to the sexual exploitation and abuse disguised by this alibi is met with a reinforcement of her systematic demonization: "Measured against the sentimental heroines of domestic novels, the black woman repeatedly failed the test of true womanhood because she survived her institutionalized rape, whereas the true heroine would rather die than be sexually abused" (34). Hence, Carby states the obvious when she writes, "the social relations of slavery [dictate that] the interests of the mistress lay with the slave master," not their female slave. The pedestal on which the former stood was supported by the institution of slavery (31), to say the least. There is surely no gender to be shared by white and Black persons in Plantation America.

There is no universal man socialized in opposition to a universal woman, or vice versa; there is a white man and a white woman specified over and against Black African "slaves," who may be described as male and female, in a greater, racist sexual opposition which Carby actually denies. She objects to the white cult of gender as if it were illogically white. Recalling the oppositional identities of slave and mistress, she asserts that the "ideology of true womanhood attempted to bring coherence and order to the contradictory material circumstances of the lives of women" (24). Yet these circumstances cannot be contradictory, for this slaveocratic concept of sex reserves womanhood for white female bodies alone. There is antagonism, in other words, not contradiction. At the outset, Carby presumes an identarian unity of white and Black women that is strictly anatomical in nature. Woman is taken for granted as a biological entity even though such biologism never grants its womanhood to Black female slaves, and biology is itself constructed to construct gender in white racist fashion. Imagining the "position of black and white women in the sexual dynamics of the slave system" as contradictory (32), rather than conflictual or antagonistic, Carby performs a womanization or feminization of the slave which is plainly not permitted by the system under study.[14] She translates a presumed physical capacity for reproduction into a sameness of subjectivity which is, crucially, belied by the social opposition between glorified motherhood and motherless breeding (30). As a result, although Carby may partially criticize the Victorian cult of true womanhood for excluding Black women, she fails to criticize the more comprehensive culture of sex or gender that constructs women as a natural and universal category.

Criticizing this culture requires a thorough interrogation of the heterosexualism undergirding white conceptions of manhood as well as womanhood. Carby's use of the term "contradiction" evidently comes from Blassingame's reading of the "dialectical relationship between the simultaneous existence of two stereotypes, a rebellious and potentially murderous 'Nat' and a passive, contented 'Sambo'" (Blassingame, quoted in Carby 1987, 21). This dialectic reflects a complex and contradictory unity internal to one subject-position, the social identity of the Black male who is enslaved. There is no biologically based unity to be contradicted across the divide between slave and master in such a case. The true manhood of the white West cannot be the property of purported beasts of burden. A "black man as slave" would be a contradiction in terms, not the marker of a contradiction within some gender shared by owner and chattel. This is no less the case for slave and mistress. Together, manhood and womanhood are manufactured for a heterosexuality of white supremacy which academic historians and critics have yet to explode.

Carby writes that the ideology of the slaveocracy claims that women should "'civilize' the baser instincts of man" and, further, that "in the face of what was constructed as the overt sexuality of the black female . . . these baser male instincts were entirely uncontrolled" (Carby 1987, 27). But it is white womanhood, not Black femaleness, which is thought to enable and elevate this manhood as the racial prerogative of white society or Western civilization. The converse is also said to be true. This other half of the equation is missed by Carby, who notes that the "slave woman, as victim, became defined in terms of a physical exploitation resulting from the lack of assets of white womanhood: no masculine protector or home and family, the locus of the flowering of white womanhood" (35). It is white manhood, not Black maleness, which is thought to enable and elevate womanhood, again as the racial prerogative of white society or Western civilization. And none of these racist concepts can be rejected as such if they are not recognized as the racist concepts of a heterosexualist empire of Occidentalism.

That Carby's basic interests lie elsewhere is revealed by her neglect of the labor identity of "the black woman as slave," not to mention the very title of her book: *Reconstructing Womanhood: The Emergence of the Afro-American Woman Novelist*. The material identity of the "black female field hand" (25) need not compete with an investigation of Black female sexuality. Another name for the cult of true womanhood is the cult of domesticity. For a real, respectable woman had to be a domesticated one who could never function as a super-exploited field worker (or even an otherwise exploited "house slave"). The persona privileged by Carby's project is, significantly, the writer or novelist, who may or may not depict this matter of labor in narrative. The Black female workers who take center stage in the texts of Claudia Jones, Angela Davis, and even Deborah Gray White are virtually nowhere to be found in *Reconstructing Womanhood*. Its attention to cultural anxiety surrounding sexual stereotypes of Black women reflects the specific concerns of an elite rather than those of the masses.

The writers Carby discusses may very well react to their exclusion from the cult of true womanhood and domesticity by seeking inclusion via the invention of a derivative discourse of Black womanhood (32). However, they may not be racially paradigmatic, except as a select social class. Carby complains that "thinking, articulate, reasoning black women were represented only as those who looked white: mulattoes, quadroons, or octoroons" (33). She will not scrutinize the politics of assimilation from the perspective of those who are still unilaterally represented as unthinking, inarticulate, and irrational, that is, most of those who were seen as simply Negro, Black, or African. The wish for a reconstructed womanhood is read in the literary corpus of the free and manumitted as if it naturally extends to the lower and lowest strata of the enslaved. The concrete examples include Lucy Delany, who speaks to the virtues of honest women, and Mary Prince, who evangelizes womanly values in a similar vein. Insofar as these writings do posit "a black womanhood in its essential difference from white womanhood," a difference which does not preclude sympathetic ties between slave and mistress (37), they testify no less to an "essential difference" between these writers and the vast majority of the enslaved. In Carby's fifth chapter, "'In the Quiet, Undisputed Dignity of My Womanhood': Black Feminist Thought after Emancipation," she allows, "As an elite, black women intellectuals could only maintain a representative black female voice if they weighed the advantages of forming an alliance against the knowledge that for the mass of black women white women were not potential allies but formidable antagonists" (118). Despite this momentary concession, she simply ignores the formation of racist class positions by the National Association of Colored Women, for example, as they adopt and adapt (61) various white-supremacist conventions for themselves. The elitist need to "forge a [moralist] culture of [true] Black womanhood" (118), akin to Carby's own aim of forging a "sisterhood of white and black women [for] feminist historiography and literary criticism" (53), is not itself interrogated as class-interested need. The elite desire for womanhood can be couched in these racially generic terms because Carby's exclusive focus on sexuality shields sexualized divisions of labor almost completely from view in *Reconstructing Womanhood*.

In short, given an investment in reconstructing (and, thereby, conserving or preserving) a reconstruction of womanhood, Carby's text ironically cannot recognize that the gender it wants to reconstruct is a social construction in the first place. Had it been able to do so, the rhetoric of reconstruction could have been put to other uses. When white supremacy reconstructs slavery as emancipation, it will also reconstruct (that is, reconsolidate) manhood and womanhood as racist social categories. This is why Carby could cite Davis in conclusion on how the "links between black women and illicit sexuality consolidated during the antebellum years had powerful ideological consequences for the next hundred and fifty years" (39). This racism of sex and gender is not merely a static carry-over from a distant period. It is a constantly reiterated feature of ruling-class machinations of empire. It is no accident that the more working-class analysis of Barbara Omolade in "The Unbroken Circle: A Historical Study of Black Single Mothers and Their Families," chapter 2 of her *The Rising Song of African American Women* (1994), describes the relationship between the past and present of racism and bondage in a much more persuasive way: "The only 'women' are those whose men have ultimate control over people of color. Thus, it becomes understood and axiomatic—to be white and female is to be 'woman' and to be white and male is to be 'man.' Black men and women are neither man nor woman; they are non-beings, e.g. chattel, niggers, underclass" (Omolade 1994, 25). The nineteenth-century cult of true womanhood was just one instance of a greater cult of gender under white Western hegemony in and beyond North America. Whether the antithesis of man and woman is rendered as chattel or underclass, the naturalization of manhood and womanhood serves a viciously political function; and this reconstruction of plantation power in subsequent colonial and neo-colonial contexts can be destroyed only when the white madness of masculinity and femininity is renounced in a vigilant and clearly revolutionary praxis.

Rape, Sexual Violence, and Chattel Slavery, Revisited

Yee's *Black Women Abolitionists* was unique in its treatment of a cult of true manhood. Histories of gender and slavery focus overwhelmingly on women, as if gender and women are coextensive and men have no gender. This observation points to a problem with the conceptualization of sex and gender across academic disciplines. For if there is a structural neglect of manhood in studies of gender, and if womanhood is misunderstood to be synonymous with gender itself, then this approach signifies an extension rather than an analysis of gender ideology, which traditionally inscribes women as being gendered and men as being generic or beyond gender. Without a doubt, this is why the cult of true womanhood is the focal point of historical writings that claim to be about gender and slavery as well as why these historical writings continue to naturalize manhood and womanhood so completely. Yet the madness of manhood or masculinity must be contested as much as the madness of womanhood or femininity in anti-slaveocratic work on gender.

A central effect of this conceptual shift would be a radical reorientation toward the topic of sexual violence. It is almost impossible to locate a text on slavery which does not construe rape as the bottom-line factor that differentiates the experience of slavery along lines of sex, or gender. Allegedly, the female can be violated, and the male cannot. This assumption is unacceptable, if not absurd, because it perversely requires heterosexuality to recognize exploitation and abuse. Not only is sexual violence reduced to whatever qualifies as rape, narrowly construed, but rape is also reduced to penile penetrations of female bodies, perhaps not even those unless they result in pregnancy and offspring. Yet to be African and enslaved in the Americas means to be barred from the gender conceits of empire, the humanity of manhood or womanhood and its Western heterosexuality. This sex could only transpire between those classified as human beings conventionally identified as men and women, not merely male and female, as non-human animals may be described. The white monopoly concept of heterosexuality will not admit any sexual activity involving chattels, beasts of burden, sexually convenient laboring animals, etc. Hence, heterosexualizing rape is especially nonsensical when it comes to the enslaved. Were heterosexuality and manhood or womanhood socially accessible to them, their sexual violation would not be systematically sanctioned by the slaveocracy. Crucially, the classification of Africans as sub-human facilitates these attacks against all Africans, since Black bodies can be abused as non-men and non-women by whites without white fears of homosexuality necessarily coming into play.[15] Ideologically outside heterosexuality proper, enslaved Africans are physically and symbolically assaulted by heterosexualism, which in racist fashion applies the concept of bestiality (and sodomy, etc.) for precisely this kind of violence.

At least two very popular literary texts counteract the historiographical repression of this reality in North America. First, in Gayl Jones's *Corregidora* (1975), the lynching bees of Southern U.S. history are described as sex circuses: "they make even that some kind of sex show, all them beatings and killings wasn't nothing but sex circuses, and all them white peoples, mens, women, and childrens crowding around to see" (125). There is no gender restriction in this show of sex and violence. Later, a female narrator recalls a plantation history that was unmentionable in Carby's "Slave and Mistress," not to mention Davis or White:

> She liked me to fan her thighs when it was hot and then one day she had me fan between her legs. Then after that she made me sleep with her, cause, you know, he

wouldn't sleep with her, and then after that something went wrong with her. She had some hot prongs she come after me with, and she told me to raise up my dress and I know where she was going to put them, right between my legs. (172)

Clearly, these hot prongs between the legs will be hidden by any logic of rape that mandates penile penetration and heterosexual copulation. A second, comparable scene of violation appears in Toni Morrison's *Beloved* (1987), when the morning rise of Paul D's chain gang is met with a series of white phallic invasions that are spoken and unspeakable at the same time: "Kneeling in the mist they waited for the whim of a guard, or two, or three. Or maybe all of them wanted it. Wanted it from one prisoner in particular or none—or all. . . . Occasionally a kneeling man chose gunshot in his head as the price, maybe, of taking a bit of foreskin with him to Jesus" (107–108). Revealing the vast array of sexual violence practiced in the name of slavery should produce a vast array of resistance tales as well. But these examples are found in Black literature, not in the discipline of history, and they come from authors whose narratives or statements have been charged with homophobia; these facts should hardly be overlooked.[16]

If the sexual abuse of males under slavery has been too taxing for historians to think or treat, this erasure is nonetheless complex. As much as "breeding" has been anxiously negotiated in North American debates, why wouldn't it count as sexual violence against all Africans, including the so-called "stud niggers" discussed by Thelma Jennings in " 'Us Colored Women Had to Go Through a Plenty': Sexual Exploitation of African-American Slave Women" (1990), for instance? An analytic escape hatch has been provided for contexts outside official U.S. colonization, as the very suggestive slave narrative of Esteban Montejo (1968) helps reveal. This narrative is cited by Rudi C. Bleys's *The Geography of Perversion: Male-to-Male Sexual Behavior outside the West and the Ethnographic Imagination, 1750–1918* (1995), which speculates on the practice of same-sex erotic activity among Africans enslaved in Cuba. It references some authoritative books on Brazil and Jamaica as well. Nevertheless, as is traditional, Bleys rationalizes any desire among and violence against males by blaming it on a shortage of females (34–35, 58). This theoretical inability to affirm racist sexual assaults on colonized males appears to be reserved for African peoples most of all, in spite of white society's infamous fetishization of Black male genitalia and physiques. What's more, the explanation that focuses all attention on male-to-female ratios narrows the scope of this practice in both time and space. Supposedly, it was only in times and places where there was a relative shortage of females that this sort of thing happened. This is in part the framework by which a whole history of sexual violence has been projected into Latin America and the Caribbean—away from North America, where, customarily, a superior balance in gender distribution is generally presupposed.

The Madness of Gender in Plantation America 47

Conclusion

Uprooting white imperialist politics of gender and sexuality here may present a unique set of intellectual problems. While certain U.S. norms or ideals may be criticized as racist, they are more rarely criticized as Western or European in origin or outlook. Barbara Bush's "'The Family Tree Is Not Cut': Women and Cultural Resistance in Slave Family Life in the British Caribbean" (1986) casually affirms, "It was in the interest of the planters to promote myths of the instability of the slave family, for this justified the exploitation and separation of slaves," who sustained "viable family forms based on African rather than European values" (126–27). Though Bush is preoccupied with proving a lack of promiscuity or immorality in her slaves, as if these evaluations were not culturally specific themselves, she directly identifies racism and white supremacy with Occidentalism. Merle Hodge's "The Shadow of the Whip: A Comment on Male-Female Relations in the Caribbean" (1974) similarly confirms a "West African matriarchalism [in] the Caribbean and indeed Black America on the whole" (116). The hegemony of the West is not ignored when Hodge inveighs against the accepted ideal of white womanhood, contending, "the revaluation of black womanhood inevitably also implies a restoration of black manhood, when the black man no longer forcibly evaluates his women by the standards of a man who once held the whip over him. It is one stage of his liberation from the whip hand" (118). If the essential vocabulary of gender is retained, the denunciation of racism does not eclipse the fact of cultural conflict from Hodge's vision. Blacks are never reduced to a social effect of some monolithic nation-state complex outside of Africa. It is not that this kind of analysis has not come forth under U.S. colonization in North America. It simply does not come forth with the support of academic commerce or colonial intellectual nationalism.

Yet the standardization of European sexual categories knows no geopolitical boundaries. Hilary Beckles's "Sex and Gender in the Historiography of Caribbean Slavery" (1995) is interesting in this respect. His engagement with well-known texts by Barbara Bush, Kamau Brathwaite, Arlette Gautier, Barry Higman, Lucille Mair, Verena Martinez-Alier, Bernard Moitt, and Marietta Morrissey leads Beckles to comment, "the post-structuralist assertion that the term woman is but a social construct that has no basis in nature has struck no central nerve, an insensitivity which says a great deal about the theoretical state of this recent historiography" (126). This statement is curious for several reasons, not the least of which is that Beckles includes his own name on the list of figures who ignore this naturalization of sex in the study of gender. The brief and odd reference to post-structuralism seems designed to scold the colonies for something like theoretical underdevelopment. But why should the demystification or denaturalization of sex and gender be classified as post-structuralist, always and automatically? On what elusive definition would post-structuralism be responsible for Toni Cade Bambara's "On the Issue of Roles" or Oyèrónké Oyêwùmí's *The Invention of Women,* for example? The "Derrida and Foucault" invoked by Beckles produce no such analysis of white racist gender or sexualities of imperialism; nor have any of their disciples, as a matter of fact. Furthermore, pronouncing something to be a social construct is not the same thing as perceiving it to be a culturally specific, Western bourgeois social construct. What is at stake in this discussion cannot be confined by any genealogy of European intellectualism (i.e., structuralism versus post-structuralism). It is a matter of colonialism and anti-colonialism, slavery and anti-slavery, imperialism and anti-imperialism.

Between British settler colonialism in the northern Americas and contemporary U.S. empire, the white racist madness of manhood and womanhood is reinforced in the past by academic literature composed in the present, even as Black radical traditions continue to erode this distinction between then and now. This is how the old world order of settler colonialism reconfigures itself in the new world order of neo-colonization. Thus, supplementing Bambara and Oyêwùmí is Sylvia Wynter's body of work on the global expansion of Western humanism—in graphically gendered terms:

> So we now see these categories emerging that had never existed before—whites who see themselves as true men, true women, while their Others, the untrue men/women, were now labeled as *indio/indias* (Indians) and as *negros/negras.* . . . You see, I am suggesting that from the very origin of the modern world, of the Western world system, there were never simply men and women. (Wynter 2000, 174)

These ultimately bourgeois conceptions (along with the heterosexuality to which they give birth) are all uncritically consolidated by conventional writing on enslaved Africans. When the particular form or content of this gender and sexuality cannot be found, their necessity is not then challenged; instead, their form and content are imposed in any possible manner, by any possible means. The contemporary U.S. domination of anti-Black, white-supremacist Occidentalism is thus naturalized or renaturalized via the culturally and historically specific categories of manhood and womanhood as well as homosexuality and heterosexuality. And enslavement to them can be presented as emancipation, once again.

All told, Deborah Gray White wrote against the weight of the Moynihan Report in an age of patriarchal revisionism. Notably, her *Ar'n't I a Woman?* came to overshadow the pioneering, politically charged essays of Angela Davis, who also wrote in the wake of Moynihan as a prisoner and high-profile activist in Black liberation struggle. Other, more conservative writers in the academy can now write as if "Reflections on the Black Woman's Role in the Community of Slaves" had never been militantly written. Darlene Clark Hine and Kathleen Thompson's patriotic *A Shining Thread of Hope: The History of Black Women in America* (1998) is a perfect case in point.[17] Davis had echoed the anti-fascist analysis of oppression and resistance written by Claudia Jones in a profoundly revolutionary post-war praxis. As Carole Boyce Davies illustrates, Jones is disappeared by citational protocols of the intellectual establishment. This erasure is extremely significant for the study of sexual politics and African enslavement since, unlike more institutionalized figures, she does not sever North America's social context from the global context of capitalist imperialism. Indeed, her framework was mirrored in Malcolm X's description of the U.S.A., at the Harvard Law School Forum of December 16, 1964, as "the racist and neo-colonial power *par excellence*" (X 1991, 167). From this standpoint, it is not nearly as easy to embrace the manhood and womanhood of empire in naturalized, nationalized terms. Writing to contest a Victorian cult of gender, while confined to an antebellum, southern region of one political state in a world system, Hazel Carby reinstated this structure of gender in a literary history showcasing a Black or "Afro-American" elite. Interestingly, perhaps paradoxically, almost all of these scholars write after the rise of the rhetoric of social construction in the West, and even though none of them besides Jones write before Bambara's 1970 "On the Issue of Roles," none of them resist the imperialist politics of sex or gender more categorically.

It is just such resistance that remains urgent all over the African world. The various insights of Bambara and Oyêwùmí should inform any angle on anti-slavery and slaveocracy, as should Wynter's extended discourse on the West. *The Invention of Women* ably criticizes a feminist rhetoric of gender, although not anatomical sex, mindful of how scholarship on gender animates a politics of gender itself (Oyêwùmí 1997, xv). This critique logically demands an interrogation of the privileged intellectual. While Oyêwùmí keeps the colonial invasion of Yorubaland distinctly in mind, personally claiming a politically exclusive royalism in the process, Bambara dissects and rejects the sexual conceits of empire as a mythology that it would be insane for Africa and its Diaspora to endorse. Her sight is deep, spanning the Black world as a whole, and it is no less sharp because of its depth. Neither Bambara nor Oyêwùmí faces the heterosexualism of the notions they otherwise debunk, while Bambara's grassroots praxis goes well with Wynter's anti-heterosexualist tracking of the bourgeois character of modern modes of domination in general.[18] For if, to date, no canonical histories of enslavement diagnose the "madness of 'masculinity' and 'femininity,'" they fail to do so in large part because they uphold sexual assimilation as a middle-class social ideal. Black history is academically packaged (explicitly or implicitly) as the pre-history of the Black "bourgeoisie," not the Black majority experience of Africans enslaved and resisting slavery, like elite domination, somewhere in Plantation America, or the whole "New World" of European empire.

3 Sexual Imitation and the Lumpen-Bourgeoisie

RACE AND CLASS AS EROTIC CONFLICT
IN E. FRANKLIN FRAZIER

It is simply not possible to use terms like "Black bourgeoisie" and "native bourgeoisie" without invoking E. Franklin Frazier and Frantz Fanon, either explicitly or implicitly. Yet these concepts are often casually used outside the critical frameworks that produced them. More generally, this vocabulary may be entirely avoided. All too few are familiar with the writings which popularized it in defiance of standard oppositions between race and class, not to mention sex and sexuality. Such learned ignorance is facilitated by the fact that the pertinent texts of both Fanon and Frazier have been more or less suppressed in favor of more comforting, less insurgent postures. Today, Frazier is less read than cited through the racist distortions of Daniel Patrick Moynihan, whose white sociology blamed Black oppression on "the Negro family" in the 1960s. Fanon is often absurdly commercialized in academia for just one part of one chapter of his earliest, most politically conservative book: that is, "L'expérience vécue du noir" in his *Peau noire, masques blancs* (1952), which was translated as "The Fact of Blackness," not "The Lived Experience of Blacks," in *Black Skin, White Masks* (1967a).[1] An institutional screening of their most profound political insights has obscured the imperative of coupling Fanon and Frazier, thinking them together rather than apart, for purposes of both comparison and contrast. This project can be initiated with a focus on the centrality of sexuality to the classic profile of the comprador elite, or "colonized bourgeoisie," across English-speaking and French-speaking contexts, from the Americas via Paris to the continental matrix of Africa.

Fanon and Frazier may be grouped with James Boggs, Amilcar Cabral, Harold Cruse, Kwame Nkrumah, Julius Nyerere, Ousmane Sembène, and Walter Rodney, for example, in reflections on the need for class analysis in Black liberation struggle worldwide. But the distinct writings of the former pay enormous attention to the role played by sex in the politics of empire, especially as it pertains to the subject of white imitation. Later on, Cedric J. Robinson examined "Euro-phoric" intelligentsias corrupted by the "sweet toxins of assimilation" in "Domination and Imitation: *Xala* and the Emergence of the Black

Bourgeoisie" (1980, 147–48); and, more recently, Ifi Amadiume derided the "continuous copycatting performance" symptomatic of "the colonized African mind" in the gendered state of neo-colonial domination (Amadiume 1989, xiv). Claudia Jones, Cheikh Anta Diop, and Frances M. Beale would add to this picture, along with the likes of Carter G. Woodson, Zora Neale Hurston, and Malcolm X (El-Hajj Malik El-Shabazz), of course. What's more, even these deft individual accounts only illustrate a greater tradition among the Black masses who have historically mocked this racist middle-class mimicry.

Both Frazier and Fanon sharpen these critiques immensely, and several aspects of their contribution may be engaged here. First, there is the need to interrogate the demand for a universal sexuality (a universal heterosexuality) as a colonizing scheme of white supremacism—for the idea that there are and can be only two true genders, natural and universal, continues to bolster imperialist missions of all kinds. Second, there is the need to stress the complicity of colonized pseudo-bourgeoisies in the social reproduction of white gender and sexual ideologies. The comprador elite's imitation of European erotic norms functions as a mark of distinction and, consequently, a medium of power in the context of Western domination. This symbolic reality is writ large in the very notion of a Black (or "native") "bourgeoisie," although it has been largely overlooked till now. In any event, no radical politics of gender and sexuality is possible without critical recognition of the colonial class aggression that sustains the culture of Occidentalism. A long-overdue recognition of the Pan-African kinship of Fanon and Frazier helps make such a Black politics possible.

"The Pathology of Race Prejudice"

An absolutely stunning identity of analysis emerges in the lifework of these two remarkable Black intellectual figures. We could even begin with Fanon's renown as a "revolutionary-psychiatrist" and connect that reputation with an early meditation by Frazier, the professed father of Black sociology. Just as Fanon considers "an authority complex, a leadership complex" in the colonizer (F. Fanon 1967a, 99), trouncing Octave Mannoni's projection of a natural dependency complex onto the colonized, Frazier himself diagnosed racism as a collective attitude in "The Pathology of Race Prejudice" (1927). The incisive thesis of this contribution to a white liberal journal of the Southern United States is that "the behavior motivated by race prejudice shows precisely the same characteristics as those ascribed to insanity" (Frazier 1927, 904). Frazier observes what he calls a "Negro-complex" in white populations en masse, while he probes the effects of an emotionally intense, dissociated system of ideas operating at every level of thought: "White men and women who are otherwise kind and law-abiding will indulge in the most revolting forms of cruelty towards black people" (905).

In most impressive form, Frazier insists that the insane are actually no less irrational than the sane. Both exploit the very same mechanism of rationalization to support beliefs that stem from a non-rational source. What separates them is the "greater imperviousness to objective fact" shown in the delusions of the mad than in those of their jailers. Hence, having noted that "when the lunatic is met with ideas incompatible with his delusion he distorts facts by rationalisation to preserve the inner consistency of his delusions," Frazier dares to state the obvious:

> The delusions of the white man under the Negro-complex . . . show the same imperviousness to objective facts concerning the Negro. . . . Pro-slavery literature denying the humanity of the Negro, as well as contemporary Southern opinion supporting lynching and oppression, utilises the mechanism of rationalisation to support delusions. (Frazier 1927, 906)

It is in fact this Negro-complex which reveals the collective lunacy of otherwise sane white men and women in the U.S.A., whether North or South, paralleling Fanon's subsequent tracking of complexes between Africa, the Caribbean, and Europe.

That this psycho-pathology is fundamentally sexual becomes most apparent when Frazier's thoughts parallel the writings of Ida B. Wells. An organic disposition to rape is routinely attributed to Africans by white supremacy or racism. The bestiality of "Judge Lynch" can therefore signify "a holy defense of womanhood" for "Jim Crow" society, which is thereby sanctified. Still, Frazier describes this sexual violence as "defense mechanisms for unacceptable wishes" and "compensatory reactions for . . . frustrated desires." Fear, hatred, and sadism combine to link the process of rationalization with the mechanism of projection, in other words:

> the Southern white man, who has arbitrarily without censure enjoyed the right to use colored women, projects this insistent desire upon the Negro when it is no longer socially approved and his conscious personality likewise rejects it. Like the lunatic, he refuses to treat the repugnant desire as a part of himself and consequently shows an exaggerated antagonism toward the desire which he projects upon the Negro. (907)

The content of this complex should take us well beyond racism or white supremacy construed as mere prejudice to a much larger, global historical canvas. For Frazier confirms Wells and her *Crusade for Justice* (1972) as he remarks that it is the white man's being "a greater menace to the Negro's home" and the white woman's bearing "unacceptable sexual desires . . . as horrible as incest" (Frazier 1927, 907) which yield the crazy projections identified as "Negrophobia" by the early Fanon, who wrote, "Are they not forever saying [in the Southern United States] that niggers are just waiting for the chance to jump on white women. . . .

Projecting his own desires onto the Negro, the white man behaves 'as if' the Negro really had them" (F. Fanon 1967a, 107; 165). Although Frazier is far from being a trained psychiatrist, his conclusion is no less profound: "The inmates of a madhouse are not judged insane by themselves, but by those outside. The fact that abnormal behavior towards Negroes is characteristic of a whole group may be an example illustrating Nietzsche's observation that 'insanity in individuals is something rare—but in groups, parties, nations, and epochs it is the rule' " (Frazier 1927, 909). In sum, "The Pathology of Race Prejudice" invokes a number of discourses, Black popular intelligence chief among them, to classify and condemn crudely expressed, attitudinal white racism as the savage sexual madness of the colonial couple in Plantation America.[2]

Rhetorically, Frazier's final allusion to Western philosophy (to Friedrich Nietzsche as a "licensed heretic") does not afford him the slightest protection from the Negro-complex; nor does his outward framework of social psychology. If, perhaps, he can ignore the possibility that a functional analysis of racism as lunacy could absolve the white lunatic, he cannot ignore the violent interjections of these lunatics themselves. The public he freely diagnoses responded with a demand for the immediate lynching of the author of this essay. Their brutish reaction served as an empirical verification of his politico-psychiatric theory of the Negro-complex, or white racist pathology, an obscene reality that would drive Frazier to change his name and domicile. His progressive engagement with psychological convention had defined insanity in practical terms as social incapacity; he contended that "the delusions of the sane are generally supported by the herd while those of the insane are often anti-social" (909). This normative delusion spells insanity and incapacity for the Black captives of a colonial imperialist order in which the dominant cultural identity is itself normally, nationally, and internationally experienced as anti-social, a destructive menace to society, home, and person. While they legally codify Blacks as "unfit for human association" (Frazier 1957a, 123), white bearers of the Negro-complex are clearly unsafe to be around, unfit to run anything or rule anyone, least of all the subjects of their racist delusions, phobias, desires, fear, hatred, and sadism. They thus forced Frazier's departure from the U.S. South as well as his tactical adoption of a new name or signature: where he had signed "The Pathology of Race Prejudice" as "Edward F. Frazier," he now identified himself as "E. Franklin Frazier."[3]

Unfortunately, Frazier would never pursue the implications of his early political psychiatric essay in his more famous academic sociology. He chose a different course of study. The insane white colonizer vanished from his reflections on U.S. race relations. Northern opinion and oppression were not incorporated into his conception of psycho-pathology. Instead, pathology was generally displaced onto another body and mind: the Black body and mind. While Fanon always insisted that the total war that is colonization yields various mental disorders in dominator and dominated alike (F. Fanon 1965, 251), Frazier's clash with the sick master class seems to vanish altogether with the violence of the white lynch mob. This may not be a cause-and-effect relation, but no more texts like "The Pathology of Race Prejudice" appear in Frazier's extraordinarily extensive list of publications. Even in the work he drafted at his career's end (Frazier 1962), when he and Fanon were being harangued by the FBI and CIA, a systematic deproblematization of white racist pathology persists throughout Frazier's passionate critique of the Black imitation-bourgeoisie.[4]

Frazier, France, and African Revolution

In the thick of what John Henrik Clarke calls the "African independence explosion" (Clarke 1992, xii), a Fanon very much at odds with the person who wrote his first book would make a new name for himself, renouncing that privileged class native to the racist rule of empire. Consider for instance his series of communiqués written for *El moudjahid* (The Freedom Fighter), the revolutionary organ of the Algerian Front de liberation nationale (FLN). Many were collected after his death with other political essays as *Pour la révolution africaine* (1964; as *Toward the African Revolution*, 1967). This Fanon makes a pivotal distinction between decolonization and independence (F. Fanon 1967b, 101); between true independence and pseudo-independence (105); between total liberation and puppet independence (196). He mocks the constitutional charade that keeps colonial structures intact:

> True independence is not that pseudo-independence in which ministers having a
> limited responsibility hobnob with an economy dominated by the colonial pact.
> Liberation is the total destruction of the colonial system, from the pre-eminence of
> the language of the oppressor and "departmentalization," to the customs union
> that in reality maintains the former colonized in the meshes of the culture, of the
> fashion, and of the images of the colonialist. (105)

Toward the African Revolution reprints his speech "Racism and Culture," originally presented in Paris at the First Congress of Negro Writers and Artists in 1956, convened by Alioune Diop's *Présence africaine*. It anticipates his *L'an V de la révolution algérienne* (1959; as *A Dying Colonialism*, 1965). In it, he incorporates sexual behavior, and erotic pleasure, into this litany for African self-determination (F. Fanon 1967b, 390). Fanon honed a new concept, too, "neocolonialism" (88), in 1957: "All the colonial countries that are waging the struggle today must know that the political independence that they will wring from the enemy in exchange for the maintenance of an economic dependency is only a snare and a delusion, that the second phase of total liberation is necessary because required by the popular masses" (F. Fanon 1967b, 125–26). The "neo" in neo-colonialism signifies regress, and the delusional complex of a functionary elite playing "progress" while their crass subservience to the white West makes matters worse for the African majority. With puppets and puppeteers so exposed, Fanon plots a fiery explosion of bona fide independence in the wake of *Black Skin, White Masks*.

Across the Atlantic, Frazier had been developing, for at least three decades, a comparable angle on the race and class that buffered white capitalist colonialism. He recognized with Lerone Bennett that "race relations in America" have always been relations between ruling elites (Bennett 1964, 25). When asked to write an essay on American Negro scholars' perceptions of Africa for an issue of *Présence africaine* edited by the American Society of African Culture (AMSAC), Frazier seized the occasion to extend the geopolitical scope of his *Black Bourgeoisie* (1957). Hence, he surveys the indirect rule of U.S. segregation in "What Can the American Negro Contribute to the Social Development of Africa?" (1958); he lambastes the Negro elite for its "uncritical imitation of white standards of behavior and the surviving values of the slaveholding aristocracy" and, subsequently, "the values of the white middle classes" (Frazier 1958, 267, 270). This group of uncritical imitators is in no position to further *any* liberation struggle, according to Frazier, whether it focuses on continental Africa or on African America:

> Africa is demanding an intellectual and spiritual leadership that has caught a vision of a new world—a world freed from racism, colonialism, and human exploitation. But the new Negro middle classes in the United States appear only to seek an opportunity to share in the exploitation from which they have been excluded and continue to be excluded except on an insignificant scale. Therefore, it becomes evident that the aims and aspirations of Africans in creating a new world cannot be limited by the narrow aims and aspirations of the leaders of American Negroes, who are merely seeking acceptance in the white man's world as it is. The American Negro is willing to pay the terrific price of the most servile conformity to the ideas and values of white Americans in order to be accepted by them. (276)

Several years before the release of Fanon's *Les damnés de la terre* (1961), published in English as *The Wretched of the Earth* (1963), therefore, Frazier reiterates his fierce indictment of the colonized elite, demonstrating again that the dossiers of Fanon and Frazier coalesce incontrovertibly, at times almost word for word, though their ultimate objectives would contrast as radically as their critiques converge.

However, in spite of his prolific intellectual output and the scholarship on the scholar himself, Frazier's political ideology remains a mystery to many or most. He may be seen as an icon of revolutionary radicalism or radical conservatism, or anything in between. Anthony M. Platt's *E. Franklin Frazier Reconsidered* (1991) captures this ambiguity in great detail:

> It is not at all easy to get a clear picture of Frazier's politics and world-view only through his interpreters. To sociologist G. Franklin Edwards, a colleague at Howard University, Frazier at one time "espoused a belief in democratic socialism." St. Clair Drake recalled that Frazier always lined up with "the communists" and was identified as a fellow traveler of the Communist Party during the 1930s at Howard University. However, Michael Winston, a former student of Frazier's, had no doubt that Frazier was "never a communist and was always openly critical of the position of the Party concerning the problem of racism in the United States." Harold Cruse went even further and located Frazier within a tradition of cultural nationalism that "cut the ground from under much of what later became Communist Party dogma about the Negro working class." Others did not even consider Frazier a leftist. Oliver Cox found in Frazier only a "red thread" of cynicism and doubt; to Pierre van den Berghe, he was one of the "establishment blacks," a darling of the white liberals; and Manning Marable, in a survey of the radical tradition of Afro-American intellectuals, damned Frazier with faint praise. It is not difficult, then, to appreciate David Southern's conclusion that Frazier was an ideological chameleon who "held a multitude of competing ideas, and which ones came forth depended on the situation." (Platt 1991, 175)

Moreover, Platt's own account of Frazier as an inveterate and uncelebrated radical (or, in the sociologist's own words, an "enfant terrible") is marred by his avoidance of the controlling theme of Frazier's academic work, assimilation,[5] which is to say, the so-called "civilization" of "American Negroes." Paradoxical as it may seem, it is this colossally conservative concern that generates Frazier's scorching criticisms in *Black Bourgeoisie*.

In a milieu as international as national, Frazier presented "The Negro Middle Class and Desegregation" (1957c) as the first MacIver Award Lecture when the American Sociological Society (ASA) honored his spectacular book *Bourgeoisie noire* (1955; as *Black Bourgeoisie*, 1957), which was actually written in France for a series entitled Recherches en sciences humaines. This had to be the version cited at the Sorbonne by discussants at the Black writers and artists conference, the proceedings of which were published in *Présence africaine* 8–10 (June–November 1956). Frazier had directed the Division of Applied Social Sciences at UNESCO from 1951 to 1953, speaking at the universities of London, Edinburgh, and Liverpool while based in Paris (Cromwell 2002, 41). Accepting his ASA award back in North America, after *Brown v. Board of Education*, amid Africa's "Independence Explosion," Frazier would address "a cleavage in the Negro community that cannot be ignored" (Frazier 1957c, 298). This social and economic schism is not to be conceived in aesthetic terms as "difference" or "diversity" or "heterogeneity," for a politics of domination is in full-blown effect;

and a polite pluralism is far from adequate to the task of confronting the class conflicts endemic to the racial antagonism that is the United States of America, super-imperialist power of a now neo-colonized world.

In some respects, by virtue of the author's status in his field, Frazier's portrait of the Black elite could be taken for granted even if its blunt political outrage is not taken seriously at the center of advanced Western capitalism today. Writing as a historicizing participant-observer in an ethnographic mode of "native sociology," Frazier redeploys the psycho-cultural angle of his text on white pathology to treat the behavior, values, and attitudes of a new Black middle class (Frazier 1957a, 13, 26). The result is equally famous and infamous. This "lumpen-bourgeoisie" (145) is characterized not only by racial subordination and socio-economic dependence, but also by systematic political collaboration, a deep-seated inferiority complex, a compensatory set of self-righteous mythologies, and a profound self-hatred exceeded only by an intense loathing of the Black masses on top of flagrant, idolatrous imitation of whites, or an abject conformity to white Western ideals. In short, a comprehensive material and subjective investment in the domestic and global status quo is in evidence.

It is actually uncanny how Frazier's analysis appears more and more accurate with the passage of time. Perusing *Ebony* or *Jet* magazine, watching the NAACP Image Awards or the multi-media charade of mainstream politics and academic discourse, we find that Frazier's insights scarcely need revision. His was a historical study or schematic, after all, and it is only several decades old; its analytic approach makes it more than an empirical study, historicist or not. Nevertheless, the presence of a Black middle class is continually touted as a completely new phenomenon, or even achievement, in North America. One can easily and without fear speak of class from this establishment angle insofar as the perspective is not one of class *critique,* since then class hierarchy and privilege will quickly become taboo subjects in conventional middle-class commentary. This is exactly why many critics can routinely use Frazier's terminology ("Black bourgeoisie," "new Black middle class," etc.) while steadfastly evading the world historicity and politics of his original articulation, which was quite radical in certain ways, and terribly conservative in others.

U.S. *Black Bourgeoisie:* "Durham" and "La bourgeoisie noire"

The issue is much older than the English edition of *Black Bourgeoisie.* Virtually all of Frazier's writings entail its socio-political economic thought, but the book's main precursors may be "Durham: Capital of the Black Middle Class" (1925) and "La bourgeoisie noire" (1928–30). Interestingly enough, these two brief essays both thematize a basically antagonistic relationship between white capital and Black pleasure. The Black masses barely appear in either piece, yet much attention is given to "the Negro." A ritual appropriation of the collective identity of the race by its narcissistic elite is performed repeatedly throughout the history of oppression and exploitation. Most egregious when executed in the public spheres of white nationalist domination, this cultural-linguistic seizure is well known, whether it is effected in the idiom of "Negroes" or "African-Americans," and Frazier is as guilty of it as the social class he scorns.

The "Durham" essay was a contribution to Alain Locke's anthology *The New Negro*. Against the elite cultural aestheticism of the Harlem Renaissance, Frazier champions an assimilationist economics. He opens with a reverse migration that takes us from a center of pleasure to what he sees as a site of abnegation, from uptown New York City to "a city of fine homes, exquisite churches and middle-class respectability . . . not the place where men write and dream; but a place where men calculate and work. No longer can men say that the Negro is lazy and shiftless and a consumer" (Frazier 1925, 333). It is here that Frazier first announces the birth of a Black middle class, the absence of which was a source of acute anxiety for those who promoted "Negro progress" in white bourgeois society. This initial sketch of Black social strata contained, on the one hand, a professional class merely imitating an actual middle class while identifying with an aristocracy; and, on the other hand, a working class comprising not skilled artisans but unskilled laborers and domestic servants, widely denounced for its racialized "love of pleasure" (333). The "New Negroes" whom Frazier hails in Durham "have the same outlook on life as the middle class everywhere. They support the same theories of government and morality. They have little sympathy with waste of time. Their pleasures are the pleasures of the tired business man who does not know how to enjoy life. . . . Middle-class respectability is their ideal" (338). The primitivism condemned in the white West as a rule and only provisionally and problematically in vogue up in Harlem is unambiguously rejected by Frazier in "Durham." For him, this city was the "promise of a transformed Negro" (339), whose professional subjection could enable psychic, economic, cultural, and political integration into "modern America" (340).

Platt's *E. Franklin Frazier Reconsidered* argues that "Durham" could not possibly reflect Frazier's true views, as Platt cannot reconcile its celebration of the middle class with Frazier's reputation for class critique (Platt 1991, 150–51). However, Frazier's politics of "culture" or "civilization" make sense of the alleged contradiction. The lack of a middle class is a real liability for white social economy in its bourgeois mode. So Frazier locates a small facsimile down South as a defense against racist cultural propaganda spread with a vengeance after pseudo-emancipation. Sylvia Wynter summons the white middle-class pathology of an earlier Frazier, not to mention Fanon, in her reflections on paternalism in "Sambos and Minstrels" (1979): "Central to the bourgeois ideology is the idea of the atomistic individual as agent. By constructing Sambo as the negation of responsibility, the slave master legitimized his own role as the responsible agent acting on behalf of the irresponsible minstrel" (Wynter 1979, 151). Accordingly, after chattel slavery is proclaimed to end in freedom, bourgeois discipline is allegedly needed to curb the pseudo-aristocratic excesses of a colored elite and the unbridled hedonism of a "reverted" African multitude. The real need, however, is to satiate a white racist psyche and to consolidate its industrial national comfort. Traditionally construed as responsibility's antithesis, Blacks are supposed to become productive and ungratified individualists, instead of ("lazy and shiftless") "Sambos" living in a savage economy of infantile pleasure. This is what it would mean to be "cultured" and "civilized" in a society of white supremacy. The always assimilationist Frazier could thus be overjoyed with the "evolved" elite of Durham, which was respectably middle-class in its work ethics and its opposition to an unmanageable Black sensuality.[6]

The promise that Frazier saw in "Durham" was never realized in the rise of a national Black bourgeoisie. Central to his own cultural-economic ideology is a distinction between old and new middle classes, a social distinction which resurfaces in his MacIver Award lecture as a nostalgia for the ephemeral charm of Durham:

> At one time the city of Durham, North Carolina . . . was regarded as a sort of capital of the old Negro middle class. As the result of the changes in the economic organization of American life as well as of changes in the Negro community, the capital of the Black middle class has shifted to Chicago or Detroit. This shift has been indicative of the emergence of a new middle class which no longer cherishes the values and social distinctions of the old middle class. The old middle class which placed considerable value upon family stability, mulatto ancestry, and thrift constituted a sort of caste in the Negro community. (Frazier 1957c, 295)

Readers of Frazier customarily ignore the fact that this new middle class, symbolized not by Durham but by Chicago or Detroit, would be the exclusive target of his sensational denunciation—this new Black "bourgeoisie" would renege on the old promise of total erotic acculturation in the West.

What distinguishes the older mock-aristocratic elites most from the newer lumpen-bourgeois class is the manner in which they mime white erotic norms in every phase of social existence. When Frazier condemns the new middle class for its uncritical imitation of white standards of behavior and value, he does not condemn racist imitation in the abstract. He condemns the socio-sexual imitation of the white racist bourgeoisie while promoting an imitation of the white colonialist slaveocracy: "The descendants of the free mulattoes became, after the Civil War, the core of a small upper class which undertook to maintain the American pattern of family life and conventional sex mores" (Frazier 1957a, 99). The older Black elite identified with the respectable pleasures of the aristocratic master and mistress, much like the exceptional elite in Durham. They always embody Frazier's all-time ideal. The new Black middle class does not cherish its racially coded models of "family stability, mulatto ancestry, and thrift." They are rebuked for a primitivized love of pleasure put on display as they uncritically imitate the unrefined (or less refined) white middle class. This historical schism between Negro elites is grounded in the greater schism dividing both Black middle classes from the masses of Black folk. The Black majority is portrayed as the essence of savagery—sexual savagery—thanks to its disrespectful repulsion of all white imitation, aristocratic and bourgeois alike.

"La bourgeoisie noire" continued Frazier's concern for a *correct* middle class, although this time in the mode of ambivalent censure. Only a couple of years after his counter-articulation of Locke's "New Negro," which was itself an elite appropriation of a militant movement slogan promoting cultural, political, and economic self-determination (Vincent 1973), Frazier exploits the conventions of middle-class critique for the readership of *Modern Quarterly*. This essay opens with a query that will dismantle some vulgar assumptions of the white Left: "Radicals are constantly asking the question: Why does the Negro, the man furthest down in the economic as well as the social scale, steadily refuse to ally himself with the radical groups in America?" To answer it, Frazier sketches Black social structure under white domination, wrecking the arrogant race and class pretensions of "radicals" who grope in ignorance: "Class differentiation among Negroes is reflected in their church organizations, educational institutions, private clubs, and the whole range of social life. Although these class distinctions may rest upon what would seem to outsiders flimsy and inconsequential matters, they are the social realities of Negro life and no amount of reasoning can rid his mind of them" (Frazier 1928–30, 379). This is to say, "race consciousness to be sure has constantly effaced class feeling among Negroes" (380), who will not function as a generic mass of wage slaves (with nothing to lose but their chains) available for political exploitation by a delusive, economically vulgar white vanguard.

Outlining the relevant marks of distinction as "property, education, and blood or family" (380), sexuality remaining tacit yet categorically graphic in each, Frazier begins by placing the majority of Black folk beyond consideration: "From ignorant peasants who are ignorant in a fundamental sense in that they have no body of traditions even, we cannot expect revolutionary doctrines" (381). "The Negro" must henceforth stand for "la bourgeoisie noire," which claims the race for itself in a fashion that preserves class hierarchy. Frazier rejects outright those whom he sees as something like a "*lumpen* lumpen-proletariat,"[7] as a prelude to his discussion of privileged Negroes and their conflictual relationship to white radicalism. White working-class racism is remarked with emphatic precision; and, in this context, so are the economic interests of the colored elite. Frazier finally observes that "la bourgeoisie noire" lacks both infrastructural riches and revolutionary desires. The history of race-class formation has left this Negro "wedded to bourgeois ideals" (382): "This group is no more to be expected to embrace radical doctrines than the same class was expected to join slave insurrections, concerning which Denmark Vesey warned his followers: 'Don't mention it to those waiting men who receive presents of old coats, etc., from their masters or they'll betray us'" (381). The presence of the middle-class respectability that was praised in Durham becomes a liability for Frazier's more or less radical audience here. The pleasure found by the new middle class in bourgeois ideals is ridiculed as perverse, while that found by the old middle class in aristocratic ones is canonized.

Never is there a violent and vengeful return of Frazier's "*lumpen*-lumpen" bodies, those "landless peasants" from whom he expected nothing. This is not the Fanon of later years. Frazier gives no more thought to those who lack proper blood, proper families (with proper genders and sexualities passed on via proper education), and property itself. Frazier's commitment to "culture" or "civilization" precludes such a reorientation, despite his offhand reference to the peasant revolt of Denmark Vesey and Gullah Jack. Till the end, a genteel class ethos remains normative and a revolutionary Negro race remains oxymoronic. Hence, "La bourgeoisie noire" culminates in the postulation of a "fundamental dilemma in Negro life." Since, according to Frazier, it is bourgeois socialization in the white racist West that makes possible the "civilization" of those whose primary struggle has been "to acquire a culture" (386), this cultural struggle takes complete priority over any and all class struggle that would threaten to subvert it. Frazier is not Amilcar Cabral. There shall be no class suicide in his universe; since one cannot ask the only "civilized" class of Negroes to revolt against the very system of their "civilization," a significant part of his dilemma is resolved in advance. The pleasures of insurrection are undesirable for Frazier, most especially among the masses of Black folk expelled from this conception of Negroes without a thought.

The Old vs. New Middle-Class Elite: Sex Mis-education

Indeed, Frazier at once performs and promotes the activity theorized by Carter G. Woodson in *The Mis-education of the Negro* (1933). Currently, Woodson may be a very safe symbol of domesticated Black history celebrations, or he may be celebrated in a different manner for the following statement:

> No systematic effort toward change has been possible, for, taught the same economics, history, philosophy, literature, and religion which have established the present code of morals, the Negro's mind has been brought under the control of his oppressor. The problem of holding the Negro down, therefore, is easily solved. When you control a man's thinking you do not have to worry about his actions. You do not have to tell him not to stand here or go yonder. He will find his "proper place" and will stay in it. You do not need to send him to the back door. He will go without

being told. In fact, if there is no back door, he will cut one for his special benefit. His education makes it necessary. (Woodson 1933, xiii)

He dissects mental (and material) slavery, during a period of nominal freedom, as a more "perfect device for control from without" (96). His text carefully considers what has come to be called "colonization of the mind," probably with far more power and precision than any text published since. For Woodson, there is no education under colonialism and imperialism, or under "slavery, peonage, segregation, and lynching" (xii), a fact which makes the school a "questionable factor in the life of a despised people. . . . Why not exploit, enslave, or exterminate a class that everybody is taught to regard as inferior?" (3).[8] Crucially, colonial schooling operates as sign and substance of social class status. The inferiority complex of the grossly mis-educated Negro produces systemic emulation of the white oppressor and a stern enmity for the Black oppressed.[9] Frazier's ultra-Westernized middle class (old as well as new) is described in Woodson's *The Mis-education of the Negro* as a "hopeless liability of the race" (xiii), decades before *Bourgeoisie noire* and *Black Bourgeoisie*. Having taught in various formally declared colonies for several years, and having struggled for much longer in the super-colony of the U.S. slave state, this father of Black history observes that "the average Negro has not been sufficiently mis-educated to become hopeless" (109). These are not the assimilationist politics of Frazier. Will we "live," asks Woodson, "or continue the mere imitation of others and die?" (180).

Black Bourgeoisie quickly proceeds to the matter of schooling because of the absence of capital in its subject's fiscal profile. The first chapter traces the Black elite's roots back to the accumulation drives of the free Negro caste before the Civil War. The Freedmen's Savings Bank exemplifies, for Frazier, "the aspirations of the Negro to conform to American ideals" (Frazier 1957a, 3). The dismal collapse of this scheme is relevant a century later, as Frazier reiterates: "the total assets of all Negro banks in the United States were less than those of a single small white bank in a small town in the state of New York" (8). The second chapter, "The Economic Basis of Middle-Class Status," shows that the Black middle class comprises professional and white-collar workers and a miniscule Black enterprise sector consisting of the smallest of small businesses adrift in a segregated service industry. There is no notable industrial or corporate capital, nor even a facade of political economic power on a national scale. Importantly, this racial privation is masked by a "myth of Negro business": Booker T. Washington dubbed his personal drudges "captains of industry" in the National Negro Business League. The amplified social as opposed to economic significance of this myth is revealed in chapter 7, "The Negro Press and Wish-Fulfillment." This rhetoric functions to "exaggerate the economic well-being of Negroes in the United States and to whet the appetite of the black bourgeoisie. . . . The white community is assured . . . that the Negro leaders who propagate the myth of Negro business are uncompromising enemies of any radical doctrines" (145). To Frazier, a "radical doctrine" is, strangely, some nebulous brand of integrationism, and his chief objection to even genuine conceptions of economic self-determination among Blacks is that they embody serious obstacles to assimilation. At any rate, the most substantial chapters of part 1 of *Black Bourgeoisie*, "The World of Reality," must rather meticulously discuss "education," the main social factor in the mobility and mentality of "lumpen-bourgeois" Negroes (26, 55).

A transition from superior to inferior middle-class dominance in Black communities is depicted as a conflict in "canons of respectability," and these canons are logically infused by distinct regimes of white colonial mis-education in North America. None of them are unconcerned with sex and sexuality; in fact, they are all said to require "a stable family life and conventional sex behavior" (109). Chapter 3, "Education of the Black Bourgeoisie," gives a partial account of the myopic dispute between Booker T. Washington and W. E. B. Du Bois, championing "industrial education" and "classical education," respectively: Frazier sides with Du Bois (whom he discounts as a self-serving snob, elsewhere).[10] The presuppositions of this debate are not critically examined. Bernard Makhosezwe Magubane sharply points out its unity of class interests in *The Ties That Bind: African-American Consciousness of Africa* (1987, 102). However, Frazier was spellbound by the fantasy of "regeneration" (Frazier 1957a, 57) previously expressed in Du Bois's *The Souls of Black Folk* (1903) as well. Emancipation is not conceived of as true and total liberation, independence, self-determination, or decolonization. It is conceived of as a cultural rebirthing of enslaved Africans in the matrix of oppression, a greater mis-education in the society succeeding official chattel slavery. Such a rebirth demands a certain sexual indoctrination. The proper embodiment of masculinity and femininity, or manhood and womanhood, is the hallmark of "civilization," a specifically erotic component of the "white man's burden." A new mind and body, new genders and sexualities would be molded in the image of the colonial mother and father, master and mistress, in the United States of America. This is racist social engineering mediated by the elitists devoted to "the making of men [and women]" out of "savages" (the doctrine associated with the classicist view of Du Bois) rather than the elitists devoted to "the making of money makers" (the doctrine associated with the industrialist view of Washington and his "Tuskegee Machine") (Frazier 1957a, 71–76).[11]

Frazier's *Black Bourgeoisie* mourns the passing of a genteel tradition in "Passing of the Gentleman and the Peasant," a subsection of chapter 5, "Break with the Traditional Background." Purportedly, there have been but two "really vital cultural traditions in the social history of the United States." The most significant is that of the sexually sensationalized peasants, the folk masses whom Frazier would desperately struggle to de-Africanize and whom he denied any traditional existence at all in "La bourgeoisie noire." The other is that of the "small group of mulattoes who assimilated the morals and manners of the slaveholding aristocracy," or "the [antebellum] southern lady and the southern gentleman" (Frazier 1957a, 98). The new middle class in Frazier actively repudiates each of these class-historical Black traditions, these colored elite and Black majority identities, at every opportunity and then some: "Through delusions of wealth and power they have sought identification with the white America which continues to reject them" (195). This piercing critique yields another conclusion extremely popular outside of academia, among "common Negroes." Writing on mate selection, bringing together "race, gender, class, and sexuality" in one motion, *Black Bourgeoisie* notes, "Since they do not truly identify themselves with Negroes, the hollowness of the black bourgeoisie's pretended 'racial pride' is revealed in the value which it places upon a white or light complexion" (28).

Nowadays, when class division in U.S. Black communities is broached, it is typically traced back to the *Brown v. Board of Education* decision of 1954, or the passage of civil rights statutes during the 1960s, or perhaps even the latest strain of Black (Republican Party) conservatism of the 1980s and '90s. Sociologically, Frazier grounds more recent social class stratification in a much earlier period. The economic shifts of World War I ignite a "Great Migration" of Blacks in the northern Americas, generating this distinction between an old middle class and a new Black "bourgeoisie" which overtakes it. There is increased occupational differentiation among Blacks as a result of increased urbanization, when the regimatic apartheid of white war industry is partially and briefly suspended with European immigration. This is not only what moved the capital of the Black middle class from Durham to Chicago or Detroit, it is also what altered the hierarchical structure of Black life. Significantly, it magnifies the importance of income relative to other marks of distinction, such as family, color, education, and property, all those marks which privileged the previous Negro elite. This process is recounted extensively by Frazier's *The Negro in the United States* (1949, revised edition 1957), even if his evolutionary, utopian integrationist optimism is entirely out of touch with realities of racism or white supremacy and empire.[12]

The sexually potent shift from old to new middle classes is presented in three stages, actually, in the spirit of Robert E. Park's "Chicago School" paradigm of social "deviance" and "pathology." The first stage may be most legible in Frazier's "natural history of the Negro family" (Frazier 1948, xix). Reprising the cultural politics advanced in "Durham," Frazier embraces those whom the masses despise as "house Negroes." They most approximate the "ideas and attitudes and morals and manners [of] white civilization" (32). Setting aside ancestral testimonies of systematic rape (53), Frazier actually endorses sexuality as the most effective means of acculturation. He claims, "Sexual relations [*sic*] broke down the last barriers to complete intimacy and paved the way for assimilation" (62), and he asserts that "the highest development of family life" was born of the "association [of] the men of the master race with the slave women" (68). For this apostle of Robert Park, the master bedroom is an ideal context for the erotic violence of "culture" and "civilization" in the white West.

Frazier's second stage involves more formal indoctrination by missionary schools erected after the Union's war for capitalist industrialization. Even less successful than the plantation in disciplining the masses, despite the use of physical as well as psychological violence (81), they could not control the "old promiscuity" of the "freedmen and -women." It was difficult, if not impossible, to replace their matrifocal "primitivism" or "motherhood outside of institutional control" (88) with patriarchal marriage or "a well-organized family under the authority of the father" (87). Yet and still, white missionaries were able to mold a select cadre of "Negroes" into "Black Puritans." They could instill in them their virtues of piety, thrift, and respectability (Frazier 1957c, 295). They could thereby reinforce the colonial traditions of colored ladies and gentlemen grounded in the plantation social economy of slaveocratic imperialism.

Frazier's third and final stage of middle-class transformation fixes the chief problematic of his entire corpus. The question is not how to recover from the sickness of psychological slavery, as it was for Woodson (1933, 16). It is how, or by which racist class system, the split Negro elite will manage to "uplift" itself from the masses. He laments the loss of virtuous Yankee missionaries that followed the "election of Negro administrators in Negro colleges," when, apparently, the standards of mis-education were somehow lowered: "in all the institutions, the canons of respectability were undergoing a radical change. Respectability became less a question of morals and manners and more a matter of the external marks of a high standard of living" (Frazier 1957a, 73). Apparently, Frazier held that the shift from a mock-aristocratic to a lumpen-bourgeois elite dominance in Black communities (after white wartime exploitation of Black collective labor) meant a reversion to Washington's "making of money-makers" and a repudiation of Du Bois's "making of men." In conclusion, *Black Bourgeoisie* criticizes the lack of a responsible elite expressing a "real interest in education and genuine culture" (193–94), which represents a culture of colonial-imperial domination, not Pan-African resistance.[13]

"Negro Sex Life" and Raw Sexual Racism

The previous white models of economy and identity which graft the piety and thrift of the second stage of mis-education onto the genteel paradigm of the first stage are crudely displaced by "The New Negro Middle Class" (Frazier 1955). Now the mis-education of the Negro, modeled on the petty and vulgar materialism of the nouveau managerial class, is hegemonic. The Black imitation of the white huckster ("Babbitt") overpowers the cultured ladies and gentlemen of the former colored upper classes. The myth of Negro business is theirs. They seek to corner the black market of North American segregation. All the same, as these middle-class genres clash, morals and manners meshing more and more with mere money, Frazier concedes that the post-war Negro is a "strange mixture [of] the gentleman and the peasant" (27). And in the end the older erotic histories have not been left behind, by any stretch. The new elite is pictured as no less a "confusion of 'aristocratic' and folk values" in *The Negro Church in America* (Frazier 1963, 81), while distinct as ever from its "great mass of less Europeanized" subordinates (77).

This renovated cult of gentility is showcased best in the obscure entry Frazier wrote in Albert Ellis and Albert Abarbanel's *Encyclopedia of Sexual Behavior,* "Negro, Sex Life of the African and American" (1961), where he makes it plain that white sociology's assimilation always refers to *sexual* assimilation, first and foremost. Theorists of evolution and integration obsess over control of the expropriated African's "raw sexual impulses" (773). This is the case whether official state rhetoric encodes racist domination as slavery, "separate but equal" segregation, or simply "America." Recycling a standard opposition between family traditions and sexual relations, Frazier sees the Civil War as subverting the quasi-discipline of the dominant culture among Blacks, at least until a "modified plantation system" brings "quasi-stability" and a "quasi-family" to "primitive peasant folk" (772–74), during white Reconstruction. The Great Migration makes matters worse. Frazier imagines an uprooted African sex running wild among roving men and women whose only culture is thought to be that of a biological hedonism. He views social disorganization as promiscuity which must be reorganized by any means. Here is the ideological basis for the "cultured Negro" and "Negress," or "man and woman of color," with no intellectual masking at all. It is from the sexual "primitivism" of Africa's Diaspora that the Negro middle class theoretically emerges, thanks to the class mechanics of each and every variety of colonial mis-education. The contrast between a "civilized" class and the "savage" mass of "ex-slaves" lays the foundation for any division between old and new elites, after global warfare, while all of the above are grounded, of course, in the greater contrast positing white over Black in general. These social distinctions center on a *raw sexual racism* that assigns raw sexual impulses to Africans in general.

A whole series of oppositional schemes of erotic or sexual identity may be witnessed in Frazier's sociology. There is the pseudo-generic model of the "natural male and female" of the West, to be embodied by the reigning white colonial couple alone; and, beyond an implied conflict between white aristocratic and white bourgeois sex, not to mention the white working class, there are the sexual antagonisms basic to Black cultural existence under white racist empire. There are "colored ladies and gentlemen," identified in strict opposition to "lumpen-bourgeois Negro manhood and womanhood." Then there is their shared identification in opposition to the erotic identities of the Black majority, the so-called common folk who menace puritanical, Victorian ways of life. There are never, ever merely girls and boys, men and women, without race and class. Analytically speaking, there are instead a legion of genders and sexualities, so to speak; and they cannot be reduced to the anatomy of any one white racist elite. This fact should serve to subvert the normative European concepts of gender and sexuality themselves, at long last. For anti-colonial readers of Frazier, expressly, there are at least twelve genders here, historically, to be read against the grain of empire; and, in the wake of this recognition, sexuality can by no means be confined to a single, simplistic dichotomy of universalized heterosexuality and universalized homosexuality. This is how Frazier's sociology can be extraordinarily useful or, rather, indispensable for political and intellectual analysis across time.

While "The Negro Middle Class and Desegregation" recalls that the despised Black masses had a reputation for being "anything but respectable" (Frazier 1957c, 295), the encyclopedia entry "Negro, Sex Life of the African and American" defines this class by its "free and easy sex life." The shift in upper-level social strata is further translated as a "sharp differentiation" of sex behavior (Frazier 1961, 774); and, crucially, this intra-elite racist sexual conflict highlights a nasty cultural politics of color. The old elite were decisively privileged by distinctions marked in *The Negro Family in the United States* as the social and economic advantages that came with white ancestry (Frazier 1948, 275). Emancipation was even resisted by many "mulatto aristocrats" who would not have their offspring schooled with "freedmen and women," whom they maliciously called "contraband" (277–78). Their blue blood is prized as *white* blood, or racially coded hereditary qualities (301). For, like mis-education, color functions as sign and substance of status in the absence of actual money or capital. *The Negro Family in the United States* confirms that the acute colorphobia of this colored caste was strongly rooted in pride in family background and a supposedly superior culture. Having a family tradition (not just conjugal relations) and cultural heritage (not just common schooling), both of which are literally and figuratively linked with whiteness, is paramount (308). Nonetheless, it is standard for U.S. discourse to restrict "color-caste" and "color-class" analysis to Latin America and the Caribbean. But this reality remains central to Frazier, from beginning to end, hence the distinction between the titles of chapters 20 and 21 of *The Negro Family:* "The Brown Bourgeoisie" and "The Black Proletariat."

If others will efface the explicit link between raw sexual racism and Black or brown "class" elitism, a centrally related matter is embraced by Western academia as if it were unrelated to these social politics of empire. It comes quickly to mind in Kwame Ture's "Howard University: Everything and Its Opposite," an early chapter in *Ready for Revolution: The Life and Struggles of Stokely Carmichael* (Carmichael 2003):

> There's one other class I have to mention. Professor E. Franklin Frazier, author of *Black Bourgeoisie* (praised be his name) died during my sophomore year. Fortunately, I was able to sit in his class before that sad event.
>
> That was a great class. Professor Frazier was funny and irreverent and I liked him. But I really disagreed with him on one issue: the presence of Africa and African cultural roots within the African community in America. Professor Frazier's position was that we were totally cut off from our African roots so that there were few if any significant African survivals in black culture in America. (Carmichael 2003, 130)

Ture could arguably be *the* ideological antidote to de-Africanization dogma, after Frazier's position is institutionalized as "Frazier's position" in U.S. intellectual spheres. He wrote in *Black Bourgeoisie* itself, "The folk culture of the American Negro developed out of his experiences on American soil. Whatever elements of African culture might have survived enslavement became merged with the Negro's experiences in the new environment and lost their original meaning" (Frazier 1957a, 100). He concedes that African culture does not of necessity disappear completely, at least among the masses. He only shows it to be resituated in a way which is impossible for sociology to grasp with its specific conceptions of culture and politics, not to mention its disciplinary devaluation of Africa and Africans as a whole. Clearly, a circular logic of white supremacy bars African cultural identity from serious scholarly consideration: In Frazier's world, "the Negro" must always mean the most assimilated caste or class. But his writing is not nearly as uniform as suggested in regard to Africa: "From this standpoint our study may have a broader significance than the group which we have studied. It may have some relevance for the study of the emergence of a middle class in colonial societies [*sic*], especially in African societies at present undergoing rapid changes" (192). Paradoxically, Frazier comes to sense a nonnational identity shared across the Atlantic by diverse populations of "Negroes," continental "African" and African "American." This global vision was brought to *Race and Culture Contacts in the Modern World* (Frazier 1957), a text and context that rarely factor into latter-day debates over de-Africanization and Frazier's own, official position on it.

By custom, he is opposed to Melville J. Herskovits and his *The Myth of the Negro Past* (1941), as Joseph E. Holloway's collection *Africanisms in American Culture* (1994) plainly illustrates. The reduction of Africa in the Americas to retentions and survivals could not have produced an All-African People's Revolutionary Party headed by Ture, who writes, "As sure as Africa is my mother, and she is my mother, revolution will come to America" (Carmichael 2003, 781).

Furthermore, Frazier's position scarcely originated with Frazier himself. The position institutionalized as his was more properly Park's Chicago School position. Its cycle of race relations (contact, conflict, accommodation, and assimilation) required de-Africanization in theory, whether or not the theory could ever be substantiated in practice. Likewise, Herskovits himself scarcely pioneered the study of African history in North America. The arguments for and research into African cultural identity are more properly associated with Woodson, his *Journal of Negro History,* and the Association for the Study of Negro Life and History, not to mention Du Bois and additional Black scholar-activists of this era, in which even white academicians had no outlet for non-racist scholarship on Africa outside of Woodson's journal. In addition, Herskovits's local and global politics of race make his installment as a white father of Africanism all the more absurd (Martin and West 1999), although a range of current African Diaspora frameworks fail to demystify the false opposition between him and Frazier.[14]

The fact is that Frazier feared that identifying "Negroes" in "America" as African would weaken prospects for assimilation and provide added rationale for Anglo-Saxon racism. Herskovits, he felt, could cavalierly ignore this danger, together with academic liberals who were themselves not Black. The greatest irony of all, perhaps, is that Frazier adopted Park's position on de-Africanization, a position Herskovits had shared in Locke's *The New Negro,* after Marcus Garvey's mass movement demanding "Africa for Africans, at home and abroad." Malcolm X, a shining son of Garveyite activists, makes this point in his Harvard speeches of 1964:

> Marcus Garvey was the one who gave a sense of dignity to the black people in this country. He organized one of the largest mass movements that ever existed in this country; and his entire philosophy of organizing and attracting Negroes was based on going-back-to-Africa, which proves that the only mass movement which ever caught on in this country was designed to appeal to what the masses really felt. (X 1991, 157)

Frazier admits in "What Can the American Negro Contribute to the Social Development of Africa?" that the fact of African origin had never been erased from American Negro minds (Frazier 1958, 263), even criticizing American Negro intellectuals who "denounced Garvey largely on the ground that he resurrected and emphasized the fact of their African origin" (273). When Frazier states for *Présence africaine* that "instead of seeking a positive identification in the traditional culture of the Negro folk in the United States or in their African origin, the middle classes seek to escape from their negative identification by becoming 'pure Americans'" (276), he again implicitly concedes the African cultural identity of Black folk in North America, concealing his own massive investment in assimilation when done in some appropriate, middle-class manner. He would never support Garvey's UNIA goals, any more than would the doctor from Chicago quoted in *Black Bourgeoisie* who joked to him that "Garvey's U.N.I.A. (Universal Negro Improvement Association) really stood for the Ugliest Negroes in America" (Frazier 1957a, 208n4). In any case, Frazier recognized U.S. "Negroes" to be every bit as African as Garvey—at the level of sexuality or "raw sexual impulses" which were supposedly all-encompassing.

What makes assimilation or white class imitation vital in this world-view is a socio-sexual discourse of "culture" and "civilization." It goes beyond Frazier's specific time, nation, and discipline, as it is a staple of European imperialism here and there, then and now, politically and intellectually. Frazier had underscored it in "The Pathology of Race Prejudice" as a madness projected onto Blacks by white supremacy (or its delusions). Wells laid it bare in her autobiography, *Crusade for Justice,* and her most militant praxis of journalism. So would Fanon, in due course. More recently, Wynter maps it out meticulously as a foundational dichotomy between rational and sensory natures in a modern Western bourgeois conception of human being. Frazier renders it visible, without challenging it, as an anti-African phobia of raw sexual impulses in imaginations of empire. It is this metaphysics of raw sexual racism that speaks through his desire for race and class assimilation in North America. Its white nationalist norms of mind and body script Frazier's "Black sociology" in supra-national environs.

Conclusion

How strange it is that E. Franklin Frazier has never been compared to Frantz Fanon at any point in either of their careers. The domestication of the former's increasingly international consideration of class surely has contributed to this separation of intellectual kin. It seemed to pain Frazier that he could not attend the conference where Fanon presented his paper "Racism and Culture" (in F. Fanon 1967b), and where *Bourgeoisie noire* was a topic of conversation before *Les damnés de la terre* (*The Wretched of the Earth*) was written. To the delegates, Frazier sent a trans-Atlantic message:

It is with deep feeling and regret that I am compelled to forgo the opportunity to attend. . . . A Conference of Negro Writers and Artists is of special importance at a time when a world revolution is in progress which will mark a new epoch in the history of mankind. This revolution is the culmination of changes which were set in motion by the scientific discoveries which led to the industrial revolution and the economic and political expansion of Europe which resulted in the dominance of the Europeans over the other peoples of the earth. . . . In Asia and Africa, where the impact of European civilization uprooted the peoples from their established way of life, new societies are coming into existence. . . . In the process of building these new societies, the writer and artist have an important role to play both in the realm of ideas and in the realm of values. They can play an important role in building up the self-respect of people of African descent outside of Africa as well as the liberation of the peoples of Africa. The artist and writer will help to determine the contributions of these new societies and nations in Africa to a new conception of human relations and of the relations of men to the resources of the world, and thus enable mankind to achieve a new stage in the evolution of humanity. (Présence Africaine Conference Committee 1956, 308)

These themes were picked up in Frazier's "The Failure of the Negro Intellectual" (1962), which was published posthumously in the year of his death. In it, he stressed "the absence of intellectual freedom in regard to national and international issues" among Negroes trapped under U.S. hegemony: "If they show any independence in their thinking they may be hounded by the F. B. I. and find it difficult to make a living. At the present time many of them find themselves in the humiliating position of running around the world telling Africans and others how well-off Negroes are in the United States and how well they are treated" (Frazier 1962, 59). It was just such FBI/CIA control that kept Black radical thinkers from attending Alioune Diop's conference at the Sorbonne.[15] Frazier could give the impression that the internationalist growth of his own thought resulted in a radical new appreciation of the Black folk majority. He refers to the sit-ins and "the revolt of Negro youth against the old respectable and conventional leadership which acted as mediators between the Negro community and the white community" (62–63), and he refers to Negro intellectual evasion of "slave revolts" and state repression: "Because of their eagerness to be accepted as Americans or perhaps sometimes because of their fear, they have written no novels and plays about Denmark Vesey, Harriet Tubman or Schields Green who went with John Brown. . . . Even today they run from Dubois and Paul Robeson" (64). Nevertheless, Frazier could never transform his thinking on the relationship between race and culture or colonial imperialist civilization. The "masses of Negroes" are always estranged from "normal family life" and "unfit for normal social life," in comparison to middle-class Negroes and white racist society as a whole (62). He believes that problems of economic and social organization must be solved before Negroes can become integrated and assimilated, and the problem is that the contemporary Black "bourgeoisie" is not up to the task (63). When the later Frazier criticizes the assimilationist elite, he does so from this ultra-assimilationist angle.

In a sense, this angle was decoded and mocked by Zora Neale Hurston in "How It Feels to Be Colored Me" (1928), which responds wryly, "Slavery is the price I paid for civilization, and the choice was not with me" (Hurston 1928, 153). Her celebration of "the Negro farthest down" (Hurston 1934, 59) supplies a fitting epigraph for any examination of erotic mimicry and empire, especially in light of Audre Lorde's distinctly African definition of the erotic: "the sensual—those physical, emotional, and psychic expressions of what is deepest and strongest and richest within each of us" (Lorde 1984, 56). Hurston equates white "civilization" with slavery and Black self-negation, affirming Black folk en masse as anything but an assimilationist minority. She scorns slavish imitation and praises "jooks" or pleasure houses in "Characteristics of Negro Expression" (Hurston 1934, 62), "jook joints" built near the very sites of labor that *The Negro Family in the United States* hoped would be camps of socio-sexual acculturation. For her the culture of "Negroes" is West Africa transplanted and open to original, ingenious reinterpretation (57–59). Her import for Pan-African deliberations on sex, eroticism, and white imitation (not "civilization") is unmistakable.

None of this is up for discussion in James E. Teele's *E. Franklin Frazier and Black Bourgeoisie* (2002), a rare academic collection devoted to his work. The third of the text that deals with the Black middle class and the Black community mostly attempts to manage the crisis Frazier provoked in a defense of the elite (and its Negro intellectuals), as if this elite (and these intellectuals) were synonymous with the community itself.[16] Anthony M. Platt's "Between Scorn and Longing" is exceptional: "With African-American businesses as marginal to the corporate economy as they were thirty years ago, with the black middle class still on the periphery of national political power, and with the New Right recruiting its first significant cadre of black neoconservatives, Frazier's insights seem as fresh and heretical as ever" (Platt 2002, 84). Here and elsewhere, others quibble with questionable details of one slice of Frazier: How exact was his definition of class? How big was the Black stratum then as compared to now? How can he be valid after the civil rights era? Yet Frazier's life-long study was not strictly empiricist but empirical, historical, and analytical. He went as far back as chattel slavery to examine social stratification within Black communities in the context of white domination, and he saw that stratification as a set of hierarchical relations, not isolated data restricted to one moment in time. He knew that the size of the elite was always exaggerated in myth and that its growth would be far from great in reality. He had seen how problematic conventional religious leadership could be, particularly when he cited student movements which took the mantle of leadership from preachers for more radical purposes, as Black Power prepared to take over from civil rights orientations.

Thus, Martin Kilson's statements that the "post-Frazier black bourgeoisie" (which is, still, no such thing) registers more "support for liberal Democratic party policies" than do white ethnic groups in America, and that "had he lived, E. Franklin Frazier would have been pleased" (Kilson 2002, 136), is truly absurd. It is an absurd validation of Frazier's insistence on the powerlessness of The Black middle class and on its compensatory power of make-believe. As Carter G. Woodson said ages ago that dependence on "two degenerate parties, being practically alike, merely contend[ing] for the opportunity to do the same thing," demonstrates "our ineptitude in politics" (quoted in Goggin 1993, 174–75). Unfortunately, Teele's *E. Franklin Frazier and* Black Bourgeoisie removes its subject from a Pan-African Black radical tradition of analysis. This tradition interrogates (or, at least, extends) rather than accepts European Marxist categories of class and their false universalization by white and some Black Marxists, not to mention capitalists. Its rejection of white racist imitation was voiced again and again by Ifi Amadiume, Frances Beale, Amilcar Cabral, Harold Cruse, Cheikh Anta Diop, Zora Neale Hurston, Claudia Jones, Kwame Nkrumah, Julius Nyerere, Cedric Robinson, Walker Rodney, Carter Woodson, and Malcolm X. Elaine Brown echoes it in her *The Condemnation of Little B: New Age Racism in America* (2002). She speaks of the "abandonment" of the Black masses by "New Age House Negroes" and "New Age House Negresses," crassly identified with "New Age Massahs" and "New Age Miss Anns." Vividly recalling Fanon as well as Frazier in her comments on Henry Louis Gates, Jr.'s 1998 *Frontline* report "The Two Nations of Black America," the former Black Panther Party minister declares, "The Gates model . . . severs all ties with his brother in the Field, hates his brother for failing to imitate him, a dark imitation of his 'white colleagues,' and would do more than snitch on his underclass brother but would, by disavowing him, join forces with racists to destroy him" (Brown 2002, 219). Teele's collection aside, in other words, there is no minimizing Frazier's terrible relevance to today's lumpen-bourgeoisie.[17]

The virtual identity of this Black bourgeoisie and Fanon's "native" bourgeoisie notwithstanding, Frazier could not champion a joyful mass destruction of white Western rule *à la* Fanon in *The Wretched of the Earth*. Whether violent or non-violent in theory or practice, a subversion of the white settler state and society is unthinkable for Frazier, who conceived of total liberation as mass assimilation led by an elite which should be as genteel as culturally possible. Often exploiting the treachery of the old middle class to reproach only the new "bourgeoisie," he betrays nostalgia for the plantation brand of comprador collaboration. Even as he maintained that the last thing the new Black middle class wanted was liberation, this sociologist of integration conceived of emancipation as liberation from Africa—that is, from a diasporized identity of African sensuality—not self-determination. A sexualized adjustment to the racist order of things is the noble but shirked responsibility of Frazier's Black "bourgeoisie," and a white patriarchal family standardizing gender and sexuality is the central offshoot of his Occidentalist ideal. No African revolution stands behind his critique of the colonized elite in North America.

Even so, the erotic embodiment of Black culture that goes beyond Frazier and the carnal dictates of empire can ignite the flames of an ecstatic politics of revolt with Fanon in *A Dying Colonialism, The Wretched of the Earth,* and *Toward the African Revolution.* For whether masculist or feminist, heterosexualist or homosexualist, European gender and sexuality remain at the center of miseducation and colonial missions, privileging comprador mimes. The naturalized and naturalizing notion that there are two universal sexes or genders which climax in one heteroerotic (or homoerotic) human sexuality is a primary resource of white bourgeois imperialism both past and present. An ideological weapon and mirage, this socio-biology underwrites the pathological projections of white supremacy along with all the slavish imitations chided and championed in *Black Bourgeoisie*. Antithetically, an anti-colonial recognition of the multiplicity of genders and sexualities, or of contentious erotic identities that dispute the normative concepts of gender and sexuality, enables the kind of radical revolution needed by the Black masses of Africa and African Diaspora in neo-colonial times. Anything else confuses the mission of true and total liberation with the sexual imitation of Frazier's lumpen-bourgeoisie, or what Fanon would call the "greedy little caste."[18]

4 Sexual Imitation and the "Greedy Little Caste"

RACE AND CLASS AS EROTIC CONFLICT IN FRANTZ FANON

Writing for *Freedomways* at the close of the 1960s, John Henry Jones would note in "On the Influence of Fanon" (1968) that his popular radicalism had more than a few forerunners in the history of Black folk struggling in North America. The classic anti-racist class critique supplied by E. Franklin Frazier might earn him pride of place on this list. Yet, other scholar-activists aside, a text like *Black Bourgeoisie* had as its goal not Black revolutionary independence but, on the contrary, white cultural assimilation. Frazier's profile of the lumpen-bourgeoisie is practically impeccable, nonetheless; and it is crucial to any examination of the erotic identities that continue to clash across the race and class context of what Fanon himself dubbed the "nation of lynchers" (Bulhan 1985, 34). Furthermore, recognizing Frazier as a significant and suppressed precursor of the author of *Les damnés de la terre* (1961; as *The Wretched of the Earth,* 1963), en route to a renewed and detailed analysis of Fanon, is essential given the fear and terror the latter's words still inspire when quoted by Black subjects of U.S. colonization. Fanon's fearsome judgments have been frequently dodged and dismissed here with a charge of geopolitical "irrelevance," as if his work could not possibly apply to this African Diasporic space, even though he only replicates, in so many respects, the prior judgments of Frazier.

The African revolution that consumes the majority of Fanon's writings was conspicuously absent from *Peau noire, masques blancs* (1952; as *Black Skin, White Masks,* 1967), typically the only Fanon trafficked today by the intellectual apparatus of the West. His graphic guerilla praxis is washed away especially when he is processed for consumption in academia, where an extremely partial, problematic, and often chronically ambivalent engagement with him is the rule. Through such post-mortem machinations, he may become a pure Freudian or Lacanian psychoanalyst, for example, a good Sartrean existentialist, a prototypical "ethno-philosopher," or a post-colonial as opposed to an anti-colonial theorist, not to mention the consummate "native intellectual" that he famously disdained and denounced. Perhaps it is a bold testament to Fanon and the work he completed in his all-too-brief life that he must be so disfigured in the service of empire—for neo-colonial counter-revolution—by selective readings of *Black Skin, White Masks.*

Decades ago, Tony Martin's "Rescuing Fanon from the Critics" (1970) remarked that most of his detractors condemned him according to European orthodoxies of Marxism. By the 1980s and '90s, however, those who devoured and then disavowed Fanon tended to do so under a similarly orthodox banner of "gender and sexuality." It is suggested that his writings are the essential, inevitable, and incorrigibly pathological effect of Black nationalism. Tellingly, this suggestion is made despite Fanon's very early mobilization for a sexually egalitarian Black radicalism in a world dominated by white nationalism: Toni Cade Bambara invoked his *L'an V de la révolution algérienne* (1959; as *A Dying Colonialism,* 1965) in "On the Issue of Roles" (1970); Angela Davis made much the same appeal in her "Reflections on the Black Women's Role in the Community of Slaves" (1971), not to mention her personal and political correspondence with George Jackson, author of *Soledad Brother* (1970) and *Blood in My Eye* (1972) and field marshal of the Black Panther Party (Aptheker 1975); and T. Denean Sharpley-Whiting recalls comparable commentary by Linda La Rue and Kathleen Cleaver, as well as bell hooks and Frances Beale, in her more recent study, *Frantz Fanon: Conflicts and Feminisms* (1998). Martin's rescue mission made an effort to reconcile Fanon to the Marxism that vilified him in death, stressing his persistent anti-capitalist stance from beginning to end. But another task remains at least as important. Most Fanon scholarship fails to acknowledge that the bulk of his corpus is committed to a radical, revolutionary dismantling of a certain colonial conservatism (simultaneously racial and sexual) which had appeared in his own name via *Black Skin, White Masks,* an anything but Black nationalist text. Cedric J. Robinson, in "The Appropriation of Fanon" (1993), observes that he devoted himself to a class suicide of the colonized elite. It can and must be added that his decided Pan-African internationalist rejection of empire also involved a scrupulous rejection of an erotics of Europe embodied by much of the first Fanon, which is only falsely presented as the definitive "Fanon" (or "Fanon, proper"), for eminently political reasons, of course.

Colonial Racism—Culture and Biology: *Toward the African Revolution*

Once, many of Fanon's more perceptive readers could notice the lack of a militant agenda in his inaugural work, often understanding his work overall as divided into several, perhaps unspecified, phases. A detailed analysis of this sort is still in order; and it might begin with a review of two documents collected posthumously in *Pour la révolution africaine* (1964; as *Toward the African Revolution,* 1967): "Antillais et Africaines" ("West Indians and Africans") and "Racisme et Culture" ("Racism and Culture"). Their juxtaposition may highlight an initial ideological movement evaded by so many readers in contemporary academia. Chronologically and otherwise, "West Indians and Africans" is closer to *Black Skin, White Masks,* which it cites in its opening line: "I mean, for example, that the enemy of the Negro is often not the white man but a man of his own color" (F. Fanon 1967b, 17). Can Black enemies of Blacks really be distinguished from white enemies of Blacks, under white colonial oppression of Blacks? What follows this statement is a genealogy and criticism of the Negritude identified with Aimé Césaire, Léon-Gontran Damas, and Léopold Sédar Senghor (as well as Paulette and Jane Nardal, among others). The political character of Fanon's criticism will transform considerably over time. For now, however, nowhere in sight is either the violent decolonization of *A Dying Colonialism* and *The Wretched of the Earth* or the cultural expression of anti-colonialism that he would imagine in "Racism and Culture," his presentation to the First Congress of Negro Writers and Artists in Paris in 1956.

"West Indians and Africans" is more concerned with explicit biological categories of race and what Merle Hodge (1972) calls the "French Caribbean New Negro." Fanon only simulates aversion to "the great white error" (F. Fanon 1967b, 27) to which Negritude was a response. While he dismisses the global culture of the Negro world as a mirage, he modestly deflects, correspondingly, only the error of scientific racism, rather than the whole "civilization" of the white racist West. That culture remains very much a mirage. He is in search of an individualism that quickly disappears in collective independence struggle, according to "Concerning Violence," the first chapter of *The Wretched of the Earth* (F. Fanon 1963b, 47). In 1955, he objects to the concept of a Negro people by insisting that "except for cultural influences, nothing is left. . . . The object of lumping all Negroes together under the designation of 'Negro people' is to deprive them of any possibility of individual expression" (F. Fanon 1967b, 17). This reduction to nothingness entails an exaggerated focus on distinctions among Africans that is never applied to the hegemonic identity of Europe. "There is as great a difference between a West Indian and a Dakarian as between a Brazilian and a Spaniard" (17), he maintains. But it is important to ask, of what West Indians and Brazilians does he speak, in this odd comparison of cities, regions, and states, some colonizing and others colonized? In what way are these geopolitical constructs critically sacrosanct, when they are equally crafted in race and empire themselves? Unnerved by a budding Negritude in Martinique, and as yet without his eventual Pan-African point of view, Fanon ignores his prior revelation in *Black Skin, White Masks:* "Against all the arguments I have just cited, I come back to one fact: Wherever he goes, *the Negro remains a Negro*" (F. Fanon 1967b, 173). Why should argument be marshaled against fact, anyway, in the face of Black cultural identification? Fanon's original critique of Negritude could be couched in a defense of French identification, culturally (if not biologically). A fundamental destabilization of France, or Europe, or what Sylvia Wynter recalls as "*Blanchitude*" (Wynter 1979, 149) is still forthcoming.

Fanon supposes that the Caribbean subject of "West Indians and Africans" has experienced metaphysics only twice, and these experiences are tied to three related historical events (F. Fanon 1967b, 21–26). "The first event was the arrival of Césaire" (21). It was the *retour* or return of Césaire *à la Notebook of a Return to the Native Land,* his *Cahier d'un retour au pays natal* (1939). As a result, Fanon can recognize a revolution in social relations, on the one hand, while upholding a status quo view of racial relations, on the other hand: "In Martinique it is rare to find hardened racial positions. The racial problem is covered over by economic discrimination and, in a given social class, it is above all productive of anecdotes" (18). A virtual democracy of race is implied, until he concedes a problem only at the trivialized level of anecdotes, and then it is covered over crudely by class. This doctrine will be rewritten quite famously by *The Wretched of the Earth.* At this point, though, "we have proof that questions of race are but a superstructure, a mantle, an obscure ideological emanation concealing an economic reality" (18). No wonder this Fanon could not welcome Césaire without ambivalence, when the latter came back to pronounce "that it is fine and good to be a Negro" (21), and "the '*big black hole*' was a source of truth" (22). The second event here is the defeat of France in Europe's World War II. It allows racist soldiers stationed on the island to be exposed, thanks to an extended German blockade, producing Fanon's "first metaphysical experience" (23). It is in this context that Césaire midwifes a local revolution in Negritude: West Indians are said to undergo a metamorphosis in their bodies and, relatedly, undertake a "valorization of what had been rejected" in their minds, namely Africa and Africans (24). The third historical event of this scheme is the delegation, by "the elections that followed the Liberation," of "two communist deputies out of three. . . . The proletarian of Martinique is a systematized Negro" (24), Fanon concludes. The problem for "West Indians and Africans" is his belief that West Indians could not possibly find acceptance in Africa after Negritude's revolution in consciousness. This unqualified and unsubstantiated rejection is supposed to produce a second metaphysical experience in the Caribbean (26).

This is all extremely ironic for a number of reasons. Of course, Fanon would himself go to Africa. He will stand for African revolution, physically and metaphysically, throughout the continent and the world at large. The West Indians who find nothing but rejection among Africans turn out to be not simply West Indians. They are not the "proletarian Negro." It is quite clear that the "Martiniquans" in "West Indians and Africans" were synonymous with those who were "neither white nor Negro" (26); in other words, they constituted a mulatto or métis middle class. The alleged lack of "hardened racial positions" is laid bare as a myth, despite the official line: "One needed only to have children by someone less black than oneself. There was no racial barrier, no discrimination." If "in Africa the discrimination was real" (26), it was also very real for those in Martinique who were not privileged by color, class, or caste. Fanon feigns a "quasi-metropolitan" ignorance in the same fashion when he mentions the colonial ranking of Guadeloupe beneath Martinique: "as people may or may not know—Guadeloupe, for some reason or other was considered a country of savages. Even today, in 1952, we hear Martiniquans insist that they . . . are more savage than we are" (20). This ranking is colonial inasmuch as Guadeloupeans are coded as darker and more African than Martiniquans under empire.[1] The Martinique of the darker, proletarian Negro is not rendered as Martiniquan or West Indian. The "West Indians" of Fanon's "West Indians and Africans" are largely the colored elite that wants little to do with Africa before and after Negritude, or 1939; and it is from the standpoint of a culturally and politically conservative, racially mixed stratum that Fanon presented African identification as "the great black mirage." Thus, Pan-Africanism was quite partially understood, in purely biological terms. Yet Césaire could clarify his position on Africa and the politics of culture in "Culture and Colonisation," his own presentation to the First Congress of Negro Writers and Artists:

> This, I submit, is what legitimizes our present meeting. All who have met here are united by a double solidarity; on the one hand, a *horizontal solidarity,* that is, a solidarity created for us by the colonial, semi-colonial or para-colonial situation imposed upon us from without; and on the other, a vertical solidarity, a *solidarity in time,* due to the fact that we started from an original unity, the unity of African civilization, which has become diversified into a whole series of cultures all of which, in varying degrees, owe something to that civilisation. (1956, 195)

This conception would make far more sense to a later, revolutionary Fanon, with the lived experiences of Martinique, France, and Algeria behind him.

In the context of *Présence africaine*'s formal declaration of Black cultural independence, Fanon surveys the bloody history (F. Fanon 1988, 31) of cultural racism (32) in "Racism and Culture," where he examines its effects upon colonizer and colonized. His profile of racist culture matches Frazier's portrait of a pathological white psyche not only because "America" is rendered synonymous with the monstrosity of racism (F. Fanon 1967b, 36), but because the whole history of European imperialism is seen to be saturated by delusions of white supremacy. While Fanon may vacillate on some matters in this watershed speech, he is unambiguous on the mechanics of Western rule. What the colonizer achieves in the colonies is not a "total disappearance of the pre-existing culture" of the colonized. Rather, a "continued agony," or "mummification," is imposed on this culture instead. The stifling nativism administered under the guise of national respect signifies, for Fanon, "the most utter contempt" and, further, "the most elaborate sadism" (34). This remarkable sadism boomerangs. Its afflictions perversely satisfy the settler's cultural superiority complex, much as the rituals of lynching satiate white colonial madness in Frazier's "The Pathology of Race Prejudice" (1927). Fanon does not confront the pathology of European culture and elite Westernization in the Caribbean so ruthlessly in "West Indians and Africans," in which his critical interest in culture was marginal, at best.

Delivered just prior to his resignation from the French civil service, arguably after his actual enlistment in the Algerian FLN, Fanon's "Racism and Culture" speech is quite a transitional text. It betrays an intense disaffection with the "metropole" that he had never before experienced, or at least recorded. It is written in a frame of mind that is decolonized or decolonizing vis-à-vis racist politics of culture as well as racial categories of biology. And it foreshadows positions formulated more radically in *A Dying Colonialism, The Wretched of the Earth,* and the rest of the political essays of *Toward the African Revolution.*

In fact, as Fanon reflects on cultural racism and the colonized, he instinctively reflects on the *assimilés* or *évolués,* the assimilationist class most acutely miseducated in the colonialist mirage of "civilization." He recalls how, infected with an inferiority complex, it strives "to imitate the oppressor and thereby to deracialize itself" (F. Fanon 1967b, 38). He insists that although this agonizing process is officially dubbed "assimilation," a more accurate description would be "alienation," for the assimilationist procedure is never wholly successful. This may be attributed to "unforeseen, disparate phenomena" as much as to the intransigent logic of racism itself (38). "Racism and Culture" hesitates to wholly affirm the power of colonized resistance to cultural colonization, the potent pleasures of this power that will explode in Fanon soon enough. Even so, the erotic character of this drama of alienation is underscored: "Having judged, condemned, abandoned his cultural forms, his language, his food habits, his sexual behavior, his way of sitting down, of resting, of laughing, of enjoying himself, the oppressed flings himself upon the imposed culture with the desperation of a drowning man" (39). While in Frazier's *Black Bourgeoisie* the elite's self-hatred (or self-aversion) indicates that they are hopelessly "becoming NOBODY" (Frazier 1957a, 28), in Fanon there is salvation of sorts for these select subjects through militant liberation struggle for bona fide independence: African revolution can save them from alienation or cultural, political, and economic mummification by white European imperialism, in conjunction with the masses of the colonized.

This anti-colonial politics of culture is so antithetical to the posture Fanon previously upheld that "West Indians and Africans" appears terribly misplaced in *Toward the African Revolution.* In his editorial note, François Maspero states that Fanon's studies put him in a privileged position to proclaim these dynamite polemics (F. Fanon 1967b, viii). But those studies entail tremendous baggage that "Racism and Culture" visibly begins to abandon in favor of FLN combat. The only major posture found in both "West Indians and Africans" and "Racism and Culture" might involve an uneven use of Marxist economics. If, at first, "questions of race are but a superstructure, a mantle, an obscure ideological emanation concealing an economic reality" (18), this reductionism is later withdrawn with the admission that "the idea that one forms of man is never totally dependent on economic relations" (40). Any accommodation to Western labor would be wrecked in *The Wretched of the Earth,* and in a way which inspires the Marxist backlash addressed by Martin: "In the colonies the economic substructure is also a superstructure. The cause is the consequence; you are rich because you are white, you are white because you are rich" (F. Fanon 1963, 40). In the essays compiled by Maspero, too, Fanon nullifies European dogma on African culture and "class consciousness" simultaneously: "In a colonial country, it used to be said, there is a community of interests between the colonized people and the working class of the colonialist country. The history of the wars of liberation waged by the colonized peoples is the history of the non-verification of this thesis" (F. Fanon 1967b, 82). More appropriately placed in this context is "Blood Flows in the Antilles under French Domination," an essay originally published in *El moudjahid* in 1960, in which the "fiction of the French Antilles" is blasted on behalf of Caribbean federation, and in which Césaire is faulted for tactical political accommodation with France rather than worldwide African identification (168). The Martiniquan masses are his focus this time (169), as are Afro-Caribbeans as a whole in "Aux Antilles, Naissance d'une Nation?" (1958). This last selection was not included in the English translation *Toward the African Revolution,* concluding as it does with the fiery Black poetry of Haiti's Jacques Roumain. Its lines were translated (by Joanne Fungaroli and Ronald Sauer) in *When the Tom-Tom Beats* (1995):

> Well, it's like this:
> we others
> negroes
> niggers
> filthy negroes
> we won't take anymore
> that's right
> we're through
> being in Africa
> in America
> your negroes
> your niggers
> your filthy niggers
> we won't take anymore. . . . (Roumain 1995, 85)

Sex and Empire, Oedipus and Negrophobia:
Black Skin, White Masks

Fanon did not voice this reversal of values in *Peau noire, masques blancs* or *Black Skin, White Masks*, in which the more or less Freudian half of an "economic-psychological system" (F. Fanon 1967a, 35) takes center stage. This Fanon fights off a primitivism that is fundamental to Occidentalism and its racializing opposition of mind and body (mind over body), without attacking the whole European approach to knowledge at the bottom of it. If, as David Caute once observed, *Black Skin, White Masks* is comparatively "heavy with scholarly references and footnotes" in an effort to establish itself as the work of an "emerging intellectual flexing his academic muscles" (Caute 1970, 29), then the carnal history of white racist empire can be probed to comprehend such an overwrought literary design.

Sexuality permeates the pages of the more naive Fanon long before the sensationalized chapters of *Black Skin, White Masks*: "The Woman of Color and the White Man" and "The Man of Color and the White Woman," besides "The Fact of Blackness." There are the cultivated phobias of the privileged *évolués*, the "evolved" elite for whom colonial reason signifies a promise of salvation. Fanon begins his discourse with a refusal to shout. "For it's been a long time since shouting has gone out of my life" (F. Fanon 1967a, 7). He strikes a placating, dispassionate pose, against politics: "These truths do not have to be hurled in men's faces. They are not intended to ignite fervor. I do not trust fervor. Every time it has burst out somewhere, it has brought fire, famine, misery. . . . And contempt for man" (9).[2] While every other Fanon book would be written most fervently, to effect explosion after explosion in the very name of humanity, the willingness to shout is explicitly recovered in *Toward the African Revolution*'s "Letter to a Frenchman": "I want my voice to be harsh, I don't want it to be beautiful" (F. Fanon 1967b, 49). "Truth" will get graphically identified with African revolution itself in the end (F. Fanon 1963, 49). By contrast, the colonized intellect of *Black Skin, White Masks* recycles the Western notion of "civilization" in which the rational is poised against all things "primitive," the emotional, the sensual, and the passionately sexual most of all.

Robinson's claim in "The Appropriation of Fanon" that *Black Skin, White Masks* takes its class-specific subject as a simple racial subject seems to be right on the mark. Still, Fanon is unequivocal in noting the cultural-economic parameters of this inquiry at the outset and in closing. The reader is initially told that what follows does not concern the "jungle savage" who lacks the appropriate metaphysical faculties (F. Fanon 1967a, 12). The "quest for disalienation" is recast, ultimately, as a purely intellectual one that is irrelevant to the worker on the sugar plantation in Le Robert, who must fight (224), since the ideal opportunity to ingest abstract values is thwarted by hunger (95–96). The discussion of class, speech, and pilgrimage to Paris in chapter 1, "The Negro and Language," is therefore telling: "In every country of the world there are climbers, 'the ones who forget who they are,' and, in contrast to them, 'the ones who remember where they came from'" (37). In short, Fanon's *Black Skin, White Masks* narrows its subject to the "attitudes that the Negro adopts in contact with white civilization" (12). It is a somewhat class-conscious and seriously class-specific study of race and racism; and, as such, it is a class-driven text whose bourgeois ambition boldly centers the colored elite as the only group fit to represent its race in any intellectually respectable manner. The masses remain swamped in the colonized world of embodiment. This is neither a mishap, nor a secret, nor much of a surprise. The elite appropriation of the majority identity is secured with the ideological aid of an empire that defines the Black majority (or its "constitution") as characterized by those same "base" sensory pleasures sublimated— or repressed—by the white racist West. Hence the old colonial humanism appears to be writ large in this Fanon's final line of prayer: "O my body, make of me always a man who questions!" (232).

Though *Black Skin, White Masks* is renowned for its contempt for the biological self-hatred invented by colonial racism, its cultural orientation stays riveted on the French identity of European colonizers. Its mythological manhood and womanhood partner to provide the model for a gendered humanity which Fanon would move to violently overthrow in Algeria's anti-colonial struggle. The sexuality of Western domination is critiqued and recast by the two chapters that follow "The Negro and Language," in which Fanon wrote, "The black man who has lived in France for a length of time returns radically changed. To express it in genetic terms, his phenotype undergoes a definitive, an absolute mutation" (19). "He is incarnating a new type of man that he imposes on his associates and his family" (36). There is no such chapter as "The Man of Color and the Woman of Color," or any other combination of the roles scripted in "The Woman of Color and the White Man" and "The Man of Color and the White Woman." As Hodge's "Novels on the French Caribbean Intellectual in France" (1972) helps reveal, an elite ethos of assimilation guides Fanon's legendary analysis of "lactification" (F. Fanon 1967a, 47), or the social dynamic of colonized subjects drinking from milk of the white "mother country's" colonization. Hodge comments that most intellectuals who journey to Paris bring as their only armor both French enculturation and an essential faith in French liberalism. She also states that the high point of this philosophy for the alienated elite is "Universal Love" (Hodge 1972, 230). This socio-sexual eros (of "Universal Man" and "Universal Woman," as it were) is idealized in the white bodies of the West alone, so Fanon entertains erotic dynamics of racism and recognition unimagined by G. W. F. Hegel. To be validated as a human being under the hegemony of Europe—*heterosexualist* Europe—this man of color must ask, "Who but a white woman can do this for me?" (63); and, likewise, this woman of color must be validated by a white man. Nevertheless, Fanon's scornful reproach of René Maran and Mayotte Capécia is hardly motivated by a hatred of inter-racial liberalism. His wish is to render these same relations more "authentic," or less "neurotic" (42, 60): "Today I believe in the possibility of love; that is why I endeavor to trace its imperfections, its perversions" (42). "This sexual myth—the quest for white flesh—perpetuated by alienated psyches, must no longer be allowed to impede active understanding" (81). The love ideal, the object or recipient of love, if not love itself, remains exclusively white in the sexual orientation of *Black Skin, White Masks.*

"Those who grant our conclusions on the psychosexuality of the white woman," Fanon continues in chapter 6, "The Negro and Psychopathology," "may ask what we have to say about the woman of color. I know nothing about her" (179–80). The white idealization of love cultivates such ignorance, for colonization itself. An abiding sexual alienation in *Black Skin, White Masks* is revealed by a footnote to "The Woman of Color and the White Man," its second chapter: "Since he is the master and more simply the male, the white man can allow himself the luxury of sleeping with many women. This is true in every country and especially in the colonies. But when a white woman accepts a black man there is automatically a romantic aspect" (46n5). An acceptance of colonial bourgeois gender conventions encourages Fanon to view relationships with white males in their crude colonial context while romanticizing relationships with white females, outside their crude colonial context. This statement is contradicted by every strand of "neurosis" analyzed throughout *Black Skin, White Masks,* especially in "The Negro and Psychopathology." What of the white woman who yearns to be driven mad by "bestial" Black male sex (171)? Or the prostitute "who told me that in her early days the mere thought of going to bed with a Negro brought on an orgasm," and "who went in search of Negroes and never asked them for money" (158)? What of the female Negrophobes of French or European empire as a whole? In her insightful essay, Hodge focuses on colonial education of colonized males, even as she envisions Michèle Lacrosil as a female version of them in the vein of Capécia (Hodge 1972, 217). She confirms that in this scenario "the natural partner of the black intellectual is the white woman" (230). This naturalization of white racist gender is not yet challenged in Fanon's castigation of Maran or Capécia, in his rationalist resistance to biological racism, or in his wicked exposé of colored cultural imitations of Western manhood and womanhood in *Black Skin, White Masks.*

Inasmuch as *A Dying Colonialism* renounces all white canonization, demystifying love and humanity in its European cast, this can be explained in terms of the itinerary of Negritude relayed by Hodge, interestingly enough: "Assimilation—Alienation—Return via Africa" (227). Beyond the flexing of hyperrationalist (and psychiatric) muscle by a student of French colonial formation,

Fanon's intellectual romance with the manhood and womanhood of the West would come to an African revolutionary end. This erotic return may be legible at first in "Racism and Culture." However, culturally speaking, a crucial sexual analysis of white racist empire still breaks through other aspects of *Black Skin, White Masks.*

Fanon's repudiation of a certain fundamentalism has not been recognized, or commodified, as a part of the academic appropriation of him in the 1980s and '90s. Labeling Freud a critical apologist for the affluent social context of Victorian Europe, Hussein Bulhan discusses Fanon's complete rejection of Freud's "Oedipal complex" in *Frantz Fanon and the Psychology of Oppression* (1985). Bulhan is aware that Fanon's refusal of such a basic principle of psychoanalysis "amounts to a serious departure" from Freud's school of thought (Bulhan 1980, 259, 254). This departure begins in Fanon's introduction, where he coins the term "sociogeny" to provide a conceptual alternative to the biological constitutionalism of "phylogeny" and the nuclear family–based individualism of Freud's "ontogeny" (F. Fanon 1967a, 11). Its development is more profound in "The Negro and Psychopathology," in which Fanon stresses the extreme disparity between Black social reality and the analytic schemas of "Drs." Lacan and Freud (150–52). This disparity is explored with particular regard to conventional descriptions of neurosis, particularly sexual neurosis. Sanctioning Black sexuality en masse, for a moment, against any pathological assessment by the West, Fanon is adamant: "A normal Negro child, having grown up within a normal family, will become abnormal on the slightest contact with the white world" (143). All "abnormal manifestations" are the product of a "cultural situation" (152), and this situation is predicated on racism. "It is too often forgotten that neurosis is not a basic element of human reality. Like it or not, the Oedipus complex is far from coming into being among Negroes. . . . This incapacity is one on which we heartily congratulate ourselves" (151–52). The sexual neurosis of psychoanalysis as well as that of the assimilationist elite of "The Woman of Color and the White Man" and "The Man of Color and the White Woman" are rearticulated as the socio-historical sickness of white colonial racism. Now Fanon refers, as he writes, to "97 per cent" of the families of the French Antilles. He even dares to exploit Bronislaw Malinowski's anthropology of "sexual savagery" and matriarchy to explain this absence of Oedipus (152), without falling prey to the fear of primitivism that otherwise envelops *Black Skin, White Masks.*

While colonial psychoanalysis makes homoeroticism and psycho-pathology perfectly synonymous, the "anti-Oedipal" Fanon troubles this association in his pre-revolutionary, most colonial-conservative work. Undermining the foundation for heterosexuality in the Freudian West, and unable to affirm an overt homosexuality in Martinique, he does not discount the overt presence of a same-sex Black eroticism, as a footnote illustrates: "We should not overlook, however, the existence of what are called there 'men dressed like women' or 'godmothers.' Generally they wear shirts and skirts. But I am convinced that they lead normal sex lives. They can take a punch like any 'he-man' and they are not impervious to the allures of women—fish and vegetable merchants" (180n44). Neither "heterosexuality" nor "homosexuality" applies exclusively, as Fanon insists on the normality of these "men dressed like women" or "godmothers" that would be damned as super-neurotic by Europe. A second instance of homoerotic Black sexual identity is located in migration. It is presented from Fanon's "sociogenic" perspective on racism, culture, and economic exploitation: "In Europe, on the other hand, I have known several Martinicans who became homosexuals, always passive. But this was by no means a neurotic homosexuality: For them it was a means to a livelihood, as pimping is for others" (180n44). The standard, static opposition between heterosexuality and homosexuality is once again a problem. Like heterosexuality, and all sexual neurosis in the West, homosexuality is a culturally specific rather than natural, universal phenomenon. And, like heterosexuality and neurosis, it can only be universalized through imperialism. It is important, then, not to erase the presence of same-sex Black eroticism and its insistent defense in *Black Skin, White Masks*. To erase it would be to endorse white sexual imperialism—whether heterosexualist or homosexualist—and its bourgeoisie. What's more, it would ignore the fact that Fanon's critique of the psycho-sexual norms of Occidentalism is far more sympathetic to these same-sex identities than his critique of Maran and Capécia is to the colored elite that imitates colonialism's heterosexuality in Martinique. These two same-sex, homoerotic cases of the Antilles are introduced precisely to preclude their assimilation; to resist, refuse, and reject the condemnation of neurosis, a pathologization which Westernization requires. "The Negro and Psychopathology" can by no means offer a full catalogue of Black sexual identity, especially when it concedes it knows nothing about "the woman of color," when its class vision is so restrictive. But neither can critics of "Fanon" who mistake his pre-revolutionary, colonial conservatism for Black nationalism, while endorsing the whole colonial framework of sexual categorization that sanctifies the culturally specific dichotomy between homosexuality and heterosexuality—a dichotomy which construes heterosexuality as natural or normal and homosexuality as neurotic by definition. Fanon's subversion of Oedipus is therefore indeed an extraordinarily radical element of *Black Skin, White Masks*.[3]

And then there is Negrophobia, the other side of pathological Oedipus. For when Black families or societies are cleared of neurosis, sexual neurosis, white families—classically enshrined by Sigmund Freud as well as Jacques Lacan—are exposed to Fanon's fresh, anti-racist analysis. The "primitivist" idea that every "intellectual gain requires a loss in sexual potential" (F. Fanon 1967a, 165) is exploded. The "civilized" and "civilizing" white family of the West is identified as a miniature of the colonialist nation, the agent of an imperialist system, and a workshop for the production of white-supremacist identities (142, 148, 149).

The Black body serves as a central "phobogenic object" (151) for all of the above. A phobia is a neurotic fear of an object or situation. The terror of racist phobias is read, customarily, as sexual revulsion. "Proceeding with complete orthodoxy," this revulsion is unmasked as a disavowed desire for "immoral and shameful things" (154–56). As a result, the "sociogenic" condition of the white family man and woman with "Oedipal-sexual neurosis" is unmasked as the psycho-pathology of Negrophobia. Black persons symbolize, for whites, "the sexual instinct (in its raw state)" and "the incarnation of a genital potency beyond all moralities and prohibitions" (177): "To suffer from a phobia of Negroes is to be afraid of the biological. For the Negro is only biological. The Negroes are animals. They go about naked. And God only knows" (165). The underside of this binary division between the intellectual and the biological is laid out, at last. The white family unit of the culture of Occidentalism is riddled with so-called neurosis, for Fanon, since the psycho-political repression of this white racist culture generates Negrophobic genders and sexualities as a rule. Their illness is never an individual ("ontogenic") affair.

This conclusion radiates from the center of Fanon's insistence that Black males are coded to "penis symbols" (159) in entire Negrophobic societies, and that Negrophobia is all-consuming in the phallic order of the West. It views these "phobogenic" victims less as human beings than as walking, stalking, human-sized erections. The sexual self-descriptions of colonial culture are thus voided as a consequence of Fanon's strategically orthodox interpretation of psychoanalytic individualism. In fact, they serve as masks for Negrophobia in *Black Skins, White Masks.* Now, neither white manhood nor white womanhood can be classified in terms of heterosexuality, "true" heterosexuality, per se. There is a racist perversion of "bestiality" at their core: "That is because the Negrophobic woman is in fact nothing but a putative sexual partner—just as the Negrophobic man is a repressed homosexual" (156). The erotic identities of the allegedly heterosexual white man and the allegedly heterosexual white woman are both anchored in Black male bodies which, because they are scripted as sub-human, cannot possibly participate in the human sexuality of heterosexuality or even repressed homosexuality, proper (as Fanon's language still seems to suggest). The genders and sexualities of the white West can in no way conform to their own social ideals or descriptions, whether officially heteroerotic or homoerotic, not with Negrophobia front and center. The myth of Black *and white* heterosexuality and homosexuality should be destroyed.

This critical perspective on homosexuality in white men is perceptive (instead of strictly phobic itself). Not confined to a stigmatized minority, it addresses white men in general. It logically accompanies the kin criticisms of sexuality in white women, as various dichotomies progressively break down. All colonial sexuality is organized around colonial racism, or this enormous Black penis hysteria of European empire. The problem with these passages in *Black Skin, White Masks* is that the orthodoxies of psychoanalysis are not flipped even further, to symbolically complement an analysis of phobias surrounding Black males with a similar analysis of phobias surrounding Black females: Negrophobia is not confined by gender, masculinity or femininity, manhood or womanhood. The history of "Saartjie Baartman," the "Hottentot Venus," at France's "Museum of Man" is instructive. The concept of Negrophobia demands completion in Fanon. It could be added that "the Negrophobic [man] is in fact nothing but a putative sexual partner—just as the Negrophobic [woman] is a repressed homosexual" with regard to Black females, who are no less construed as hyper-sexual by white racist imperialism. But the terms must differ. A white man cannot literally be a repressed homosexual vis-à-vis Black male bodies or a heterosexual aggressor vis-à-vis Black female bodies. A white woman cannot literally be a heterosexual aggressor vis-à-vis Black male bodies or a repressed homosexual vis-à-vis Black female bodies. The repressive, racially exclusive formulation of heterosexuality and homosexuality is reserved for white bodies only—even if the way that white heterosexuality and white homosexuality function as white masks for Negrophobic reactions to Black skin is ignored: Black people are barred from this category of human being and its specious categories of modern, human sexuality. This follows from what in Fanon is a first principle of white colonialism's "civilization," whose violence is neither heterosexual or homosexual; to be precise, it is "Euro-sexual."

The most radical insight of the pre-revolutionary Fanon's *Black Skin, White Masks* must provide much-needed context for his widely publicized line: "Fault, guilt, refusal of guilt, paranoia—one is back in homosexual territory" (183). For the context is Negrophobia. It is the assimilationist fear of the "primitive" which produces a more problematic line, at any rate: "I have never been able, without revulsion, to hear a man say of another man: He is so sensual" (201). This is Negrophobia also, internalized by a colonized elite. "The Negro and Psychopathology" finds this Fanon evidently exhausted by such a routine and fading fast from its many ramifications. His point of view in "West Indians and Africans" suddenly appears, in advance: "The Martinican is a Frenchman, he wants to remain part of the French Union, he asks only one thing, he wants the idiots and the exploiters to give him a chance to live like a human being" (202). Few contemporary Fanon scholars ever confront these unraveling lines, and it is not to their credit: "I am a Frenchman. I am interested in French culture, French civilization, the French people. We refuse to be considered 'outsiders,' we have full part in the French drama. . . . I am personally interested in . . . the French nation." (203). This is a part of *Black Skin, White Masks*. But it is only a small part of Fanon, who would pursue the radical implications of his work to Africa, leaving his colonial assimilation progressively, impressively behind.

New Ways, New Attitudes, and New Modes of Action: *A Dying Colonialism*

After examining the alienated elite in "Racism and Culture," with an emphasis on erotic enjoyment, Fanon later revisits the sexual aggression of Europe in *L'an V de la révolution algérienne* (1959; as *A Dying Colonialism*, 1965). Here he amplifies considerably his previous treatment of psycho-pathology and gender. He has again the chance to confirm imperialism's penile obsessions, as is made clear by the madness explored earlier in "The 'North African Syndrome,'" an essay written in 1952 and reprinted in *Toward the African Revolution*, in which white phallic hallucinations of rape and prostitution as well as homosexuality run wild (F. Fanon 1967b, 11–15). Nevertheless, the erotic focus of Fanon's first full-blown revolutionary book, drafted in the embattled terrain of Algeria, deliberately privileges the female population of the popular, colonized masses. They had left the writer of *Black Skin, White Masks* virtually speechless.

Importantly, Fanon's earliest call for "a new humanity" is found not in *The Wretched of the Earth*, but in *A Dying Colonialism*. It is militantly identified with a new sexual egalitarianism, an anti-colonial sexual egalitarianism for theory and practice (F. Fanon 1965, 28). The opening chapter is "Algeria Unveiled." Instantly, it marks the stylization of bodies as the most definitive aspect of any cultural identity. The imperialist project of "cultural destruction" craves a penetration of the veil as the consummation of its charge. So sociology and ethnography move in to apprehend "a basic matriarchy," obviously non-Oedipal in nature, beneath the surface or veneer of universal male entitlement. The historic mission of the French regime in Algeria is decided accordingly: "If we want to destroy the structure of Algerian society, its capacity for resistance, we must first of all conquer the women" (37–38). Fanon diagnoses the mobilization of bourgeois femininity and feminism in the social work of "destructuring Algerian culture" (39) as a sexual compulsion, or a haunting dream that the "matrilineal essence" of a subject people will prove to be an ally in colonial patriarchal annihilation, not the matrix of indigenous cultural resistance (37, 40). Five years into revolutionary struggle, there is no hint of vacillation, as there was in his "Racism and Culture" speech of 1956: "the occupier, smarting from his failures, presents in a simplified and pejorative way the system of values by means of which the colonized person resists his innumerable offensives" (41). Mass resistance is center stage, and, ultimately, the gender dynamics of this resistance generate a sexual revolution within a revolution which—in the face of French colonial psycho-pathology—Fanon will champion as an African national reality as well as a bedrock political *ideal*.

He finds the French obsession with exposing the veiled to be a microcosm of the "sadistic and perverse character" (40) of the colonial relation. The white sexual violence writ large in Negrophobia reemerges vis-à-vis colonized women, who are shrouded in a romantic exoticism "strongly tinged with sensuality" (40). This is a missionary project of erotic conversion. It becomes apparent to Fanon that the colonizer sees the wrenched-aside veil as revealing a hyper-sexualized body, one not at all unlike the "black male-penis" in intensity: "Her timidity and her reserve are transformed in accordance with the commonplace laws of conflictual psychology into their opposite, and the Algerian woman becomes hypocritical, perverse, and even a veritable nymphomaniac" (46). Unveiling is equated with "breaking her resistance, making her available," and reducing her to an object of possession (41–42). The fantasies that Fanon analyzes in the dream materials of French men contain maximal violence. This much is specified not for women generically, but for the colonized female in particular: "there is possession, rape, near-murder" almost always. This racist erotic aggression is manifest in persons classified as both "normal" and "neuro-pathological" in the West. Once again, "para-neurotic sadism and brutality" is conveyed as the socio-historical essence of European sexuality, after colonialism, in and for colonialism (44, 46).[4] "A normal [white] child, having grown up within a normal [white] family, will [be exposed as] abnormal on the slightest contact with the [colonized] world," *A Dying Colonialism* seems to say.

The white female "neurosis" observed in Algeria further clarifies the political scheme of integration for Fanon, as the erotic metamorphosis of a few unveiled women incurs an excessive and envious animosity from a number of French women. Although the refusal to unveil arouses an aggressive frustration in these settlers, an assimilationist unveiling elicits the same hostile reaction. The "saved" Algerian woman (42) is projected as "amoral and shameless," and obscenely "offensive." She is seen as a threat to the heterosexuality of empire, her symbolic "evolution" aside. The "evolved" subject of colonization can only "evolve" given a process of trans-racialization that is concurrently a process of trans-sexualization, and this process is never-ending. *A Dying Colonialism* clearly deciphers the cultural and biological politics of accommodation, beyond *Black Skin, White Masks:* "Integration, in order to be successful, seems indeed to have to be simply a continued, accepted paternalism" (44n8).

The sexuality of integration is at issue in all of Fanon's work. The game of cultural seduction backfires in "Algeria Unveiled," igniting a social transformation of the most militant sort. The women of the colonized majority do not activate their own destruction. They participate in the violent struggle for national liberation. Their determination abides despite the "legendary ferocity" of a colonial regime designed to promote psychological despair (100): "The leaders of the Revolution had no illusions as to the enemy's criminal capacities. Nearly all of them had passed through their jails or had had sessions with survivors from the camps or the cells of the French judicial police. No one of them failed to realize that any Algerian woman arrested would be tortured to death" (49).

The white racist "neurosis" constitutive of the empire culture of the West ensures that the torture recounted in Fanon will routinely be a sexual torture. This is the context in which he esteems Algerian women's militancy, repeatedly, as an interior revolt of enormous magnitude (48–51).

He champions the colonized women who penetrate, interestingly, "the flesh of the Revolution" (54), counter to the integration desired by France, and despite its dreams of seeing them "penetrated, martyrized, ripped apart" (46). Their absolutely central rather than auxiliary participation in the FLN is traced through an "instrumentalization" of the veil which engenders massive socio-sexual change on unequivocally anti-colonial terms. Fanon remarks that evasion had formerly been a traditional mode of resistance, and that this practice, along with social restrictions placed on female mobility, made their latest mode of activism phenomenal. He stresses the revolution in subjectivity, erotic in nature, vital to any liberation from imperialism: "The absence of the veil distorts the Algerian woman's corporeal pattern. She quickly has to invent new dimensions for her body, new means of muscular control. . . . The Algerian who walks stark naked into the European city relearns her body, re-establishes it in a totally revolutionary fashion" (59). Moving from the immobilized "native [*sic*] quarters" to the city of the conqueror requires a release from the gendered terrain of colonial psychology: "She must consider the image of the occupier lodged somewhere in her mind and in her body, remodel it, initiate the essential work of eroding it, make it inessential, remove something of the shame that is attached to it, devalidate it" (52). This uprising must destroy the self-image of the colonizing couple as well as the wretched image of colonized identities against which Western narcissism is defined.[5] Whether the white standard is metropolitan bourgeois manhood or womanhood, the revolutionary subjects of *A Dying Colonialism* should reject sexual assimilation and integration, much as the Black masses repel Oedipus in "The Negro and Psychopathology." Moreover, "this couple that brings death to the enemy, life to the Revolution" (57) is decidedly not a romantic couple at all, but an extended, inclusive family or community of revolt.

There is another, considerable, and almost completely ignored evaluation in this chapter: "It is the white man who creates the Negro. But it is the Negro who creates negritude." Fanon infers "one of the laws in the psychology of colonization" with thoughts of Césaire, Damas, and Senghor in Algeria: "In an initial phase, it is the action, the plans of the occupier that determine the centers of resistance around which a people's will to survive becomes organized" (47). The matter of sexual imitation is vital in the colonial conflict over the veil. For while colonialist unveiling is refused, a militant anti-colonialist unveiling is marvelously deployed; and a momentary, tactical reveiling is also deployed, well beyond its original context, toward the same revolutionary goal of independence or self-determination. Fanon recalls strategic imitations of two distinct colonial personas: the female militant's practical transformation into "a European woman, poised and unrestrained, whom no would suspect" is about to blow up the settler complex; and her stereotypical animation of the veiled woman who looks "so much like a 'fatma' that the [French] soldier would be convinced that this woman was quite harmless" (57, 61). Neither category is to be internalized, however; a radical sexual transformation takes place outside these options. It is with this versatility of this insurgent in mind that Fanon mentions that the anti-colonialist abandonment of the veil would be provisionally and self-consciously reversed when the French resumed their "old campaign of Westernizing the Algerian woman." Spontaneously, the women of the colonized "who had long since dropped the veil once again donned the *haik,* thus affirming that it was not true that woman liberated herself at the invitation of France and of General de Gaulle" (62). While Fanon himself is critical of veiling in its traditional dimension because of the politics of a rigid separation of the sexes, he affirms this symbolic act of veiling that is at once beyond a repressive tradition and against the thrust of empire (63). What does not go unrecognized in the psychology of colonization is a most important fact. Any sexual transformation that does not willfully transpire on fiercely indigenous, anti-colonialist terms is only a racist pretext for cultural destruction, whether this pretense is staged in heteroerotic or homoerotic, masculine or feminine fashion.

Fanon expressed these sexually insurgent politics in *El moudjahid* and a *Résistance algérienne* communiqué appended to "Algeria Unveiled," in which he wrote that "revolutionary war is not a war of men" (66). Collected in *Toward the African Revolution,* "Decolonization and Independence" states that "the FLN defined its program: to put an end to French occupation, to give the land to the Algerians, to establish a policy of social democracy in which man and woman have an equal right to culture, to material well-being, and to dignity" (F. Fanon 1967b, 102). The drive is toward a new society (103). "Algeria Unveiled" itself closed with this call: "It is the necessities of combat that give rise . . . to new attitudes, to new modes of action, to new ways" (F. Fanon 1965, 64). This simply cannot entail old genders and sexualities or families. "There is not occupation of territory, on the one hand," under colonialism, and "independence of persons on the other," Fanon insists: "French colonialism has settled itself in the very center of the Algerian individual" (65). There shall be new persons, too, new bodies, souls, and minds. The radical erotics of a new society, not confined to the space of conjugal relations, extend to a series of metamorphoses. The father's son is transformed into the militant, and the "woman-for-marriage" into the "woman-for-action," for instance: "The young girl was replaced by the militant, the woman by the *sister*" (108). Reflecting on the "new values governing sexual relations" among the colonized (109), Fanon considers "revolutionary love" (115) and "the united militant couple" (112), along with the daughter's incitement of the father's own militant transformation (110). Rethinking the foundation of sexual relations (114), he underwrites this paternal joy at the daughter's new personality (109) as a part of his revolutionary, sexual-political conversion (105) in chapter 3, "The Algerian Family." Fanon's own advocacy of this twin birth of "a new woman" and "a new nation" (107, 112) is at the center of his popular advocacy of a new humanity. The French assimilationist's eclipse of sexual violence against colonized women is significantly redressed by the African revolutionist: "In stirring up these men and women, colonialism has regrouped them beneath a single sign. Equally victims of the same tyranny, simultaneously identifying a single enemy, this physically dispersed people is realizing its unity and founding in suffering a spiritual community which constitutes the most solid bastion of the Algerian Revolution" (119). (Here, Toni Cade Bambara and Angela Davis can be heard, loud and clear.) A new Fanon would sum up in *Résistance algérienne,* finally—and it is not the elite man or woman of color of whom he speaks—"Side by side with us, our sisters do their part in further breaking down the enemy system and in liquidating the old mystifications once and for all" (67).

Revolutionary Violence—Ecstasy and Nakedness: *The Wretched of the Earth*

Recently, Nigel Gibson has looked at a range of Fanon's writings in *Fanon: The Postcolonial Imagination* (2003), although he considers the politics of sexuality only in "Algeria Unveiled." He takes stock of the decontextualization of the revolutionary's writings in a now counter-revolutionary age. Today's politics produce a condemnation already laid out in *The Wretched of the Earth:*

> He has been damned by both sides. For example, it has been argued that Fanon is uncritical of "tribal chiefs," on the one hand [Jack Woodis], and that he was a political authoritarian who ran roughshod over ethnic difference, on the other [Christopher Miller]. It is argued that Fanon overestimated the degree of change taking place in gender relations [Marie-Aimée Helie-Lucas], or that he was a cultural conservative upholding traditions like the veil [e.g., Mervat Hatem]. Some conclude that Fanon, away from the political center, had very little influence on events in Algeria [James Le Sueur]. Others damn Fanon for having too much influence [e.g., Irene Gendzier]. (Gibson 2003, 11)

On this score, Gibson's introduction to *Rethinking Fanon: The Continuing Dialogue* (1999) is similarly interesting:

> Fanon's public entrance into the Algerian revolution came at its most radically articulated moment, that is, with the Soummam Platform. The moment continued to affect the theoretical issues explored in *A Dying Colonialism* and *The Wretched of the Earth.* With forty years' hindsight we can criticize Fanon's optimism, but was

he wrong to think that revolution could strip away retrograde social relations? Grounded in a conception of culture and consciousness as changing and changeable, a revolution in values is what he experienced. (Gibson 1999, 28–29)

But how is it that hindsight is what neo-colonialism and fundamentalism offer? Should Fanon's polemic be reduced to a question of optimism or pessimism? *A Dying Colonialism* in particular, his second book, embodies a neglected genre of text. It is a rhetorical propaganda of ideals. It propagates values for a new society at the same time that it argues that they are already in existence, in embryo, as evidence for the idea that colonialism is decadent and decolonization is long past due—a dying colonialism, indeed. This is poesis. Gibson writes that the degeneration of the revolution in Algeria "does not negate its truth; it simply makes Fanon's critique of its pitfalls all the more compelling" (Gibson 2003, 14). While this is certainly true, the perception is undercut by any notion that Fanon's thesis (or optimism) was "subverted" in "post-colonial Algeria" (147). *A Dying Colonialism* upholds a new set of ideals while it continues its struggle to make its words flesh, a historical *fait accompli*, as the author himself had already embraced them. This evokes Fanon's statement in "Concerning Violence" that "all decolonization is successful" (F. Fanon 1963, 37). If it is not successful, it is not decolonization. Likewise, when the tide of revolution is turned back, the situation is no longer revolutionary; it is retrogression, as Fanon effectively prophesies. The degeneration of sexual revolution in the degeneration of the Algerian revolution is itself a perfect illustration of Fanon's future tracking of colonialism as neo-colonialism in *The Wretched of the Earth*. Hardly Fanonian, Gibson's rhetoric of "post-coloniality" hampers this insight. So does the relegation of "race" issues to *Black Skin, White Masks* in *Fanon: The Postcolonial Imagination* and its general decontextualization of Algeria's revolution from Fanon's Diasporic insistence on African revolution. This is ironic, given Gibson's concession of the importance—and elision—of early scholarship on Fanon by "African and African American radicals" (Gibson 1999, 14), not to mention Sharpley-Whiting's *Frantz Fanon: Conflicts and Feminisms*.

Sharpley-Whiting is incisive and systematic in her survey of anti-Fanonism and its politics of gender, deftly undoing what she deems "a postmodern mythology—Fanon as a misogynist" (Sharpley-Whiting 1998, 48). It all begins with Capécia's *Je suis martiniquaise,* both her racist-sexist Negrophobia (48) and its strange recovery by mostly white feminists in U.S. literary criticism and Cultural Studies. If the majority of critics never read Capécia themselves, they claim her from the pages of Fanon in "a dangerous feminist politics" (49) that essentially identifies anti-colonialism with misogyny, while "ignoring Capécia's re-inscription of sexually racist stereotypes of black women" (48): "Capécia would be immortalized in feminist writings as the lamb at Fanon's sacrificial altar, rather than the complicit victim of the sexploitive, antiblack woman colonial condition" (49). The class and color dynamics of colonized elites would expand this reading significantly. Still, Sharpley-Whiting faults feminisms almost as much as certain feminists fault Fanon. She refuses to ignore "a recurring antiblack male bias" in feminist theories which "appropriate indiscriminately the equally masculinist, oftentimes virulently racist-sexist thought of Freud, Lacan, Foucault, and Nietzsche . . . even as they aggressively critique Fanon for his 'misogyny'" (19). Moreover, this "Fanon" is almost always equated with *Black Skin, White Masks,* which in turn is almost always misread as a Black nationalist treatise. Sharpley-Whiting has *A Dying Colonialism* more in mind when she notes "Fanon's radically humanist profeminist consciousness" (24), differentiating various feminisms throughout. There are neo-colonial or colonialist feminisms, white feminisms, and those without "an anti-racist/anti-capitalist agenda" (19); and, she adds, "while linked by ethnicity and sometimes class, not all black feminists are radical; just as not all Euro-American lit-crit feminists are liberal. Some black feminists are ideologically liberal or conservative" (22).[6] But the official idealization of feminism as the only possible, nameable alternative to sexism or misogyny, the only imaginable framework or language for sexual politics, theory, and practice—in the history of the world, not even the history of the white bourgeois West—this is never challenged. In fact, *Frantz Fanon: Conflicts and Feminisms* assumes that feminists must be against homophobia by definition, as if there are not homophobic and anti-homophobic or lesbian expressions of feminism. It accepts the crude description of Fanon's "latent homophobia" by critics of *Black Skin, White Masks* (10), as if its critique of Negrophobia could not be read otherwise; as if his defense of Black male "godmothers" does not exist; and as if this one Fanon text is exemplary of or interchangeable with all others. Could *A Dying Colonialism* not destroy the gender-conservative basis for colonial homophobia as recycled by certain passages of his first, most colonial and conservative book? Why is *The Wretched of the Earth* constantly effaced in academic representations of "Fanon," over and over again, despite its one-time canonical status among "African and African American radicals" or Black Power revolutionaries in Pan-African revolt?

Fanon's final and most famous work would note how Western empire is refurbished with pseudo-independence, or the complicity of a comprador caste whose historic mission is to wear the "mask of neo-colonialism" (F. Fanon 1963, 152). These white masks in *The Wretched of the Earth* reveal how the socio-sexual culture of Negrophobia is mimed, globally, by what Frazier dubbed a "lumpenbourgeoisie." In *A Dying Colonialism,* Fanon wrote that the only colonized who could be identified with a French radio before its revolutionary appropriation were those of the "developed bourgeoisie" (F. Fanon 1965, 69), and that the function of the colonized intellectual was to be "an active agent of the upheaval of the colonized society" (41). *The Wretched of the Earth* tracks the class lines of erotic violence under European imperialism with a precision unseen since Frazier cloaked his own critique in the exact same colonial tongue as *Bourgeoisie noire* (1955).

"The Pitfalls of National Consciousness," the third chapter of Fanon's third book, profiles the "colonized bourgeoisie." Like Frazier's elite, this "underdeveloped middle class" (F. Fanon 1963, 149) lacks the key ingredient of the economic identity it parrots: money (178), together with the power it brings. Narcissistically, it aims to occupy the place of those who inferiorize it. It harbors a quasi-neurotic wish for identification that matches the caste propaganda of "the Negro press" analyzed by Frazier (1957d, 178). Having "totally assimilated colonialist thought," it embodies a "will to imitation" (F. Fanon 1963, 161) which manifests itself in the worst way; it uncritically clones the white-supremacist bourgeoisie of the West not even in its reputed stages of exploration or invention, but in its period of negation or decadence (153). Frazier argued that his Black elite could only behold their oppressors in the situations of leisure. Fanon's heuristic application of Western economics ignores a fact that "Concerning Violence" decided "not to overlook . . . any longer" (96). The myth of bourgeois history, of its inventive exploration as well as its decadent negation, is entirely founded on the exploitation of enslaved and colonized Africans. The white ruling class pillages the majority peoples of the world, their material technologies and natural resources. It doesn't explore out of largess. It pirates for domination. Fanon will reconfirm the "unutterable treason" (167) of its imitators, detailed by Frazier for decades, as the "gaudy carnival" sponsored by colonial empire. Unlike Frazier, however, Fanon does not long for a better incarnation of this cultural prototype of Western humanity (163), on either side of the Atlantic. There is no Black or colonized "bourgeoisie," in truth; "there is only a sort of little greedy caste, avid and voracious, with the mind of a huckster, only too glad to accept the dividends that the former colonial power hands out to it. . . . It remembers what it has read in European textbooks and imperceptibly it becomes not even the replica of Europe, but its caricature" (175). The second phase of Fanon's African revolution must liquidate this "useless and harmful middle class," if life is to begin (311).

The blistering castigation of the "greedy little caste" in "The Pitfalls of National Consciousness" culminates in "On National Culture," chapter 4, which was Fanon's speech to the Second Congress of Black Artists and Writers, in Rome in 1959. Its topic is "the native [*sic*] intellectual [who] has thrown himself greedily upon Western culture" (218). This figure is a symbolic representative of the comprador elite in Fanon; and it surely resonates with the character animating much of *Black Skin, White Masks*. Negritude again provides a point of departure. This Fanon is not the same writer who identified as a Frenchman in

"The Negro and Psychopathology," when he asserted his desire to be a man of no past (F. Fanon 1967a, 203; 226). The climax of "Racism and Culture" represents a radical shift from the mindset that slighted Alioune Diop, conference organizer and founding editor of *Presence africaine,* as some sort of pro-primitivist "self-segregationist" (185–86).[7] Fanon recognizes that "the plunge into the chasm of the past is the condition and the source of freedom" (F. Fanon 1967b, 43). This ideological transformation is deepened in "On National Culture," in which an easy critique of "passionate research" (F. Fanon 1963, 210) on the Black past is jeered as a sign of colonial investment:

> The passion with which native [*sic*] intellectuals defend the existence of their national culture may be a source of amazement; but those who condemn this exaggerated passion are strangely apt to forget that their own psyche and their own selves are conveniently sheltered behind a French or a German culture which has given full proof of its existence and which is uncontested. (209)

Fantastically, all colonized minds are morally and politically compelled to "strip naked" and study the history of their bodies—such a study is presented as a necessity, not a luxury (211).

This is an amazing unveiling for African revolution at large, beyond gender and any one part of the continent, at any given time. Fanon had maintained in *A Dying Colonialism,* "The Algerian woman who walks stark naked into the European city relearns her body, re-establishes it in a totally revolutionary fashion." There is an experience of nakedness thanks to the phenomenal significance this veil has for her socio-historical identity or consciousness. "One must have heard the confessions of Algerian women or have analyzed the dream context of certain recently unveiled women to appreciate the importance of the veil for the body of the woman." Initially, the militant "has an impression of her body being cut up into bits, put adrift; the limbs seem to lengthen indefinitely. . . . The unveiled body seems to escape, dissolve" (F. Fanon 1965, 59). "On National Culture" holds that this experience is imperative for all colonized people, and for colonized intellectuals in particular, so revolutionary does Fanon consider the model of these female revolutionaries for all of us. The "primitivizing" mind-body dichotomy of Western empire can be undone when colonized minds undergo a transformation as radical as the transformation of militant women in "Algeria Unveiled." Without question, these intellectuals must relearn their bodies, reestablish them in a totally revolutionary fashion, even to the point of feeling "cut up into bits and put adrift," until a new, revolutionary humanity is brought into being. The alienating European intellectual tradition is their (imperialist) veil. This anti-colonial stripping is central to the "turn[ing] over of a leaf" (316) Fanon so famously promotes in conclusion: *A Dying Colonialism* is thus reprised as *The Wretched of the Earth* reasserts "the fact is that everything needs to be . . . thought out anew" (F. Fanon 1963, 100).

Fanon then affirms "African-Negro culture" in a class analysis of colonization. He deplores the elite assimilation of bourgeois culture and bourgeois interpretations of African culture. He celebrates the culture of the subjugated masses, who produce and practice it for self-preservation and self-determination, in spite of the forces of colonial destruction. Therefore, "cultured individuals" (F. Fanon 1963, 208) should reveal their commitment to African culture not in sterile words aimed at their oppressors, but in struggle, fighting to liberate this besieged culture with "body and soul" (232): "I say again that no speech-making and no proclamations concerning culture will turn us from our fundamental tasks: the liberation of the national territory; a continual struggle against colonialism in its new forms; and an obstinate refusal to enter the charmed circle of mutual admiration at the summit" (235). When he claims that "every cultural is first and foremost national" (216), Fanon may illustrate an anti-colonial adage he quotes a few moments later: "It is always easier to proclaim rejection than actually to reject" (219). There will be no complete rejection of colonialism without a rejection of the boundaries set up and imposed by colonialism on the African world. On the whole, Fanon militates for Pan-Africanism and internationalism, toward a new humanity, with a strategic emphasis on national liberation rather than nationalism as conventionally understood and administered in Europe—bourgeois Europe, to boot. In any case, his ultimate embrace of Black culture as Black *popular* culture is energized by his revolutionary commitment to the masses: "Adherence to African-Negro culture and to the cultural unity of Africa is arrived at in the first place by upholding unconditionally the peoples' struggle for freedom" (235).[8]

This freedom would be a liberation from the psycho-biology and kidnap of "mother-country" thought. "On National Culture" explains how colonialism teaches the colonized that decolonization would result in "'barbarism,' degradation, and bestiality." The so-called civilizing mission or white man's burden was to put an end to this projected "savagery," which is largely sexual. Fanon denounces this propaganda of paternalism, disputing any maternity of empire: "On the unconscious plane, colonialism therefore did not seek to be considered by the native [*sic*] as a gentle, loving mother who protects her child from a hostile environment." Colonialism *is* that hostile environment, a would-be mother of another kind or species. The parent of colonial racism "unceasingly restrains her fundamentally perverse offspring from managing to commit suicide and from giving free rein to its evil instincts." The children of colonialism can evidently only be cured with oppression: "The colonial mother protects her child from itself, from its ego, and from its physiology, its biology, and its own unhappiness which is its very essence" (F. Fanon 1963, 211). These are the thoughts of empire that must be stripped from the minds and bodies of the colonized in the name of a revolutionary mother who is African, not European, "bloodthirsty and implacable" (145).

Whereas *A Dying Colonialism* deploys strategic imitations to detonate colonial compounds via sexual revolution, *The Wretched of the Earth* denotes a class-stratified divide between an erotics of violence based on elite mimicry and an erotics of violence based on mass militancy, Black militancy in mass revolt. There is in "Concerning Violence" a totalizing psycho-affective violation that surrounds and immerses the colonized. In the following chapter, "Spontaneity: Its Strength and Weakness," Fanon continues to demand colonialism's demise in a no less violent frenzy organized by the charged body of African revolution. He says that "the settler keeps alive in the native [*sic*] an anger which he deprives of an outlet" (54), a "violence which is just under the skin" (71), and an emotional sensitivity that is fixed on the skin's surface "like an open sore" (56). This is the "peaceful violence" (81) that is channeled by the privileged caste in the manic aggression of colonial assimilation (60). That caste's pleasure as an elite becomes the corrupt pleasure of the colonizer. It facilitates the colony's function as the brothel of the Western world (154). This violence among the masses, "at one and the same time inhibitory and stimulating" (53), is channeled as the frustrated aggression directed at those who should be called "brother, sister, friend" (47). This is before rebellion: "This is the period when the niggers beat each other up" (52). The choice between collective annihilation and armed resistance will eventually be made by the African majority, and, outside comprador privilege, it knows that "only violence pays" (61). The "disalienation" that preoccupied *Black Skin, White Masks* can only be accomplished in an erotics of violence that is the revolutionary violence of the masses: "life can only spring up again out of the rotting corpse of the settler" (93). And, for the Black masses described in zoological terms by white racist empire (42), bona fide decolonization is the radical remedy that destroys the material and symbolic economy of Negrophobia, its empire. The purpose of struggle is "to allow the accumulated libido, the hampered aggressivity [of "peaceful violence"] to dissolve as in a volcanic eruption." The "fulfillment of this eroticism" is the driving force of liberation (57), literally the ecstasy of revolt in Fanon.

His rebel erotica cannot be captured by the current academic rhetoric of gender and sexuality, even though *The Wretched of the Earth* does reiterate the insurgent sexual militancy of "Algeria Unveiled" and "The Algerian Family":

> In an underdeveloped country every effort is made to mobilize men and women as quickly as possible; it must guard against the danger of perpetuating the feudal tradition which holds sacred the superiority of the masculine over the feminine. Women will have exactly the same place as men, not in the clauses of the constitution but in the life of every day: in the factory, at school, and in the parliament. (202)[9]

A spiritual community is advanced and idealized, in lieu of the "greedy little caste," toward the practical political construction of a new society and a new humanity. "Come, then, comrades, the European game has finally ended. . . . We today can do everything, so long as we do not imitate Europe. . . . Let us decide not to imitate Europe; let us combine our muscles and brains in a new direction" (312–13). Against the sensory complex of the colonizer and the "nauseating mimicry" (311) of the colonized elite, the violent transformations of *A Dying Colonialism* guide the movement of *The Wretched of the Earth*, a thrilling culmination of Fanon's revolutionary lifework.

Conclusion

Frantz Fanon is without a doubt unparalleled in his trailblazing thought and his translation of this thought into action, or radical political commitment. His life was all too brief, indeed. Yet the life of his mind was not only prolific but dynamic enough to include extreme theoretical movement and growth. The content, scope, and purpose of his complex, practice-driven ideas prove to be too much for the intellectual order of the West, which he sought to undermine along with the political institutions of Western imperialism, to be sure. Questions of embodiment are absolutely central for considerations of his praxis, especially in the present or the future which he forecast with such extraordinary vision.

All too many scholars rigidly associate Fanon with selective fragments and interpretations of a single text, *Black Skin, White Masks;* and even then the radical implications of his work on Negrophobia and empire are ritually evaded— *Negrophobie*, by Boubacar Boris Diop, Odile Tobner, and François-Xavier Verschave (2005), notwithstanding. Most critics seek to preserve the sexual categories of colonialism (heterosexuality and homosexuality, Oedipus, etc.), which it helps significantly undermine. The colonial contradictions of Fanon's prerevolutionary book are exploited to scapegoat him for his colonization in a more or less white nationalist discourse on Black nationalism, a nationalism which *Black Skin, White Masks* scarcely represents. The bulk of Fanon's writing represents not his initial concerns, those of an intellectual elite, but the concerns of the masses and African revolution. This Pan-Africanism, internationalism, and humanism produces *A Dying Colonialism, The Wretched of the Earth*, and *Toward the African Revolution* beyond the distortion, misappropriation (exploitation) and demonization of *Black Skin, White Masks* (or a few quotations from "The Fact of Blackness"). On the whole, Fanon understands and endorses a new humanity ("new attitudes, new modes of action, new ways"), a revolutionary new orientation toward gender and sexuality, mind and body, ecstasy and eroticism, and an undeniably indispensable dissection of the entire cultural, psychological, and political economic world of white Western imperialism. The world of colonialism and neo-colonialism and its "greedy little caste" would suppress this Fanon—both his personal revolutionary transformation and his revolutionary articulations in print. It must repress his insistence on the nasty pathology of empire, here and there, then and now.

In what seems like another season, Ayi Kwei Armah published "Fanon: The Awakener" in *Negro Digest* in October 1969. He surveys the complete Fanon, aesthetically and politically, with urgency. He does not fail to notice inconsistencies (Armah 1969, 32) in what the author wrote when he was twenty-five years old (29), piercing as he is about *Peau noire, masques blancs:* "His delusion of belonging in a white French society should not be strange to black people who still consider themselves Americans" (8). Armah appreciates what this first, but nonetheless insightful, Fanon had to offer: "a complete picture of the integrationist personality stripped of all pretenses, with all clothes removed, bare and naked right down into bones and guts" (29). The nakedness of class suicide is something else altogether, even if the "decision to turn his back on a successful career, a brilliant past, present security and a professionally promising future was not an easy one" (34). Since, as Armah says, so many of us "are ill with the intellectual laziness Fanon called the special disease of us educated slaves," he advised a return to *L'an V de la révolution algérienne,* "the most misunderstood and most misused of Fanon's works" (35). Conversely, he characterizes *Les damnés de la terre* as "the greatest statement made about today's world" (39). Resisting white power, white European power, and "pimp power" (40), and scornful of misguided searches for masculinity and femininity, Armah closes "Fanon: The Awakener" in line with *Pour la révolution africaine:* "The question for any individual African, Afro-American, Afro-Caribbean or any other kind of African-related intellectual is whether to decide to go along with this useless and destructive parasitical bourgeoisie élite or to rack our brains to find a way to be useful not to the system that oppresses our people but to our people themselves" (41).

"What significance, then, does the fate of the black bourgeoisie in the United States have for the bourgeoisie of [others] that have come into existence as the result of the expansion of western civilization and European capitalism?" (Frazier 1957a, 28). Frazier posed this question at the end of his introduction to *Black Bourgeoisie.* An international comparison of Fanon's and Frazier's writing on this comprador class is key, therefore: North America may try to protect itself from Fanon's massive anti-colonialism, but Black Power intervenes and Frazier's sociology subverts any attempt to deny their common critique of Black elites. Between Fanon's political economic, philosophic, and psycho-cultural perspective and Frazier's historical, sociological, empirically rich perspective, virtually no distinction emerges. The lumpen-bourgeoisie and the "greedy little caste" are pictured as twins, so to speak, separated at birth by Western empire and plantation slavery. The difference lies not in the portrait. It lies in the politics of the perspective. Frazier modifies his vision over time in some respects, yet not nearly as much as Fanon, whose revolution was rather total, Pan-Africanist, and militantly erotic. This movement is broadcast in the title of his brother Joby Fanon's book, *Frantz Fanon: De la Martinique à l'Algerie et à l'Afrique* (J. Fanon 2004); and, crucially, the socio-sexual imitation of the colonized elite was renounced as a part of this African revolution that is still to come.

5 Colonialism and Erotic Desire— in English

THE CASE OF JAMAICA KINCAID

Two years after his untimely and apparently CIA-facilitated death, Frantz Fanon could again be heard in Simone de Beauvoir's autobiography *La force des choses* (1963; as *Force of Circumstance,* 1992). Though the metropolitan pair of Beauvoir and Jean-Paul Sartre spend much time dodging charges of colonial complicity in their conversations with Fanon, the African revolutionary breaks through the French voice of white liberal imperialism. Beauvoir recalls his emphasis on the role of socio-economic structure in the formation of psychoses, citing his belief that all "political leaders should be psychiatrists as well":

> He described several curious cases, among others that of a homosexual who, at every successive stage of his psychological deterioration, took refuge in a lower social stratum, as though he were aware that anomalies of behavior visible at the top of the social scale may be easily confused, lower down on it, with irregularities due to extreme poverty; his psychosis progressed in this way until finally he was living in a state of semi-dementia in the colonies, just one bum among all the others. By then his social disintegration was so complete that his mental deterioration was scarcely noticeable. (Beauvoir 1992, 318)

This account is no doubt mediated by Beauvoir. There is mention only of poverty, and a much-too-casual reference to homosexuality, never of the political economy of racism. Nevertheless, Fanon doubtlessly exposed the cultural racism which permits the nationality of the colonized to be identified as a state of deranged or degenerate subjects, a physical or geopolitical and psychological place where all the bums and derelicts of Europe are guaranteed to pass for normal, no matter what. The colonizer can conceal his or her degeneration in general and hide from colonial homophobia in particular within the race and class context of the colonies since the colonies are supposed to be a site of complete sexual savagery. While Beauvoir writes as if the cause of Western madness may lie in the mere fact of homosexuality itself, even the earliest Fanon (of *Peau noire, masques blancs* [1952; as *Black Skin, White Masks,* 1967]) names Negrophobia as the culprit in the carnal violence of colonialism. No conventional distinction between heterosexuality and homosexuality could explain the constitutional pathologies of white supremacy. All of the sexual identities of white "civilization" are necessarily "neurotic" (whether male or female, gay or straight), in the traditional terms of the West. For this reason, Fanon's psychiatric revolt can and should be mobilized to attack Occidentalism in each and every one of its erotic forms.

It is with this overall project in mind that another African-Caribbean author ought to be read today. In direct contrast to Fanon and a range of others, Jamaica Kincaid would not celebrate the death or downfall of Europe or North America in any form. Her literary enterprise is centrally defined by the erotic dictates of an old "civilizing mission," even if contemporary critics manage to ignore such a monumental fact. To be sure, *My Brother* (1997) recycles a moralizing rhetoric of AIDS in a fashion that reiterates classically racist politics of sex and empire: Black people en masse signify a mortal anatomical danger to the proper heterosexual living of the modern bourgeois world, a world of "culture, development, and civilization." But Kincaid's entire corpus encodes a mind and body tragically captured by Western colonization. *My Brother*'s official classification as a memoir makes it graphically continuous with work Kincaid began in *At the Bottom of the River* (1983), *Annie John* (1985), *A Small Place* (1988), and *Lucy* (1990), not to mention publications that follow it. This literature proves to be as homoerotic as it is politically conservative, on the whole, and, as a case study of sorts, it begs to be read in a way that recognizes the hegemonic social project of "heterosexualization" as a historical project of white colonial imperialism.

Tragedy, Sexuality, and Kincaid

Together, Zora Neale Hurston and Simone Schwarz-Bart can provide a perfect point of departure for a Pan-African interpretation of Kincaid. Hurston's folk writings, set in the U.S. South, are founded on a basic distinction between the average Negro and the mis-educated elite. As she notes in "Characteristics of Negro Expression" (1934), the former belongs to a Black popular majority that transplants the genius of West African culture into a new context, while the latter is a member of a self-despising middle class that scorns anything Negro unless it is approved by white society in advance. Famously, Hurston would disdain all political ideologies mired in the ethos of assimilation, dismissing them outright as "the 'tragedy of color' school of thought" (Hurston 1955, 740).[1] This school sees slavery as progress, more or less, and it associates Blackness with sin, shame, and regret. Hurston's reply in "How It Feels to Be Colored Me" (1928) is another story, of course:

> I am not tragically colored. There is no great sorrow dammed up in my soul, nor
> lurking behind my eyes. I do not mind at all. I do not belong to the sobbing school
> of Negrohood who hold that nature somehow has given them a lowdown dirty deal

and whose feelings are all hurt about it. . . . No, I do not weep at the world—I am too busy sharpening my oyster knife. (Hurston 1928, 153)

Defining Blackness in ethnological instead of simply biological terms, Hurston distinguishes between two forms of imitation in her rejection of imitation-as-assimilation. There is the slavish imitation of the privileged elite that apes all things European in a practice of self-annihilation. For them, being "Negro" or "colored" is a tragedy without end. Then there is the art of mimicry enacted by Black masses everywhere, irrespective of colonial geographical borders. This artful mime is not performed to assimilate or become that which is emulated; it is performed for the sheer pleasure of the act itself, often with great irony instead of tragedy, in a manner which, as a matter of fact, reinforces Black cultural identity. All art is mimicry or a "modification of ideas," according to Hurston, and she is adamant that Africans have absolutely no equal in this arena of culture (Hurston 1934, 59–60).

A comparable Black world portrait of the Caribbean can be observed beyond Hurston's *Tell My Horse: Voodoo and Life in Haiti and Jamaica* (1938) in Simone Schwarz-Bart's novel *Pluie et vent sur Télumée Miracle* (1972; as *The Bridge of Beyond,* 1974). Its heroine begins her testimony with an anti-colonial self-affirmation that resonates with the colorful Hurston:

A man's country may be cramped or vast according to the size of his heart. I've never found my country too small, though that isn't to say my heart is great. And if I could choose it's here in Guadeloupe that I'd be born again, suffer and die. Yet not long back my ancestors were slaves on this volcanic, hurricane-swept, mosquito-ridden, nasty-minded island. But I didn't come into the world to weigh the world's woe. I prefer to dream, on and on, standing in my garden . . . till death comes and takes me as I dream, me and all my joy. (2)

Once again, a more or less pitiful response to the persistence of colonial racial oppression is rejected in favor of a joyful identification with the culture of resistance: Télumée's or Schwarz-Bart's oyster knives are wielded with dreams of liberation. There is no call for assimilation (or white Westernization) in any terms. If there is tragedy as a result of colonialism, there is no tragedy of color. Her protagonist's vision is as Pan-African as Schwarz-Bart's approach in her six-volume collection *Hommage à la femme noire* (1988; as *In Praise of Black Women,* 2001).

This convergence of cosmos and ideology in Hurston and Schwarz-Bart is significant but may attract much less attention than writing which supplies what is in essence another version of "the 'tragedy of color' school of thought." Kincaid fits this genre to a T. The great country of Schwarz-Bart's Diasporic island is commercially eclipsed by the symbolics of Kincaid's *A Small Place.* Kincaid uses a discourse of primitivism to classify Antigua, or the Caribbean at large, as a place populated by children, even lunatics, who are unable "to give

an exact account of themselves," and who are incapable of "careful consideration" (Kincaid 1988, 52–57). For Schwarz-Bart, this point of view manifests
symptoms of a small heart. Moreover, Kincaid's "memoir" narrates her migration to the center of neo-colonial empire not only as an escape from a supposedly small place, but no less as an escape from a specifically sexual place which
would have inflicted upon her "ten different children by ten different men," or
an AIDS-related death like her brother's (Kincaid 1997, 28, 41). It is this imperialist conceit of a savage, small-minded sexuality that holds the key to any
analysis of the tragic yet (in many cases) esteemed text of Kincaid.

Sylvia Wynter has offered a profound theoretics of sex both in the immediate
context of Caribbean women's writing and in the African world more globally.
Outlining the metaphysics of humanism which articulates modern European
imperialism, her "Beyond the Word of Man" (1987) observes that the historicization of modes of subjectivity often associated with the name of Michel Foucault was first effected by Aimé Césaire and then by Fanon, Edouard Glissant,
and George Lamming, to name a few. Unlike Foucault, however, these Black and
Antillean figurations expose the centrality of race to the ideal self advanced in
the philosophies of empire (Wynter 1987, 640). In "the Greek . . . esthetics of
the post-Enlightenment bourgeoisie," after the dogma of Christianity is countered by the doctrine of humanism, the "native" or "nigger" is thought to occupy the inferior half of the dichotomy of rational and sensory nature that
grounds the social order of colonization. Blacks are posited as enslaved, not to
a bipolar order of Occidentalism, but to a "lower sensory nature" that must be
"mastered and mistressed" by the logic of white supremacy (641). This middle-
class model of desire and being promotes the illusion that universal reason is
the essence of Europe: according to this evolutionist scheme, African peoples
must become "auto-phobic," physically and culturally self-negating, to approximate humanity (643). The specter of a "savage, sensory nature" and sexuality,
unchecked by "higher civilization," defines race, racism, and empire.

Wynter treats the political effects of this mind/body split further in "Beyond
Miranda's Meanings: Un/Silencing the 'Demonic Ground' of Caliban's 'Woman,'"
an "After/Word" Wynter crafted for Carole Boyce Davies and Elaine Savory
Fido's *Out of the Kumbla: Caribbean Women and Literature* (1990). Here she
particularizes the universalizing discourse of feminism and firmly situates it,
with Marxism and liberalism, as the latest and last variant of the Western "Word
of Man" (Wynter 1990, 363). Her effort to move beyond all these frameworks
of domination, while indulging William Shakespeare's *The Tempest* (1611),
continues to unveil what has come to be termed "the social construction of gender" as well as the social construction of "an allegedly natural erotic preference"
(365). What Wynter calls the "stigmatization of homoerotic preference" (370)
has to place the concept of a universal heterosexual in the genealogy of white
racist power along with the universal man of liberalism, the universal proletar-

ian of Marxism, and the universal woman of feminism. Her recognition of this heterosexualism as colonial also enables us to unmask the current gay and lesbian counter-discourse of the West and its universal "queer," which has appeared as the latest, though not necessarily last, embodiment of the humanist imperialism of Europe.

Such an anti-colonial politics of sex and sexuality is crucial for the study of Kincaid. In a review of *Lucy*, which is typically considered an at least semi-autobiographical sequel to *Annie John*, Opal Palmer Adisa pinpoints the theme that would continue to perplex Kincaid's readership. Without fail, the narrator strives to sever all connections to her roots or ancestry, her past, including the West Indian family and community she so frantically disavows. Speaking on the mother-daughter conflict in particular, Adisa ultimately concludes, "I am still not sure I understand or even know the source of her pain, real as it is" (Adisa 1991, 57). Indeed, the authorial figure remains enigmatic for many or most. Yet an erotically focused turn to *Annie John* and the primary relations of this tale can clarify what is always at stake in Kincaid. The conservative charge of her work is similarly clarified as a result.

From *At the Bottom of the River* to *Annie John*

In "A Walk to the Jetty," the eighth and final chapter of *Annie John*, the title character navigates a complex emotional landscape as she makes her way with her mother and father to the ship which will take her to England and far away from all that she has ever known. Before embarking, however, she contacts her former friend, Gwen, in a moment that boldly reiterates the controlling theme of her childhood existence. As the two meet, Annie John is filled with sexual shame, conceding, "when I saw her now my heart nearly split with embarrassment at the feelings I used to have for her and the things I had shared with her." Gwen feels this embarrassment as well before she announces her recent engagement to a boy from her hometown, anxiously seeking her girlfriend's approval. With disdain and disgust Annie John replies, "Good luck." The sardonic temper of this retort is lost on Gwen, who expresses no small relief in turn: "Thank you. I knew you would be happy about it." Tellingly, the soon-to-be migrant concludes this passage by saying, "We parted, and when I turned away I didn't look back" (Kincaid 1985, 137). What kind of closure could these words represent?

This indisputably homoerotic tryst is anything but new to the narrative at this point. Gwen's last appearance was just two chapters before, when she herself proposed a certain kind of marriage to Annie John, perhaps like the one announced in their final encounter: "I think it would be nice if you married [my brother] Rowan. Then, you see, that way we could be together always" (93). Already by chapter 6, this relationship is producing feelings of shame and embarrassment in Annie John. She is left dazed, confused, and almost speechless by Gwen's proposal, even though it comes from someone she once described as "the love of my life" (129):

> I stopped and stood still for a moment; then my mouth fell open and my whole self started to tremble. All this was in disbelief, of course, but, to show how far apart we were, she thought that my mouth fell open and my whole self started to tremble in complete joy at what she had said to me. And when I said, "What did you just say?" she said, "Oh, I knew you would like the idea." I felt so alone; the last person on earth couldn't feel more alone than I. I looked at Gwen. It was Gwen. The same person I had always known. Everything was in place. But at the same time something terrible had happened, and I couldn't tell what it was. (93)

The thing that is terribly different now is discernable only a few pages earlier as a shift in the social expectations centered in the schools of British empire. Not long before "the love of [her] life" propositions her with the idea of a cover marriage, Annie John is taken out of the class she shares with Gwen and placed with girls two or three years older, who "didn't offer the same camaraderie of my friends in the second form" (90). Prior to this promotion, the friendly intercourse in the chapters of *Annie John*'s memoir devoted to schooling is driven by an explosive female homoeroticism, which is graphically scripted as the pleasure of paradise.

In the chapter entitled "Gwen," in which Annie John marks the moment "we fell in love" (46) and observes that "other girls were having the same experience" (48), Annie John boasts, "I would then laugh at her and kiss her on the neck, sending her into a fit of shivers, as if someone had exposed her to a cold draft when she had a fever. . . . I said that I could not wait for us to grow up so that we could live in a house of our own. I had already picked out the house" (50–51). In the next chapter, named after the Red Girl, a sort of tomboy figure with no regard for protocols of gender, Annie John celebrates "the perfection of [a] new union" (60), while bracing herself for a "future of ridiculous demands" (53) that will hamper the loves and desires of the passionate schoolgirl setting. This future is synonymous with dread, since she knows she will be expected to abandon Gwen, the Red Girl, and "every other secret pleasure" (61) she enjoyed before the coming of shame and embarrassment, or their general cultural enforcements. Nonetheless, and as usual in *Annie John*, there is virtually no heteroerotic desire in this particular universe of meaning.

Still, despite the intensity of the adolescent female attractions felt by the protagonist, the *true* true love of *Annie John* is not a schoolgirl at all. She lies behind the various pubescent faces used to mask her. After all is said and done, it is Annie, the fabled mother, who is the permanent and paradigmatic love in Kincaid's erotic life-script. This is an extraordinarily basic fact that a slew of psychoanalytic interpretations have managed to repress. Much of this relation is prefigured in *At the Bottom of the River*, and not only in the section entitled "My Mother." For "In the Night" gives voice to yearnings that will pervade subsequent narratives no less:

> Now I am a girl, but one day I will marry a woman—a red-skin woman with black bramblebush hair and brown eyes, who wears skirts that are so big I can easily bury my head in them. . . . This woman I would like to marry knows many things, but to me she will only tell about things that would never dream of making me cry; and every night, over and over, she will tell me something that begins, "Before you were born." I will marry a woman like this, and every night, every night, I will be completely happy. (Kincaid 1983, 11–12)

Likewise, at the outset of her tale, Annie John revels in the erotic bond between this insatiable daughter and the doting mother who tells her stories about the time "before I was born" (Kincaid 1985, 20). As plain as day, and far from the schoolyard, the original libidinal paradise is found in the maternal body. *Annie John*'s second chapter, "The Circling Hand," comprises detailed and ecstatic descriptions of the ritual baths and everyday affections shared by Annie and Annie John, as well as animated accounts of the mother's physical beauty, a beauty that leaves the daughter spellbound.

In the midst of such pleasure, the narrator makes it clear that nothing is like the love of a mother, who in her eyes functions, always and for everyone, as the primary focus of erotic attachment. Of her orphaned father, whose bodily appeal is explicitly ranked beneath that of his mate (18), Annie John says, "I loved him so and wished I that I had a mother to give him, for, no matter how much my own mother loved him, it could never be the same" (24). The rapture of the maternal love bond is also manifest in her initial response to Gwen: "When I first heard from her that she was one of ten children, right on the spot I told her that I would love only her, since her mother already had so many people to love" (74). Indeed, Gwen and other schoolgirls appear as objects of Annie John's affection only when her mother distances herself from her newly maturing daughter, after deciding it is time to make a "young lady" out of her (26–27). This ceremonial act is depicted as absolutely earth shattering, even criminal, by Annie John, who is never, ever able to recover from it, even by story's end. In fact, it is the heartbreak of this distancing that drives her to find an escape from her mother and her "mother's land," motivating her final walk to the jetty.

In Kincaid's *Lucy*, the main character is still unable to resolve this problem. Three years older than Annie John, she has the haunting maternal presence still in mind, and insists, "for ten of my twenty years, half of my life, I had been mourning the end of a love affair, perhaps the only true love in my whole life I would ever know" (Kincaid 1990b, 132). Could any text be any clearer on this score? Why has such clarity been lost on literary critics?

Unequivocally, this mother-loaded passion is the source of the very real pain and alienation discerned by Adisa in her probing review, "Island Daughter." But the prevailing take on Kincaid disregards this central erotic conflict in resorting to Nancy Chodorow's object relations theory and its psycho-social analogues. The subject of *Annie John* as well as *At the Bottom of the River* and *Lucy* has been forced into a transcendent tale about all mothers and all daughters, who always have the same difficulty separating from each other psychologically, en route to the promised land of Western or Westernizing individualism. In the sociological Freudianism of *The Reproduction of Mothering* (1978), Chodorow reinscribes the normative myth of bio-anatomical sex with a developmentalist account of nuclear family drama. She argues that, in the shadow of Oedipus, boys and girls assume two distinct gender personas over time, thanks in large part to the sexual dynamics of conventional mothering. Mothers identify more heavily with daughters than sons, and vice versa, thanks to sex identification itself, in a tautological twist that was supposed to explain how gender and sexuality materialize in the first place. With the social production of sex in the racial context of empire ignored, Chodorow can claim that her generic girl child normally has trouble differentiating herself from her mother before reaching a trans-cultural, trans-historical state of womanhood.

Though much of this framework has been gravely disputed, even within the colonial intellectual confines of North America, its main ideological assumptions are casually applied to situations that should easily undermine it altogether.[2] For example, among early and prominent essays on Kincaid published in Selwyn Cudjoe's *Caribbean Women Writers: Essays from the First International Conference* (1990), Donna Perry invokes "the recent pioneering work by Nancy Chodorow" (Perry 1990, 252) and Helen Pyne Timothy cites it as "evidence for a metatheory that has universal application" (Timothy 1990, 234). Elsewhere, this orthodoxy is writ large in Wendy Dutton's "Merge and Separate: Jamaica Kincaid's Fiction" (1989) and Roni Natov's "Mothers and Daughters: Jamaica Kincaid's Pre-Oedipal Narrative" (1990). The Chodorow doctrine was further enshrined in the European canon of "French feminism" by Giovanna Covi in an essay in *Out of the Kumbla* (1990), after which Wynter began "Un/Silencing The 'Demonic Ground' of Caliban's 'Woman.'" Covi would go on to edit *Jamaica Kincaid's Prismatic Subjects: Making Sense of Being in the World* (2004). June Bobb (1988), Diane Simmons (1994), and Mary Helen Washington (1991) continue this critical trend, along with Lizabeth Paravisini-Gebert's *Jamaica Kincaid: A Critical Companion* (1999).[3]

Nevertheless, despite this standard resort, the problem in Kincaid is never a cognitive separation from the mother's ego at all. It is instead the erotic detachment from her love and affection that fires the text at every turn. What separation-individuation anxiety is manifest when Lucy mourns the end of "a love affair, perhaps the only true love" she may ever have? Or when the girl in *At the Bottom of the River* proposes to marry a woman who can tell her stories that only her mother knows? The shame felt by Annie John as she greets her old girlfriend for the last time is especially revealing when it is grasped both how fully Gwen signifies a displaced and disavowed desire for Annie, the beloved mother for whom Annie John is named, and how fully the sexual subject of "Annie John" will be reincarnated as "Lucy Josephine Potter."

Until she is "launched into young ladyness" (Kincaid 1985, 45) at the age of twelve, Annie John lives with her loving mother in perfect harmony and erotic bliss. Though this daughter certainly identifies with her beloved mother, the identification itself is not portrayed as problematic. It is indicative of a profound matrilineal tradition, a fact which the characters of Ma Chess and Ma Jolie plainly illustrate. After puberty, the "new order of things" (29) institutes a crisis of romantic desire, not ego identity, in which Annie John yearns for the bodily liaison that was once considered natural and innocent. When she wins a certificate for being "the best student" at Sunday school, she rushes home to "reconquer" (30) her mother like the spurned lover she feels herself to be. Upon arrival, she is appalled to witness the sights and sounds of the bedroom shared by mother and father as husband and wife, where there is no space for an adolescent child. In the wake of this sexual encounter, the narrator not only keeps a jealous distance from her father, but also pretends it is actually she who rejected her mother, with whom she is nonetheless obsessed (32). It is then that Gwen and the Red Girl enter the picture as secret girlfriends who are guarded from mother Annie as if she would really, jealously disapprove. The inseparable love ethic once shared with the maternal figure is henceforth transferred to the homoerotic haven of the schoolyard. In compensation for an unbearable loss, the budding "young lady," forced from her mother's arms so that she may one day be the "mistress" of her own house (28), now imagines with Gwen "a house of our own" (51) and dreams of retreating with the Red Girl to an island all their own (71).

These displacements prove to be futile, especially with the passage of time. Before Annie John develops a literal love sickness in the chapter called "The Long Rain," she admits, "I missed my mother more than I had ever imagined possible and wanted only to live somewhere quiet and beautiful and with her alone, but also at that moment I wanted only to see her lying dead, all withered and in a coffin at my feet" (107). A certain bitterness and hatred (26) has consumed her ever since the original erotic rift. Her father, whom she once loved platonically and with pity, no longer receives compassion as a motherless child: "I could not believe how she laughed at everything he said, and how bitter it made me feel to see how much she liked him" (83). The mother is hated constantly but only in order to do away with overpowering feelings of love. Recanting the death wish hurled at the object of her affection, Annie John reflects, "suddenly, I had never loved anyone so or hated anyone so. But to say hate—what did I mean by that?" (88). Reading this conflicted animosity as evidence of a cognitive struggle, as critics have done, only duplicates the daughter's strategy of self-deception. The mother-loaded passion of *Annie John* dictates the entire narrative, including the need for some kind of emotional release in the end. The walk to the jetty is, consequently, a frantic attempt to escape this heartache through a salvation naively (and tragically) identified with the metropolis. The move is from mother to so-called "mother country."

Between *Annie John* and *Lucy*

Lucy picks up where *Annie John* leaves off, except that Lucy's destination is now, fittingly, neo-colonial America instead of old England. The mother of the title character is still named "Annie." She remains the chief focus of the text despite the physical distance separating her and her daughter. With a personal history already familiar to readers of Kincaid, Lucy arrives to assume the role of "au pair," dissociating herself from the more racialized position of "the maid" (Kincaid 1990b, 9), as she generally aims to become "a part of the [white bourgeois] family" that she has many occasions to criticize. Although repeatedly disavowed, her old blood relations mediate her response to the new relations of her immigrant life, and the love-torn protagonist's rescue mission ends as tragedy.

Though Lucy describes her Caribbean family as a millstone around her neck (8) and, like Annie John, says that she scorns Annie as an overbearing mother (36), this self-presentation is constantly betrayed by *Lucy,* the narrative: "Whenever [Lewis] heard me speak of my family with bitterness, he said that I spoke about them in that way because I really missed them" (47). Mariah, wife of Lewis and mistress of the house, is exposed for her complicity with a sociopolitical status quo. She is showered with love and affection nonetheless, in a scenario that paints Mariah as a white-faced version of Lucy's own Black mother: "The times I loved Mariah it was because she reminded me of my mother. The times that I did not love Mariah it was because she reminded me of my mother. . . . Mariah reminded me more and more of the parts of my mother that I loved" (58–59). If she sees her love for her real mother as insufferable, Lucy "grow[s] to love" the Mariah rendition of Annie "so" (46). This love co-exists with similar feelings for the children in her charge. Lucy says of Mariah's daughter, "I loved Miriam from the moment I met her. . . . She must have reminded me of myself when I was that age, for I treated her the way I remembered my mother treating me then" (53). Revealingly, this love for Miriam enables her to relive the "age when I could still touch my mother with ease" (54). When Lucy meets her eccentric girlfriend, Peggy, she is especially pleased that Mariah disapproves; Mariah's disapproval recalls Annie's disapproval of the Red Girl as imagined by Annie John (Kincaid 1985, 63).

The Peggy character should be viewed as an older version of the passionate young loves of a previous life. Predictably, in this more adult alliance, the inescapably homoerotic displacement of the maternal romance is veiled by a more or less artificial male presence. In the chapter dubbed "Tongue," Lucy first recounts her sexual escapades with Peggy as involving a search for boys which almost always results in an act that includes no boys at all: "We were so disappointed that we went back to my room and smoked marijuana and kissed each other until we were exhausted and fell asleep" (Kincaid 1990b, 83). On the same page, Lucy recalls with significant anxiety, "there was a girl from school I used to kiss, but we were best friends and were only using each other for practice" (83). Just as Annie John's girlhood experiences would make a mockery of this heterosexualist posture, the balance of Lucy and Peggy's relationship tells a different story. When a man named Paul enters the story on Lucy's arm, the love triangle becomes more than a little tense. Peggy explodes with jealousy: "This had never happened before. We had never quarreled. I had never chosen the company of a man over hers. I had never chosen anyone over her. . . . I immediately imagined our separately going over the life of our friendship, and all the affection and all the wonderful moments in it coming to a sharp end" (101). The girlhood eroticism recounted in joyous detail by young Annie John, before the embarrassing farewell to Gwen, is far too dangerous for the grown-up Lucy to embrace without shame. However, Lucy also expresses a commitment to her girlfriend in explicitly conjugal terms: "Because Peggy and I were now getting along, we naturally started to talk about finding an apartment in which we could live together. It was an old story: two people are in love, and then just at the moment they fall out of love they decide to marry" (109). This privileging of the female love relation comes as no surprise. In each and every remotely erotic encounter with men that appears in *Lucy*, the narrator makes a point of telling the reader that she is "not in love" (48, 67, 70, 101, 118, 156). For Annie John and Lucy, as well as the narrator of *At the Bottom of the River*, love is an erotically charged emotion reserved for the mother and her same-sex replacements alone.[4]

Lucy is devoted to mourning this unrequited love, a mission cloaked by the image of her family as a millstone around her neck, and this mourning is foretold by Lucy's response to letters sent by her mother from the Caribbean: "I thought of opening the letters, not to read them but to burn them at the four corners and send them back unread. It was an act, I had read somewhere, of one lover rejecting another, but I could not trust myself to go near them. I knew that if I read only one, I would die from longing for her" (91). Compelled to open the letters later by the news of her father's death, the lover pens a response designed purely to inflict pain, to turn the table on rejection, yet again to no avail: "To all this the saint replied that she would always love me, she would always be my mother, my home would never be anywhere but with her. I burned this letter, along with all the others" (128). Lucy admits that she thought she might die trying to be alone and away from the site of her pain. The "feeling of bliss, the feeling of happiness, the feeling of longing fulfilled" which she thought "would come with this situation was nowhere to be found" (158). This story terminates with the title character opening a book and writing her name, "Lucy Josephine Potter," along with the statement "I wish I could love someone so much that I would die from it" (164). The final line produces tears of "shame" (164), the emotion that shook the mature and migrating Annie John in the face of her childhood passion. Literally erasing these last words of confession with her crying, Lucy can neither live nor reject the love that makes death desirable and undesirable all at once.

This family romance repels the explanations of Kincaid's more "cognizing" critics who, concentrating on bonding, magically eclipse the subject of desire. Interestingly enough, *Lucy* opens with a striking comment on Freudian presumption: "Poor Visitor" recounts a night at dinner when the narrator shares one of her dreams and an indigenous interpretation of it in the tradition handed down by her mother. Both Lewis and Mariah are offended; they distort Lucy's dream and remain hostile to her matrilineal analysis. The neo-colonial couple negates the message placed before them by subsuming it under an alien system of meaning: "Their two yellow heads swam toward each other and, in unison, bobbed up and down. Lewis made a clucking noise, then said, Poor, poor Visitor. And Mariah said, Dr. Freud for Visitor, and I wondered why she said that, for I did not know who Dr. Freud was" (15). Rhonda Cobham sidesteps the critique implied by this passage in a review dubbed "Dr. Freud for Visitor?" (1991), delving further into orthodoxies of Oedipus. But other critics could have reconsidered their indulgence of Chodorow vis-à-vis *Annie John*.

Ostensibly, and paradoxically, psychoanalysis is the Western doctrine that concedes the existence of erotic dynamics between parent and child, even as it is some version of this very doctrine that is used to shield or repress these dynamics in Kincaid. Before Freud was able to give the girl of his Victorian scenario an Oedipus complex, however, he had to make her shift the site of her pleasure both from her clitoris to her vagina and from her mother to her father. He writes in "Femininity," "the phase of the pre-Oedipus attachment is the decisive one for a woman's future" (Freud 1933, 107), and he spends much speculative energy trying to secure this last gender assignment in particular: "Unless we can find something that is specific for girls and is not present or not in the same way present in boys, we shall not have explained the termination of the attachment of girls to their mother" (103). Freud would have the girl first redirect her desire to the father, and only then to other males, on the way to social and psychological "normalcy." For a normal femininity to develop, along with normal masculinity, to produce a normal heterosexuality that will lead to a civilized world, Freud's girl must mount an enormous constitutional struggle to surrender the "bisexual disposition" of every child; and, most of all, she must surrender her strong, abundant "sexual relations" with her mother (99). The father of psychoanalysis meets this challenge with "penis envy." The fallacy of this concept is conceded at the moment of its articulation: "If you reject this idea as fantastic and regard my belief in the influence of the lack of a penis on the configuration of femininity as an *idée fixe,* I am of course defenceless" (106). He offered nothing else to sever the girl's primary sexual attachment to the mother, an attachment that "could leave behind so many opportunities for fixations and dispositions" (100) and one that is, according to Freud, especially remarkable in "the primitive child" (102). Of course, neither Chodorow, nor "French Feminism," nor psychoanalytic criticism in general thinks to interrogate this primitivism (or his sexist sexual racism).[5]

Freudianism and Chodorow aside, the anti-colonialism of Césaire (the foremost figure cited by Wynter in "Beyond the Word of Man") has a neglected counterpart in Léon-Gontran Damas. The Guyanese poet blasts the socio-sexual violence of empire in his 1937 poem "Hoquets," or "Hiccups," his favorite work, which prefigures the young ladyhood discourse in Kincaid. The select colonized male child is besieged with a host of gendered imperatives which yield the refrain "Talk about calamity / talk about disasters / I'll tell you." There are whole verses lamenting the fact that the speaker's "mother wanted her son to have good manners at the table," to cultivate a "well-bred stomach" and a "well-bred nose," "to have the very best marks," to speak "the French of France . . . the French that Frenchmen speak . . . French French" (Damas 1972, 15–16). In this self-conscious context of the "colonized bourgeoisie," if the male child doesn't know the history of the "mother country," his mother won't let him go to mass the next day in his Sunday suit. The grueling production of a "young gentleman" for the order of the colonizer is powerfully portrayed:

My mother wanted her son to be a mama's boy:

> You didn't say good evening to our neighbor
> What—dirty shoes again
> And don't let me catch you any more
> playing in the street or on the grass or in the park
> underneath the War Memorial
> playing
> or picking a fight with, what's-his-name
> what's-his-name who isn't even baptized. (16)

This furious incantation ends with the child being reprimanded for skipping his violin lessons and daring to prefer the banjo and guitar. The racist ethic at the core of all the sexually specific dictates mediated by the mother is made most explicit in the final line: "They are not for *colored* people—Leave them to *black* folk" (17). In fact, the entire poem reads as a reverse diatribe against the tyranny of comprador elite socialization. In a translation of "Pour Sur" ("Surely"), which appeared in Keith Warner's "New Perspectives on Léon Damas" (1973), the stance is very much the same. Although Damas writes in advance of *Black*

Skin, White Masks and *The Wretched of the Earth,* the poem is more Fanonian than Freudian: "Me / I say to them / shit / and other things as well. Then / I'll stick my foot in it / or quite simply / grab by the throat everything that shits me up in capital letters / COLONISATION / CIVILISATION / ASSIMILATION / and the rest" (quoted in Warner 1973, 3).[6]

With its searing and precise lyricism, the Damas poem is also evoked by a much later work entitled "Girl" from Kincaid's *At the Bottom of the River:*

> is it true that you sing benna in Sunday school?; always eat your food in such a way that it won't turn someone else's stomach; on Sundays try to walk like a lady and not like the slut you are so bent on becoming; don't sing benna in Sunday school; you mustn't speak to wharf-rat boys, not even to give directions . . . this is how to behave in the presence of men who don't know you very well, and this way they won't recognize immediately the slut I have warned you against becoming; be sure to wash every day, even if it is with your own spit; don't squat down to play marbles—you are not a boy, you know. (Kincaid 1983, 3–5)

But while the mother of the boy in "Hiccups" is rendered as a race and class subject of the "mother country" she ventriloquizes, "Girl" does not explicitly condemn this colonial order. Many critics have assumed Kincaid to be writing an autobiography of personal, psychological rebellion. Yet the cultural politics of Damas aren't remotely conceivable in her aesthetic world-view. While in "Hiccups" the wrath of the child was focused on the colonizer beyond the colonized parent of the colonized elite, the child in Kincaid remains attached to the culture of colonialism as she rages against the mother who withdraws her erotic affection.

From the start, Annie John is proud to be privileged as a target of colonial mis-education in English. Her storied childhood trunk is stuffed with good report cards and certificates of merit from primary and Sunday school (Kincaid 1985, 21). With the onset of "young ladyhood," she takes piano lessons and instruction in manners so she can "meet and greet important people in the world" (27–28). At her new school, there is Latin and French to be studied in addition to English (29). It is with an award for best student in Bible class that she tries to regain her lost mother-love (30). The tradition in which she thrives includes texts such as *Roman Britain* (73), *A History of the West Indies* (73), *The Schoolgirl's Own Annual* (75), and, naturally, "an elaborately illustrated edition of *The Tempest*" (39). The first of these books Annie John wins as a result of being made prefect of her class (73). She had gladly seized the responsibility for overseeing the class in the teacher's absence at an earlier point as well (49). By the time she is ordered to copy Milton's *Paradise Lost* as a punishment for defacing a textbook, in the chapter entitled "Columbus in Chains" (82), her literary Anglophilia is already firmly established.

Hence, in a moment of passionate revelation, Annie John tells Gwen that she wishes she had been named "Enid, after Enid Blyton, the author of the first books I had discovered on my own and liked" (51). Blyton is the author of a series of racist children's books available throughout Britain's colonies. Furthermore, as the narrator seeks a final escape from her attachment to her mother, she begins to daydream about a different life ("Somewhere in Belgium"). She finds herself identifying with "Charlotte Bronte, the author of my favorite novel, *Jane Eyre*" (92).[7] England is the destination Annie John desires, when all is said and done. It is a place which promises to rescue her from every ill of her psycho-social reality. What is lost on her is the fact that her missionary schooling by England is responsible for the sexual shame and embarrassment she feels before Gwen during their last goodbye; that a colonial ideology of sex and sexuality is responsible for the erotic dictates enforced by her mother; and that a bodily trip to the metropolis is likely to make matters worse. The occasional posture of rebelliousness notwithstanding, Annie John remains a well-bred product of British mis-education who learns to loathe the feelings of love she has for her mother and her sex.

A Small Place—To or Fro

This "civilized native" conceit is reproduced elsewhere. Between *Annie John* and *Lucy*, pseudonymous memoirs by another name in the minds of most, Kincaid published *A Small Place*. This was autobiographical polemic: Moira Ferguson in *Colonialism and Gender Relations from Mary Wollstonecraft to Jamaica Kincaid* (1993) calls it "*Annie John*, Part 2." For *A Small Place*, Kincaid returns home as Kincaid, or an acidic tour guide for the *New Yorker*, in what is often read as a critique of the current state of Antigua.

When attention is drawn less to what Kincaid says explicitly to white tourists, and more to what she says about Black Antiguans, her political outlook is exposed for its crude conservatism. The natives are said to hate the tourists because they themselves are too poor to travel and turn their boredom into pleasure (Kincaid 1988, 19). Behind the hatred reported by Kincaid as a native informant is her own apparent envy of tourists from Europe or North America. The prime example of national corruption after pseudo-independence is located in the colonial archive: "Oh, you might be saying to yourself, Why is she so undone at what has become of the library, why does she think that this is a good example of corruption, of things gone bad?" Her only reply is to invoke "the beauty of us sitting there like communicants at an altar, taking in again and again, the fairy tale of how beautiful you were, are, and always will be; if you could see all of that in just one glimpse, you would see why my heart would break at the dung heap that now passes for a library in Antigua" (42–43). Earlier, Kincaid claims to understand some people's desires to "blow things up" (i.e., "terrorism") as an act of social outrage. She gives the example of Barclays Bank, which was built on chattel slavery (26), but imagines no such desire to destroy the "splendid old colonial library." Instead, she recalls going there with great joy every Saturday afternoon as a child, often "walk[ing] out with books held tightly between [my] legs" (45–46). This aesthetic (and erotics) of empire is reiterated in her elitist statements on Black Caribbean speech. Before she states that the formerly enslaved have no tongue to describe the crimes of history (31), she remarks that police in Britain had to get "a glossary of West Indian bad words" to identify abusive language hurled at them by Afro-Caribbean migrants (25). Kincaid clearly does not consider "Creole" a respectable form of expression. She can berate Antiguan youth for being "almost illiterate" (43) in what she dubs "their native tongue of English" (44), as if her chosen English could be their native tongue and their actual tongue counts for nothing. With the discourse of the library exalted and these other languages demeaned, the message is obvious: Kincaid wants Antiguans to speak "English English," and it is better to be colonized in a beautiful way than to be left outside the high cult of England altogether.[8]

The semblance of protest in *A Small Place* is directed against the author's exclusion from Anglophile "civilization"; it is not an actual, rebellious rejection of it. Ferguson could be no more off the mark when she affirms that the library is "a cultural institution that has been one of the sole and free instructors of the people" (Ferguson 1993, 136). Its usual function under colonial imperialism is what Carter G. Woodson studies in *The Mis-education of the Negro* (1933). This is how Kincaid can come to classify her native land as a small place. Tellingly, Western geography does not describe the British Isles or the North American suburbs as small places in like fashion. The metaphysics of smallness is meant for certain people who "cannot see themselves in a larger picture, they cannot see that they might be part of a chain of something, anything" (Kincaid 1988, 52) and those who "have no interest in the exact, or in completeness, for that would demand a careful weighing, careful consideration, careful judging, careful questioning" (54). Completing this standard portrait of primitivism, Kincaid writes that these small folk do not have a proper sense of time (54) and that they are prone to corruption (55), melodrama (56), and childlike behavior (54–57). This is precisely the colonial framework Wynter debunks in "Un/Silencing The 'Demonic Ground' of Caliban's 'Woman'" and "Beyond the Word of Man." Thus, *A Small Place* can close with the author's desire to be "just a human being" (81), despite the racialization of the globe which this rhetoric of humanism implies. The tragedy of color for Kincaid is that her native cannot become the tourist, or the colonized cannot become the colonizer, after all, in a world history that continues to be dominated by the latter.

When *Annie John* is rewritten as *Lucy* to mourn the maternal love affair without end, the cultural hegemony of the white West is no less evident. In the jargon of the colonial surveyor, Lucy states, "I was born on an island, a very small island, twelve miles long and eight miles wide; yet when I left it at nineteen years of age I had never set foot on three-quarters of it" (Kincaid 1990b, 134). When a group of white partygoers chatter about their latest trip to "the islands," Lucy is not angered but embarrassed: "somehow it made me ashamed to come from a place where the only thing to be said about it was 'I had fun when I was there'" (65). She describes the Caribbean not merely as hot; its weather has to have a divine moral purpose: "It was a heat that bore down on you, first as a warning, then as a punishment, for sins too numerous to count" (52). As the narrator, now in the bosom of U.S. empire, continues her flight from her love for her mother, she is running from the history of Black colonization in the Americas as well: "I thought that if I could put enough miles between me and the place from which that letter came, and if I could put enough miles between me and the events mentioned in the letter, would I not be free to take everything just as it came and not see hundreds of years in every single gesture, every word spoken, every face?" (31). Even when this approach flounders, the illusion is what counts. Amnesia and individualism remain optimal: "I had begun to see the past like this: there is a line; you can draw it yourself, or sometimes it gets drawn for you; either way, there it is, your past, a collection of people you used to be and things you used to do. Your past is the person you no longer are, the situations you are no longer in" (137).

This desire to "escape" is again defined by literary phantasms of English. When the title character looks at her signature, "Lucy Josephine Potter," she contemplates renaming herself just as "Annie Victoria John" did: "In my own mind, I called myself other names: Emily, Charlotte, Jane. They were names of the authoresses whose books I loved. I eventually settled on the name Enid, after the authoress Enid Blyton" (149). In *Annie John,* the protagonist is one day horrified by her Blackness as a clear result of schooling: "My skin was black in a way I had not noticed before, as if someone had thrown a lot of soot out of a window just when I was passing by and it had fallen on me." Catching a glimpse of herself, she remembers a painting entitled *The Young Lucifer* which represented him as "charred and black," with "coarse" features (Kincaid 1985, 94). When the next Kincaid character displaces her love for her mother in an alien environment, the erotics of this exchange land on the blue eyes of an assortment of white bodies, whether Mariah (Kincaid 1990b, 39), Paul (99), or Peggy (100). Eventually, when all psychological resistance proves futile, she concludes, "The stories of the fallen were well known to me, but I had not known that my own situation could even distantly be related to them. Lucy, a girl's name for Lucifer" (152–53).

Before and after *A Small Place,* what we read in Kincaid again and again is not so much a critique of the "young ladyhood" ideology of imperialism as its extremely tragic confirmation. With the coming of puberty, the daughter is divorced from her maternal passion, not to mention its same-sex analogues, by the force of convention ordained by Britain in its colonies. Although resenting the sexual dictates that demand this separation, the heartbroken child assumes a normative posture thanks to the discipline of missionary instruction. A severe habit of Anglophilia is formed as the literature of conquest provides a release from forbidden and unrequited love. The more Kincaid's character seeks relief in the daydream material of colonial aesthetics, the more she internalizes the mores that condemn her unladylike desires. An acute frustration is born of this resentment, which has no oppositional politics to speak of. The daughter aims to hate the mother as a means of coping with the attraction that continues throughout her adult life, and all this emotion is directed against the colonized mother and, by extension, her mother's land.

On *My Brother,* etc.

In an interview conducted by Selwyn Cudjoe for *Caribbean Women Writers,* Kincaid frames *Annie John* in a fashion identical to the fashion in which it has been received by critics: "The feelings in it are autobiographical, yes. I didn't want to say it was autobiographical because I felt that that would be somehow admitting something about myself, but it is, and so that's that" (Kincaid 1990a, 220). No doubt, *Annie John* reprises *At the Bottom of the River* and is "sequeled" by *A Small Place* and *Lucy.* The intertextual consistency is as precise as its convergence with Kincaid's own life history.[9] And the story continues. After *Lucy,* there was *The Autobiography of My Mother* (1996), which was the first Kincaid book to be commercially classified as a novel. In certain respects, it could represent a break in the personal narrative beginning with *At the Bottom of the River.* But its general thematic conforms to the rest of her corpus, as the title boldly illustrates. *My Garden (Book)* (1999) will maintain the textuality of imperialism, not unlike *A Small Place,* and *Among Flowers: A Walk in the Himalaya* (2005a) will even be published by National Geographic. *Mr. Potter* (2002) will turn to paternal genealogy as a compliment to *The Autobiography of My Mother* and everything that precedes it. This is not to exclude her edited projects, *My Favorite Plant* (1998) and *The Best American Travel Writing* (2005b), or the publication of *Talk Stories* (2001), a collection of her *New Yorker* columns from 1978 to 1983. With whatever license, Kincaid's long autobiography is extended by various means; regardless of classification, every new offering builds on the foundation set "fictively" or not so "fictively" before.

Following *The Autobiography of My Mother, My Brother* (1997) would pick up the mission of *At the Bottom of the River, Annie John, A Small Place,* and *Lucy,* arguably as a climax of this earlier work. The pandemic of AIDS and HIV brings sexuality to the fore in a manner critics cannot possibly ignore. Still, most if not all continue to ignore Kincaid's own sexual orientation, her relationship to sexual identity—personally, intellectually, and politically—as she graphically objectifies the reported sexual orientation of her sibling. At once homoerotic and heterosexualist in focus, this is a memoir that is not supposed to be really about her or her sexual morality, no matter how much her discourse is a discourse of projection; and no matter how much her maternal fixation remains firmly in place.

My Brother concerns the youngest of the writer's three brothers, "Devon," a "homosexual," who died of AIDS on January 19, 1996, according to the book jacket. However, consuming this narrative as such would implicate its readers in a series of subterfuges. Kincaid not only insists that she did not love the brother for whom her book is named; she also concedes that she did not know him very well at all. She left Antigua when he was three years of age; she only made contact with him again during the last three years of his life; and she has since done little to familiarize herself with his person. An extreme ignorance of the politics of HIV and AIDS also permeates this text so thoroughly that Kincaid's opinion on the matter is rendered completely suspect. It is in the second half of this account that Devon is suddenly declared a "homosexual," based on Kincaid's brief encounter with a strange white woman at a Chicago bookstore (Kincaid 1997, 156–61). Much as the erotic term-concepts of the West are presupposed to be universal, this posthumous sexual categorization is embraced as an unquestionable truth. Henceforth, Devon can be defined as homoerotic in sexual orientation or preference while his chronicler steers clear of any such designation herself. Could this be more odd, coming from the author of the autobiographical feelings of *Annie John, Lucy,* etc.? Why should Kincaid's own sexuality not be declared and marketed in similar terms?

From beginning to end, she depicts Devon as a pathologically mothered son coming from a pathological motherland. When she hears of his medical condition, she imagines a lifestyle that would explain all disease: "he lived a life that is said to be typical in contracting the virus that causes AIDS: he used drugs (I was only sure of marijuana and cocaine) and he had many partners (I only knew of women). He was careless; I cannot imagine him taking the time to buy or use a condom. This is a quick judgment, because I don't know my brothers very well" (7). As this one of Kincaid's brothers appears to quickly become all "brothers," these reckless assumptions reveal much about her conception of HIV. She thinks of it as a moral plague that results from moral laxity, which requires moral discipline. Typically, in *My Brother* drug use and sexual promiscuity, not the exchange of bodily fluids, are thought to produce infection. But in truth neither smoking marijuana, nor snorting cocaine, nor having multiple sex partners is primarily at issue. What is includes intravenous injection and sex with but one partner, *if* either sex or injection involves a viral infection; and these are simply two possible means of transmission; there are others. Kincaid's rhetorical slide is not inconsequential. A conservative, pathologizing discourse of AIDS is employed to condemn the "sinful sensory nature" of someone she does not care to know, whoever he might be or have been.

Dying as opposed to living with AIDS in *My Brother*, Devon is rather luridly pictured as a rotting penis, anus, and oral cavity waiting to expire—for all intents and purposes, as a consequence of "Antiguan sex." The exploitative and voyeuristic nature of this account of his ailing Black body is disguised by Kincaid's claim that her own sexual life is a "monument to boring conventionality." She writes, "I wanted him to tell me what his personal life had been like. He would not do that. Antiguans are at once prudish and licentious" (41). The common media image of a "mad and monstrous contaminator" is unleashed as Kincaid inveighs against "sexual irresponsibility," pure and simple. Her stated fear is that Devon continued to have sex with unwary and unprotected partners. Beyond this posture of epidemiological concern, she is repelled by his erotic practice in general (at least as she imagines it). So she mocks his self-expression in Black popular music of the Caribbean as she fails to understand his boasting: "Me nar joke, mahn, when me sing, gahl a take ahff she clothes" (68). "Girls to take off their clothes when they hear him sing? What could that mean?" (70). She must forget the passage in *Lucy* where her alter ego desires to do this very same thing:

> Mariah placed the flowers before me and told me to smell them. I did, and I told her that the smell made you want to lie down naked and cover your body with these petals so you could smell this way forever. When I said this, Mariah opened her eyes wide and drew in her breath in a mock-schoolmistress way. . . . This was the sort of time I wished I could have had with my mother, but, for a reason not clear to me, it was not allowed. (Kincaid 1990b, 60)

Kincaid herself plays the "schoolmistress" in *My Brother*. She insists that had she not ruthlessly rejected family and nation as a young woman in her teens, she might have "known" a man just like her mother's son, Devon. This sort of sexual character "must account for the famous prudery that exists among a certain kind of Antiguan woman [*sic*]," or "the English-speaking West Indian woman" at large (Kincaid 1997, 69). Somehow, this reference to Anglo-Saxon prudery is not meant to refer to the puritanical mores of British empire. The colonial ideology of "young ladyhood" is justified here with a vengeance. Despite the pain effected by her mother's discipline, or distance, Kincaid can embrace it in this context since she might otherwise "have ended up with ten children by ten different men" (28); and, she adds aghast, no woman who did would be ostracized where she comes from (40).

Upholding nuclear family values which uphold racism and patriarchy in Europe and North America, Kincaid opens her memoir by saying she is surprised to discover her love for her brother (20); then, after this initial selling point, *My*

Brother proceeds to repeat that she has never loved him or his people at all (51). She declares that she thinks of all three of her brothers as her mother's children as opposed to siblings of her own (21). Later, when a Black woman activist from Britain asks why Kincaid doesn't take Devon to the United States for medical treatment, the author is horrified. She responds in defense of herself: "I have a family" (48). Coded as a threat to the very concept of family, like all that is Antiguan, Caribbean, or African, Devon appears to be a brother to Kincaid for literary-commercial purposes exclusively.[10] Any affiliation with what he represents would be dangerous to her mission. Her trip to see him before his death reverses the migration narrated in *Lucy* as an escape from her mother and her Black cultural identity: "When I was sitting with my brother, the life I had come to know was my past, a past that does not make me feel I am falling into a hole, a vapor of sadness swallowing me up" (23). There is a historical past that refers to the abyss of the collective history of African Diaspora, and for her, individually, there is a more contemporary past that refers to her life in New York or Vermont. She experiences her Black "past" as misery, or sadness—tragedy. She envisions freedom from this Black past, family, and culture as freedom itself in the white bourgeois West.

The market-oriented title of *My Brother* notwithstanding, Kincaid zeroes in on the demonic mother, once again, as much as on Devon and her mother's land. When the daughter sought to lose herself in English novels as a child, the mother was hostile enough to this practice to actually burn these books (197), in a symbolic protest against "slothfulness" (44) and perhaps a great deal more. No political analysis of this act is entertained. For her mother signifies an entirely negative matriarchal presence that is ruinous for male and female children alike. Devon is believed to be pathological and unproductive because he never abandons his mother's house to reproduce his own household, as did Kincaid. This decree is delivered in support of a bizarre work ethic that could have killed someone in his state at the time: "It is hard for us to leave our mother, but you must leave; this one thing you should do before you die, leave her, find your own house as soon as you are well enough, find a job, support yourself, do this before you die" (78). This wish is written as if Kincaid comes back to Antigua to effect a divorce between mother and brother (or brothers), who until now was written out of her rapturous tales of mother and daughter. She blames her mother for shaping the sexual identities of all her children with an "infectious" kind of love; a perverse ("primitive") love which colonial literature and migration can never overcome; and a love "unequaled I am sure in the history of a mother's love" (17), Kincaid concedes, as she recasts this problematic love theme from *At the Bottom of the River, Annie John,* and *Lucy* to *My Brother,* etc.

By and large, Devon conveniently functions as a Black deformation of both white heterosexuality and white homosexuality throughout *My Brother,* while the erotic dynamic is downplayed and distorted with regard to his sister, Kincaid, who will only compare herself to him in her capacity as a writer. Being a writer (of English) is comparable to being a homosexual or having AIDS, living with AIDS, and dying from AIDS. And with her brother "outed" in death, as a sexual counterpoint, Kincaid can unsuccessfully attempt to revise her own writings and present her maternal conflict as if it had no erotic element whatsoever. The love affair of *Lucy*, the sexual shame and embarrassment of *Annie John*, the marriage proposal of *At the Bottom of the River*, etc., are all meant to disappear from consciousness in the demonization of *My Brother*. Born after an erotic paradise when her mother was "really beautiful" (71), Devon and his death from AIDS allow Kincaid to deflect the self-implicating sexual preoccupations of virtually everything she has ever written in the shadow of British colonial literature.

Conclusion

Dionne Brand's short story "Madame Alaird's Breasts," collected in her *Sans Souci* (1989), is much like *Annie John*. It concerns an all-girl cohort and their erotic fascination with a schoolteacher's anatomy: "We discussed Madame Alaird's breasts on the way home every Tuesday and Thursday, because French was every Tuesday and Thursday at 10:00 a.m. . . . . [H]er breasts were huge and round and firm. . . . Madame Alaird's breasts were like pillows, deep purple ones, just like Madame Alaird's full lips." The descriptions are lush and lusty, unquestionably lovelorn. The narrator testifies, "Her breasts gave us imagination beyond our years or possibilities, of burgundy velvet rooms with big-legged women and rum and calypso music. Next to Madame Alaird's breasts, we loved Madame Alaird's lips. They made water spring to our mouths just like when the skin bursts eating a purple fat mammy sipote fruit" (Brand 1989, 80). Almost oblivious to boys, the thirteen-year-old girls experience jealousy only when a gloomy mood comes over their buoyant teacher, and they imagine that her husband is to blame: "Cheeups! You don't see he could use a beating!" (82). Her breasts, "hidden in dark green knit," suddenly become "disappointing" for "months until, unaccountably, her mood changed. . . . Madame Alaird was back to herself and we lapped our tongues over her breasts once again, on Tuesdays and Thursdays" (83). The story closes with the unrepentant schoolgirls lowering their eyes before her, as if "penitents" at an altar of voluptuous flesh and blood (84). Without a doubt, critics can read this unabashed same-sex eroticism *as* same-sex eroticism because Brand is labeled a Black lesbian writer, unlike Jamaica Kincaid.[11]

Inge Blackman offers another Kincaid counterpart in her film *Paradise Lost* (2003). Touted as a personal journey and a documentary on "gays and lesbians in Trinidad," it ironically invokes the Milton with whom Annie John was punished in "Columbus in Chains." After twenty years of hiding and feeling like an alien, Blackman recalls a host of good grades and high prizes in her well-

schooled background. But she is no longer proud, noting that her good-girl performance was nothing short of a prison. She too tried to find an escape in England. She speaks of her mother as someone who "demonstrated all the complexities of someone brought up in the colonial era." This mother is not
decontextualized, nor are her complexities. Of her father, the filmmaker states,
"I wanted to be like him and marry a beautiful woman!" In time, Blackman
"chooses life over damnation" and terminates her twenty years of hiding behind
a repressive mask, reuniting on camera with her African-Caribbean family, Black
mother and father, as her father insists, "You always love your child." *Paradise
Lost* closes with Blackman continuing a search for erotic resources in the more
socially liberating masks of Carnival, while lamenting her present status as
something of a cultural outsider, having been away in Britain too long. This
narrative also converges with Kincaid's erotically as much as it diverges from it
politically, all critical evasions aside.

In Kincaid, who is too often read alone, apart from other Black and Caribbean writers, it is the sexual crisis of a Black mother's daughter in the context
of British colonization which drives the discourse, not in just one or two texts
but in her lifework as a whole. The girl-child is totally enraptured by the woman,
who turns out to be irreplaceable in the passionate psyche of adolescence and
adulthood. When this same love administers a new order of body relations, determined specifically by British colonial relations, the loving child is nothing
short of crushed. As she strives to turn her bitterness into hatred in order to
cope with the loss of this childhood romance, she escapes into a world of fantasy
supplied by the colonizer. The daughter is quick to surpass the mother in her
adoption of alien norms. She is not like the boy-child in Léon-Gontran Damas's "Hiccups." The girl-child in Kincaid never repudiates "COLONISATION /
CIVILIZATION / ASSIMILATION," or the cultural violence of empire. Internalizing the colonial ethos that makes her desires unbearable in any form, she
comes to experience her "native" identity as a global historical curse. Being born
Black in Antigua or the Caribbean is seen as a tragedy that only further Westernization can assuage. There is no joy in mass resistance for Kincaid, as there
could be for Zora Neale Hurston and Simone Schwartz-Bart and Damas. There
is instead a severe Anglophilia spun from England to North America, and a
sharp alienation from her African past, which is conceivable only as a past that
should vanish entirely.

The silence on her politics of sex has been monumental, to say the least,
among academics and non-academics alike. A special issue of *Callaloo: A Journal
of African-American and African Arts and Letters* on Kincaid in 2002 did not
change the course of her critical interpretation. The autobiographical basis of
Kincaid's fiction and non-fiction may make it awkward or costly for conventional critics to perform serious criticism when compulsory heterosexuality is
threatened. She can therefore reap the benefits of a career of autobiographical

writing, taking extraordinary liberties with the lives of others, without being subject to a candid critique herself.[12] This is how literary criticism is compulsorily complicit with heterosexualism, especially since much of Kincaid might have been read as "pure fiction" from the outset rather than uncritically praised as autobiography or memoir. Such complicity should come as no surprise at all. This compulsory heterosexuality is colonialism's heterosexuality. What Kincaid's literature exposes more than anything is how literature has been employed to colonize desire for white racist empire—for what Sylvia Wynter charts as "The Word of [Western] Man."

If the sexuality of motherhood compounds matters for some, Elaine Brown counters this reticence in her autobiography, *A Taste of Power: A Black Woman's Story* (1992). She had no problems writing, non-fictively,

> We would go to sleep at night, my mother and I, in our back room, and she would hold me and stroke my "beautiful hair" like a lover. . . . A woman who was "nothing" wrapped her strong arms around my skinniness and protected me from unknown, deadly beasts. When she held me, her large breasts were comforting, and sometimes sensual. We were one against the world. (Brown 1992, 22)

Further on in her narrative, Brown reflects on her "maternal cocoon" (71): "She was my one and only mother, my rock, whom I really loved. But suddenly I saw that I had to leave her, to climb out of her or cast her out of me" (90). This mother-daughter saga provokes neither homophobia nor anxiety about incest. But this is not Kincaid or her critics. It is Elaine Brown, anti-puritan militant and former leader of the anti-colonialist, anti-imperialist Black Panther Party.

Finally, we should recall Audre Lorde's "biomythography," *Zami: A New Spelling of My Name* (1982), to address what has gone completely unaddressed in Kincaid. On her mother's island of Carriacou, *Zami* is "a name for women who work together as friends and lovers." "There it is said that the desire to lie with other women is a drive from the mother's blood" (Lorde 1982, 255–56). Black and Pan-African in ideology, this is the kind of analytic that can confront Kincaid's "'tragedy of color' school of thought." When the main character in *Lucy* realizes that "my past was my mother," she remembers being told in a distinctly female tongue, "You can run away, but you cannot escape the fact that I am your mother, my blood runs in you, I carried you for nine months inside me" (Kincaid 1990b, 90). This overpowering love consumes the daughter in Kincaid precisely as the lore of *Zami* would prescribe. A reliance on psychoanalysis and its primitivism is infinitely less compelling. It exploits the taboo drama of incest to standardize a heterosexuality that is thought to be a mark of white supremacy, or Western "civilization." Lorde's *Zami* rejects heterosexual as well as homosexual formations of Europe and North America. It assumes the sexual significance of the mother; and, for daughters, it assumes the elemental vitality of "homoerotic" replacements of "mother love."[13] These same-sex alternatives, by which a routine desire for mothers would be routinely redirected, are treated as non-existent or unviable in Kincaid. The mother-driven "desire to lie with women" is denied altogether so that no other adequate release for this first emotional attachment can be found. In fact, all Black eroticism is rejected in favor of an aesthetics of English, as if English were something we could not live without.

Lorde knows that the mis-educated subject who renounces mother and motherland in a system of self-negation designed by Europe is bound to live a tragic existence. The early Frantz Fanon classified the pseudo-Oedipal "neurosis" of the colonized elite in exactly this light, just as the later Frantz Fanon observed in *The Wretched of the Earth* how the violence of colonialism is recycled and aimed at those who should be called "brother, sister, friend" before the ecstasy of African revolution. In order to grasp the function of the mother-daughter relation in Jamaica Kincaid, and to resist the erotic schemes of colonial and neo-colonial power, the controlling categories of masculinity and femininity, heterosexuality and homosexuality must be exploded beyond belief. Although her body of writing is no cause for political celebration by the colonized, it provides a near-perfect case study for a revolutionary analysis of race, sex, and empire that could one day help take us from tragedy to victory.

6 Neo-colonial Canons of Gender and Sexuality, after COINTELPRO

BLACK POWER BODIES/BLACK POPULAR CULTURE AND COUNTER-INSURGENT CRITIQUES OF SEXISM AND HOMOPHOBIA

Any work on the topic of this text must begin in the present neo-colonial situation, precisely as it revisits prior historical realms, and in the end it should explicitly return to the current time-space of Western imperialism. The subject of sex and sexuality can be engaged with the conceits of empire or against them, as is the case with any other subject, in point of fact. Whether the reigning regime of white supremacy is more North American or continental European in focus may be less important than whether or not this racist world order is mystified or demystified in theory and practice. However, the hegemony of U.S. Occidentalism today is disguised by a rhetoric of post-coloniality which shields the reality of neo-colonialism from view. A resulting dubious ignorance of white Western domination could only produce a sexual discourse that is continuous with this domination, locally and globally.

A revolutionary activist and scholar, Walter Rodney is world-renowned as the author of *The Groundings with My Brothers* (1969), *A History of the Upper Guinea Coast, 1545–1800* (1970), *How Europe Underdeveloped Africa* (1972), *A History of the Guyanese Working People, 1881–1905* (1981), *People's Power, No Dictator and The Struggle Goes On* (1981), and *Walter Rodney Speaks: The Making of an African Intellectual* (1990), among many other publications; and he was almost inarguably *the* militant critic of neo-colonialism in the Pan-African world. In "Problems of Third World Development" (1972), an *Ufahamu* article of the utmost importance, he notes that the current era of "constitutional independence" (Rodney 1972, 34) is clearly a counter-revolutionary epoch (30, 41). This is the age in which imperialism develops new forms of political manipulation and the cultural and economic subjugation of the colonized by the colonizer is confirmed. Since colonialism is colonialism, in all its various guises, it could be asked why the prefix "neo" is necessary in the neologism of "neocolonialism." But, for Rodney, the "neo" in neo-colonialism refers to the need for renewed anti-colonialism in this latest phase of empire as well as the recent creation or consolidation of a petty bourgeois elite in the pseudo-independent states of the colonized world, in Africa and elsewhere. This complicit class of white racist power is ordered to oversee the recolonization of subject peoples who rebelled against "raw colonialism," or colonialism in its older forms. It includes "Third World" intellectuals mesmerized by years of "First World" mis-education (38). Responding to and resisting the more or less indirect rule of our time, Rodney exposes how imperialism turns retreat into success (43) in the period after political emancipation (34), so-called.

It is hardly surprising that he presents the "nasty history" of tourism (31) as a prime example of "dependency" and "underdevelopment" in this counter-revolutionary era of empire. The power politics of sex are writ so large in the practice of tourism that the phrase "sex tourism" seems redundant. The Black radical figure most routinely identified with Rodney, C. L. R. James, recognized these politics himself in "Towards the Seventh: The Pan-African Congress—Past, Present, and Future" (1976). He called for the abolition of the European nation-state, the Black comprador elite, and the social ethos of patriarchy in the struggle against neo-colonization at home and abroad. This call was first voiced by Claudia Jones in "An End to the Neglect of the Problems of Negro Women!" (1949). Beyond James, further, Rodney was actually more likely to invoke Frantz Fanon's *The Wretched of the Earth* (1963) and its critique of the "greedy little caste" which helped "set up its country as the brothel" (154) of the Western world. It was this Fanon, champion of the sexual revolution in Algeria and the African revolution at large, whom Toni Cade Bambara cited in her own rejection of the white "madness of 'masculinity' and 'femininity'" in "On the Issue of Roles," her brilliant polemic published several decades ago in her edited collection *The Black Woman: An Anthology* (1970; reprint, 2005).

Yet, over the last several decades, commercialized gender and sexuality talk in Western academia has had little or nothing to say about the neo-colonial context in which it is produced. The material and symbolic condition is instead embraced as an ordinary fact of life. This geopolitics of empire may be best illustrated by the vilification of nationalism (or nationality) in now-standard discussions of sexism and homophobia. The nationalism vilified is typically the nationalism of the colonized, not the colonizer who invents nationalism as a bourgeois form of rule. Hence, many people come to see *Black* "nationalism" as synonymous with any given evil, even though the rhetoric of nationalism is itself of European origin and, in this case, a common misnomer for Black militancy of various ideological kinds. White nationalism is never conceived or mentioned as such, by contrast, let alone castigated as the ruling force of the globe. Why is this canonical criticism of sexism and homophobia couched as a criticism of colonized "nationalism," in its insurgent mode? And where "Black nationalism" is vilified, its Black popular culture is never far behind: Black people may be castigated en masse as sexist and homophobic, out of colonial context, with Black militancy now mentally and militarily destabilized. This counter-insurgent articulation of gender and sexuality would repress revolutionary articulations of the matter at hand. For a bourgeois commercialization of sexual discourse bolsters the neo-colonial conceits of U.S. (or North American)–led Occidentalism; and, it shall be seen, this sexual politics of white power is visible in Western academia's recent institutionalization of "Black gay men."

Cheryl Clarke: Anti-Homophobia, Pro–Black Revolution

A fiercely radical, anti-colonial analysis of sex was available at the center of world empire as late as the early-to-mid 1980s. Cheryl Clarke's "The Failure to Transform: Homophobia in the Black Community" (1983) is exemplary. A contribution to *Home Girls,* the landmark anthology edited by Barbara Smith, the essay opens with the following line: "That there is homophobia among black people in America is largely reflective of the homophobic culture in which we live." Some "venomous" legislation before the U.S. Congress is then quoted to confirm the ruling class's "fear and hatred of homosexuals," homosexuality, and the homoerotic "potential in everyone." Even so, as the ultimate source of sexual violence is situated with precision, what never gets lost is "our responsibility to transform ourselves," despite white supremacy, in the interests of Black liberation (Clarke 1983, 197).

Crucially, when Clarke targets the power and prestige of the ruling class, she also provides a class critique of the colonized elite that emulates the ruling race. It was this specific social stratum, its "intellectuals and politicos" in particular, who most "absorbed the homophobia of their patriarchal slavemasters," and they attempt "to propagate homophobia throughout the entire black community" (198). Clarke's readers cannot ignore the cultural limitations of the West. She condemns the colossal pressure brought to bear on "men, women, and children to be heterosexual to the exclusion of every other erotic impulse." Likewise, she condemns the "insular, privatized," and "male-dominated" nuclear family promoted by state and society alike (200). If Black people have been violated as a whole by this history of white sexual repression, Clarke can nonetheless recognize how the Black middle class cultivates Occidentalism with a vengeance. Her survey of homophobia in the Black community reveals its decidedly bourgeois character. She indicts the writings of Ed Bullins, Calvin Hernton, and LeRoi Jones as the work of an intelligentsia, for their support of a certain sexual conservatism in the male mode. "Black bourgeois female intellectuals" are indicted, too, as Clarke goes on to read the work of bell hooks, Michelle Wallace, and Mary Helen Washington for their own heterosexualist politics (203). "Black homophobia" cannot be examined outside the class mechanics of white colonization and oppression in "The Failure to Transform."

Clarke's consciousness of "petit-bourgeois" politics allows her to put the sexual attitudes of the masses of Black folk in perspective. She remarks that the poor and working class, "historically more radical and realistic" than the "reformist and conservative" middle class ("bourgeois nationalists" included), have often "tolerated an individual's lifestyle prerogative, even when that lifestyle was disparaged by the prevailing culture." While classic, this observation is scarcely uncritical. It avows that if lesbians and gay men were actually exotic subjects of the masses' curiosity, they were accepted as part of the community, at any rate; and "there were no manifestos calling for their exclusion." The substance of this tolerance should form the basis for the transformation that Clarke desires. She affirms that poor Black communities have "accepted those who would be outcast by the ruling culture," upholding this humanity as a kind of paradigm for contemporary political movements (206). The historical function of these communities as a space of refuge for sexual outcasts, white as well as non-white, leads Clarke to preface her survey of homophobia with an anti-racist reproach: "I sometimes become impatient with the accusations hurled at the black community by many gay men and lesbians, as if the whole black community were more homophobic than the heterosexist culture we live in. The entire black community gets blamed for the reactionary postures of a few petit-bourgeois intellectuals and politicos" (205). In other words, Black people get scapegoated for homophobia in general, not only by a Black intellectual elite, but also by white "bohemians" who exploit Black communities for sustenance when white bourgeois society has shunned them.

There is no question about what sparks Clarke's erotic thought. Her aims are expressly and enthusiastically revolutionary. The "custodians of white male privilege" remain the major object of scrutiny even as colonized mentalities are scrupulously probed (198). We are told that "time and again, homophobia sabotages coalitions, divides would-be comrades, and retards the mental restructuring, essential to revolution, which black people need so desperately" (200). "Homophobia divides black people as allies," Clarke continues. "It cuts off political growth, stifles revolution, and perpetuates patriarchal domination" (207). Finally, this statement is rephrased and reiterated in the spirit of collective responsibility: "The more homophobic we are as a people the further removed we are from any kind of revolution" (208). To press the issue outside this imperative would be pointless at best, or highly suspect. Absolutely, sexual transformation must take place against the status quo of white supremacy and its patriarchy. In the wake of the Black Power movement, after neo-colonialism's counter-revolutionary rise, Clarke promotes an anti-homophobic practice of Black revolutionary politics against these United States of America.

Joseph Beam: "In the Life," after *Zami: A New Spelling of My Name*

Three years later, a similar outlook would inform Joseph Beam's introduction to another landmark anthology, *In the Life* (1986). "Leaving the Shadows Behind" opens with a strong, stock indictment of homosexual racism: "*All the protagonists are blond; all the Blacks are criminal and negligible. By mid-1983 I had grown weary of reading literature by white gay men who fell, quite easily, into three camps: the incestuous literati of Manhattan and Fire Island, the San Francisco cropped-moustache-clones, and the Boston-to-Cambridge politically correct radical faggots*" (Beam 1986, 13). Beam does not hesitate to state the obvious: "We ain't family. Very clearly, gay male means: white, middle-class, youthful, nautilized, and probably butch" (14–15). Barbara Smith repeats this verdict almost verbatim in "Homophobia: Why Bring It Up?" (1990). Analyzing an armed police attack on a Black working-class bar in Times Square, she notes, "'Gay' means gay white men with large discretionary incomes, period" (Smith 1990, 101). This connection between them is far from coincidental; Smith coedited, with Gloria T. Hull and Patricia Bell Scott, *All the Women Are White, All the Blacks Are Men, But Some of Us Are Brave* (1982). Beam reports that he could find little to sustain himself in Giovanni's Room, the gay, lesbian, and feminist bookstore where he worked in Philadelphia, its terribly ironic naming after the James Baldwin novel notwithstanding. Beam "devoured *Blacklight* and *Habari-Daftari*; welcomed *Yemonja* (which later became *Blackheart*); located and copied issues of the defunct newspaper *Moja: Black and Gay*—but they simply weren't enough. How many times could I read Baldwin's *Just above My Head* or Yulisa Amadu Maddy's *No Past, No Present, No Future?*" In the meantime, he was fed by Smith's *Home Girls*, Audre Lorde's *Zami: A New Spelling of My Name* (1982), and other works in what he calls the "Womanist" and "Zami" tradition (Beam 1986, 14). The rich matrix out of which Clarke wrote "The Failure to Transform" resounds throughout *In the Life*, from beginning to end.

A paragraph placed as an inset before Beam's introduction defines the idiom employed by an oral tradition in African Diaspora: "*In the life*, a phrase used to describe 'street life' (the lifestyle of pimps, prostitutes, hustlers, and drug dealers) is also the phrase used to describe the 'gay life' (the lives of Black homosexual men and women)." Next it is stated that, for the purposes of this collection, "*in the life* refers to Black gay men" (12). The white bourgeois terms of "homosexuality" and "gay identity" grounded in the cultural historical specificities of the West appear here merely to be erased, in a sense, by the cultural historical terms of Black community, poor and working-class Black community most of all. As a book, *In the Life* is inadequately described by its subtitle, *A*

Black Gay Anthology, just as "in the life" as a phrase is inadequately defined as "Black homosexual men and women." It is the hegemony of Europe or Eurocentrism, and nothing else, which dictates that Black and non-Western bodies be contained by the erotic codes of a colonial middle class. Much like Lorde's *Zami,* if not exactly like *Zami, In the Life* represents a "new spelling" of our name. An erotics of Pan-Africanism is writ large throughout Beam's "Leaving the Shadows Behind." Carole Boyce Davies recalls Lorde's revision of the Carriacou word "Zami" ("women who work together as friends and lovers") in *Migrations of the Subject: Black Women, Writing, and Identity* (1994); and she remarks that this *patois* term has yet to gain acceptance in the halls of Western academia (Boyce Davies 1994, 18).[1] She upholds its usage elsewhere, among Black activists in Britain, when she writes "From 'Post-Coloniality' to Uprising Textualities: Black Women Writing the Critique of Empire" (in Boyce Davies 1994). But Lorde's and Beam's vernacular is suppressed by the same structure of power that could paradoxically appropriate "In the Life" (*à la Giovanni's Room*) as the title of a white majority middle-class newsmagazine on U.S. public television.

In any case, the counter-revolution of neo-colonialism is palpable in Beam's introduction: "This is not an easy time to be a Black man, nor a Black woman." What explains the "invisibility" of his contributors in the gay white market of conspicuous consumption? He answers in the hard language of "power, racism, conspiracy, oppression, and privilege" (Beam 1986, 15). He berates the municipal bombing of the MOVE organization in Philadelphia as the murder of eleven Black men, women, and children. He condemns the brutality of state violence in apartheid South Africa and compares it to the effects of U.S. domestic colonialism or empire: "We are dying in prisons, on drugs, in the streets, by the hands of the state and our own" (16). This is what frames Beam's treatment of sexuality. "In 1985, we are still radicals," he insists, thanks to the homophobia sharply recast by Clarke: "We are even more susceptible to the despair, alienation, and delusion that threatens to engulf the entire Black community" (17). In direct opposition to this deadly order of things, toward Black revolutionary change across the board, Beam offered *In the Life* as an organized effort to live and love against the grain of neo-colonialist desires (18).

So where are the likes of Beam and Clarke in the academic production of sexual discourse today under white racist imperialism? Texts written in the vein of "The Failure to Transform" and *In the Life* are virtually nowhere to be found in prevailing treatments of sexism and homophobia in North America and beyond.[2] There may have been no other time period during which sex and its politics could be discussed with such public, intellectual ease. The institutional presence of Women's Studies as well as Gay and Lesbian Studies suggests as much. However, no one is encouraged to ask what kinds of discussions have been approved by and for what kind of publics in this intellectual scene. Its commercialization of gender and sexuality as new and gainful objects of study is highly selective about the past and present work it promotes, not to mention the past and present work it obscures.[3] Although precious little space is made for Beam's and Clarke's Black radicalism, sexually speaking, ample space is made for Black politics of another sort as they coincide with the current, counter-revolutionary mission of Western empire. Two filmmakers, Isaac Julien and Marlon Riggs, achieve prominence in this context insofar as the revolt against white supremacy promoted by other critics of "homophobia in the black community" is almost totally disregarded. No necessary threat to Occidentalism is to be posed and its bourgeois mission is to remain intact.

Isaac Julien: "Darker Sides" and "Snow Queens"

As Lewis Gordon comments in "Black Skins Masked: Finding Fanon in Isaac Julien's *Frantz Fanon: 'Black Skin, White Mask*'" (1996), "it is indicative of the political climate at the close of the millennium that films by such luminaries as Charles Burnett, Haile Gerima, Julie Dash, and Euzhan Palcy are not greeted as major cultural events." He observes further that Julien's film on Fanon was showered with academic attention, by contrast (Gordon 1996, 148). The politics of this filmmaker's popularity are on full display. For Julien is not concerned with the revolutionary Fanon. This Fanon may be found in *A Dying Colonialism* (1965) and *Toward the African Revolution* (1967) in addition to *The Wretched of the Earth*. As the title of this film indicates, it is the early and assimilationist Fanon who is screened by Julien. Even that more ambivalent Fanon is frozen on a few selected pages of *Black Skin, White Masks* (1967), while the bulk of his radical life-work is downplayed or repressed. This fact can be used to reveal the neo-colonial sexual politics of other works of Julien's, namely *The Darker Side of Black* (1994) and "Confessions of a Snow Queen: Notes on the Making of *The Attendant*" (1994).

The titles of these texts demand scrutiny themselves. While the name of the film, *Frantz Fanon: "Black Skin, White Mask,"* shows that Julien will not focus on Fanon's African revolution, the titles of the film *The Darker Side of Black* and the essay "Confessions of a Snow Queen" show that Julien remains trapped in the cultural symbolics of imperialism. *The Darker Side of Black* claims to be a documentary on homophobia in dancehall and hip-hop, African Diasporic expressions of the musical Black masses. The "darker" side of Black is already coded, then, before the first frame, as its "lower-class" side, the underside of societies headed by neo-colonized Black or brown elites. The genres of hip-hop and dancehall will be negated entirely, in a metaphorical system equating all things Black (and all Black people) with "darkness," or metaphysical evil. Since Africa is supposed to be the "dark continent" for the white West, what other side could Black people possibly have? What would a lighter side of Black look like in Julien?

In "Confessions of a Snow Queen," he continues the color complex expressed in *The Darker Side of Black*. A "snow queen" is the opposite of a "dinge queen" in the racial ideology of gay white culture. White men are said to be dinge queens when their sexual practice fetishizes Black males. Black males are said to be snow queens when they respond in kind. Black bodies are erotically slurred as dinge, the dirt associated with the dark by the logic of white supremacy. White bodies are pictured as "pure as the driven snow." Julien calls his piece a "confession," but it is far from repentant. He glorifies in his own identification as a snow queen in a simple celebration of "inter-racial desire" which does nothing to dismantle the rigid, caste-like hierarchy in which such inter-racial racialism is embedded (Julien 1994a, 126). The sexual games of power and racism are by no means confined to the sadomasochism of *The Attendant* (1993). A complex of color was also obvious in the aesthetics of Julien's *Looking for Langston* (1989), in which the desirability of Black bodies is graphically determined by gradations of light skin. Investing all eroticism euphemistically in "inter-racialism," meaning Black and white sexual commerce, Julien plays with white supremacy and preserves it as if it is synonymous with pleasure itself. According to "Confessions of a Snow Queen," nothing should be done to challenge it as a structure of colonial domination.

Promotional ads for *The Darker Side of Black* included a review from the U.S. gay white press which claimed in a boldfaced caption, "Homophobia in Hip-Hop Is More Powerful Than the New Right," a statement ascribed to the self-identified Black British filmmaker and a sentiment born out by his interview with Jon Savage in "Queering the Pitch: A Conversation" (1994). Julien makes a distinct reference to dancehall artists Buju Banton and Shabba Ranks: "there's a real limit to them infiltrating the 'pop' market place in countries like America and Britain if they're going to hold on to and promote homophobic points of view; controversy will ensure that a price to be paid by them hurts them financially and I think it denotes the sort of power that gays and lesbians do have in the market place" (Julien 1994c, 12). How telling it is that homophobia is thought not to have a market in the old and new centers of white (heterosexualist) empire; that the class power of gay, white consumerism chided by Joseph Beam, Cheryl Clarke, and Barbara Smith is championed by Julien; and that the racist economy which enables this exercise of power is completely endorsed. One wonders if Julien would say homophobia in Black communities in Britain is more powerful than British xenophobes, racists, and imperialists in England.

The Darker Side of Black begins by musing on the memory of slavery in the most abstract and aesthetic terms, making no comment on present-day modes of enslavement and colonization. Julien's narrative is given voice by Paul Gilroy, who quickly reduces the Black power of music and dance to terror and brutality. African culture has no creative power of its own that would supply Africans with the power to resist terror and brutality under slavery, colonialism, and neo-colonialism. The lyrics of Buju Banton's "Boom By-By" are criticized via a stereo-typical split between the dancehall of today and the reggae of yesterday, a split which construes the latter as entirely hopeful and the former as hedonistic. This move ignores the truth that reggae artists and dancehall artists have often been one and the same, as is the case with Banton himself. It disregards, moreover, the vital production of reggae after the death of Bob Marley; and it reproduces a pacifist, puritanical domestication of Rastafarianism by and for white West-ern middle-class consumption. These visibly counter-insurgent gestures guide the first segment of Julien's film, which is preceded by the caption "*GUN-CULTURE.*"

Thankfully, as *The Darker Side of Black*'s narration refuses all anti-colonialist explanation, there are many Black subjects in the frame who work to subvert the official story. They know full well that the sudden fear of guns reinscribed by the film appears the second they are taken up by the dispossessed, the darker sons and daughters of Africa, in Jamaica and elsewhere. The Geto Boys' Bush-wick Bill is insistent: "The world was built on straight gangsterism, because when Columbus came over here, the queen of Spain sent with him nothing but people from the dungeons that were nothing but criminals and rapists and mur-derers and all that. That's what this country was built on." Ice Cube recalls more than "slavery" when asked to explain why rappers include guns on their album covers: "We do drive-bys. But that's on a small scale when you compare the drive-by on Iraq. . . . We do car-jackings. But that's small when compared to *country*-jackings, when America goes into Panama, takes out its leader and puts in its own leader. So we do things on a small level and America does it on a big level. . . . It ain't just us. White people do everything we do."[4] This is the global historical context in which the subject of violence (sexual and non-sexual) should be confronted. So other, non-rapping voices come to counter the voice of Gilroy and its ignorance of empire. Florizelle O'Connor of the Kingston Legal-Aid Clinic explains that guns became a part of the political culture in Jamaica after the plans of politicians backfired, when they lost local control over the weapons as the people tried to usurp this symbol of authority in order to feed themselves. A lawyer, Richard Hart, reminds us that "the introduction of new and high-powered weaponry into this country" stems from U.S. interven-tion in Jamaica when Michael Manley's administration was on the verge of rec-ognizing the revolutionary socialist government of Cuba. Manley himself ap-pears to add that international drug trafficking must be factored into the equation as well. Still, this is not the tale of the gun told by Julien and Gilroy under the rubric of "*SEX* CULTURE" in the second section of *The Darker Side of Black*.

The narration maintains that "bad dreams are turning into violent reality for some, but most don't seem to care." It goes on to contend that "the lyrical gun" of dancehall and later hip-hop has found "a new enemy target" in "queers." What is grossly irresponsible about this approach is that barely a handful of songs are summoned for cinematic questioning. Most of the focus falls on one single lyric, Buju Banton's "Boom By-By." Nonetheless, Banton and all Black popular music are scripted as somehow single-handedly responsible for all sexual violence since slavery. A serious hypocrisy must be stressed at this point. For the exact same relationship between reality and representation posited by *The Darker Side of Black*'s sweeping indictment of dancehall is summarily dismissed by Julien's "Confessions of a Snow Queen" and *The Attendant,* in which the filmmaker fights for the right to enjoy the racialized violence of sadomasochism without censure. For Julien, no greater drama of domination or structure of power calls for critical interrogation of any sort; he considers these representations harmless and without any necessary relationship to reality. The handful of dancehall and hip-hop artists questioned by *The Darker Side of Black* all deny that they promote or wish to promote sexual violence with Julien's "lyrical gun." More importantly, when they thwart the filmic construction of their lyrical productions as mere anthems for gay-bashing, the exchanges always degenerate into a question of whether or not a given artist personally and publicly promotes homosexuality. This repeated scenario is analytically quite absurd, for why should a simple study of attitudes about sexual preference restrict itself, in a racist world order ruled with a heterosexualist, homophobic hand, to the individual opinions of a few dreaded Black males, whether Brand Nubian or Shabba Ranks or Buju Banton?

The answer is underscored by Inge Blackman, another powerfully resistant voice in the film. She is identified as the director of *Ragga Gyal D'bout!* (a film which plainly does not inform Julien's standpoint). Her insights are sharp and reminiscent of Clarke's "The Failure to Transform": "Most of the prominence has been given to Black people who are homophobic and so then Black culture is being painted as a homophobic one. What you don't hear are the more complex issues raised by Black people who are not homophobic and who are also avid fans of ragga." The matter of sexuality is often raised not in order to deal with it, in other words; it is deployed to destabilize Black culture and its popular musics of resistance. Blackman says that during the making of her own film, "Ragga women were saying very important things which were not usually aired in the mainstream media," such as that "Boom By-By" was homophobic and should be condemned, "but what they resented was the way that the gay press campaigns about ragga and how the mainstream media had taken up the homophobia in ragga and painted the whole of ragga as homophobic." The false distinction between bad (and dangerous) dancehall and good (and safe) reggae is never viable for Blackman. She broaches a criticism of gay white groups that is routine when it comes to hip-hop as well: Black people are grossly overrepresented in their targeting of homophobia, a targeting that permits the homophobic press of the white ruling class and the gay white middle-class press to coalesce in North America. This neo-colonial coding of sexual politics conceals how, as Blackman recounts, "Black lesbians actually do participate in dancehall culture." "Dancehall culture," she continues, "particularly in England, acts as a celebration of women's sexuality and it's a way in which Black women can bond with each other on the dance floor. This is very, very strong. Black women can be sexual with each other, can dance in a very sexual, in a very lustful way on the dancehall in ragga culture." Of course, no white culture anywhere promotes celebration of any Black sexuality, in any form.

Blackman's appearance in *The Darker Side of Black* is predictably brief. The sheer radicalism of her intervention is overshadowed by the gay liberalism of Donald Suggs, a convenient Black spokesperson for the practice criticized in her *Ragga Gyal D'bout!*[5] Blackman's remarks do force Julien's film to concede, for only a moment, that dancehall celebrates women, or the bodies of Black women more specifically. Author of *Noises in the Blood: Orality, Gender, and the "Vulgar" Body of Jamaican Popular Culture* (1995), Carolyn Cooper speaks in support of this position.[6] This is after female deejay Lady Saw (author of the 1996 "What Is Slackness?" and other brilliant songs) explains, patiently, "Men deejay, right? You got some men, they will go and diss the ladies. But I'm not for that, right? I'm for the *ladies*. I go there and defend and hold it down, right?" This intervention is instantly mobilized against hip-hop, once dancehall's avowed sibling. The narration states that its masculist premises "dismiss women" wholesale as "bitches and whores." Chuck D of Public Enemy will interject that Black people didn't invent this language. But what about its reinvention? No one comparable to Lady Saw or Cooper is interviewed when Julien's camera goes up northward on this side of the Atlantic. Only one female rapper gets to talk, Monie Love, whose base was in Britain and who says she'd revalue the term "bitch" were she ever labeled one. This tokenizing inclusion is not itself supposed to be sexist. There is absolutely no trace of the early rap tradition that culminates in Lil' Kim, self-dubbed and undisputed "Queen Bitch" of hip-hop. She performs what dancehall calls X-rated or "dirty reality" lyrics when they are sung by Lady Saw. The title of her solo debut, *Hard Core* (1996), refers to both rap and sex, with extreme and ecstatic violence, as racist sexist conventions are turned on their head at the center of the empire that created them. Artistically, she embodies "*GUN* CULTURE" and "*SEX* CULTURE" to scandalize colonizing and colonized elites in North America, just as Lady Saw and others do in the Caribbean. This is one crucial example that defies *The Darker Side of Black*'s crude masculinization of hip-hop, which is to say Julien's own submission to conventional colonial categories of masculinity and femininity when it comes to the culture and music of the Black masses.

The closing line of the film steers clear of anti-imperialist analysis, consistent with its opening line and its narrative in general. There is a short and final section subtitled "FAITH," in which the non-Christian dismissal of Christianity as "the backbone of 'white supremacy'" is treated as cause for alarm and dismay.

Disbelief in the West, decried as Babylon, is also dismissed as nihilism. Ultimately, there is this query: "Would it be too simple to say that something of the violence of slavery has been internalized and lives on in these Black musical cultures, that it reappears, here and there, in these coded popular forms, providing a perverse remedy for today's miseries?" "Simple" would be an inappropriate description of this claim. It rhetorically erases the existence of older Black musical forms, many of which were produced in direct opposition to slavery and do not fit this pathologization of hip-hop and dancehall. It would be far more appropriate to ask if Julien's "Confessions of a Snow Queen" internalizes and resuscitates the violence of slavery, in light of its uncritical exaltation of all sadomasochistic "inter-racial desire" in *The Attendant*. *The Darker Side of Black* began with a shackled and faceless Black body on a Caribbean beach, which is known to be the sexual playground of white tourism in the current epoch of neo-colonial empire. Why retreat into a distant, exotic period of domination in reference to today's miseries, or a slavery that is seemingly without masters since Black people are supposed to be solely responsible for perpetuating its violence?

It is not old slaveocratic imperialism, per se, but neo-colonial imperialism which manufactures misery today. This is what the resistant voices in *The Darker Side of Black* stress in spite of Julien's narration; and for them slavery is by no means a thing of the past. Michael Franti, a former member of Disposable Heroes of Hiphoprisy and lead vocalist of Spearhead, makes a point endlessly elaborated throughout hip-hop. Declaring his undying love for Black music and Black people, he regrets the commercialization of the genre by white racist forces that pressure many artists to conform to media constructions, including homophobic and masculist constructs of the mainstream. This commerce of Western culture and capital is not targeted by Julien's filmmaking, or by the public service campaigns of white gay and lesbian liberalism, which regularly put a Black face on homophobia under U.S. nationalist empire. That is why interviewers in *The Darker Side of Black* fail to understand how devotees of hip-hop and dancehall can love its musical culture of African Diaspora and critically engage it at the same time, mindful of neo-colonial conditions, without ever wanting to trade it in for any Occidentalist erotic.[7]

Marlon Riggs: Celebrating Class "Difference" and Anti–Black Nationalism

Most of the basic problematics of Julien are reproduced in Marlon Riggs's *Black Is . . . Black Ain't* (1995). Its opening credits proclaim that the filmmaker "challenged racism and homophobia with his work and his life." The celebrity Riggs acquired after the release of *Tongues Untied: Black Men Loving Black Men* (1989) is an apparent consequence of this challenge. The topic of sex or sexuality is no less central to *Black Is . . . Black Ain't*, whose title is taken from a fictional sermon in Ralph Ellison's *Invisible Man* (1948). *A Personal Journey through Black Identity* is Riggs's subtitle. His personal struggle with AIDS and his unsuccessful effort to finish this film before his death receive extensive coverage. Regrettably, if he may not match Julien eye for eye regarding race and class politics of sex, Riggs's text exudes a Western bourgeois orientation at any rate.

Black Is . . . Black Ain't aims to demonstrate how Black identity constrains Black people because of social definitions that exclude specific segments of the population. However, as the film's "gumbo" metaphor reveals, a conventionally white nationalist construct of ethnicity (or "liberal pluralism") guides the critique Riggs presents. He returns at the outset to his familial roots in Louisiana. A curious consideration of color and class immediately ensues. Riggs remembers there being Black folk of every shade in his background; then he notes that his family in Baton Rouge was distinctly darker than his family in New Orleans. The family in New Orleans is described as "light enough to pass." Several other speakers enter the scene to confirm the existence of a mulatto group of Creoles and their legendary hostility toward black skin, Black folk, and Black self-identification. The film never produces a critical analysis of color-caste or the cultural history of white supremacy, which could benefit from the portrait of the brown middle-class elite writ large in E. Franklin Frazier's *Black Bourgeoisie* (1957) as well as his *The Negro Family in the United States* (1948). The cursory treatment of the issue in *Black Is . . . Black Ain't* restricts the social significance of color to the confines of Louisiana. Riggs himself claims this highly stratified structure of race and color was not significant enough for him to notice. Despite his dark complexion, which the Creoles actually point out on screen, he concludes his reflection with these words: "I didn't even think about it." Evidently "every shade" of black is appreciated, even the shades of those who adamantly oppose any inclusion in this category; and "every shade" is apparently appreciated outside the system of domination that crafts it. Hence, however obscene, the social politics of what others call a "pigmentocracy" can be relayed through a metaphor of "gumbo" despite a pecking order of white and Creole anti-Black racism.

Black Is . . . Black Ain't is dedicated to criticizing Black people who criticize this process of racist class formation (whether the character of this criticism is problematic or not). Riggs recalls his days at Harvard University and his inability to speak "Black English." Barbara Smith unilaterally defends her elite schooling and standard English, with the additional support of Angela Davis and Michelle Wallace. The unjust privilege of white and bourgeois power will not complicate the film's discussion at all. The complaints on these matters of class mimic those of white racists who reduce race to a simple matter of melanin when faced with the charge of racism: "I can't help that I'm white." One can "help" being a white racist, however, and one can "help" a cultural and economic system of class domination. Essex Hemphill endorses the flight to the suburbs made by "some of us," those who have "moved up" on "the socio-economic ladder," eschewing the "inner city" as a "frightening" standard of Black identification. This elite class narrative was evident in the extremely talented poet's *Ceremonies* (1992). In Riggs's film he is extremely anxious about the inability of some to "constantly" keep up on "hip" fashion, music, and language. This class of experts take scant pleasure in Black popular culture and its resistance to the white bourgeois culture of empire. For the most part, they are intellectuals who do not find it frightening when the suburb-based elite sets the social standards of Black identity over the poor and working-class majority; that is, when it is they who hegemonize Black political life and perform an academic appropriation of Black culture in white racist public spheres. Their class domination of Black communities is presumed, while a critical vocabulary of class is studiously avoided throughout the film. One "non-intellectual" witness explicitly identifies his African American middle-class affiliation as a source of pride, as if this ranking says nothing of the Black masses ranked beneath him. In the end, the celebration of difference championed in *Black Is . . . Black Ain't* is always coded as a celebration of *class* difference in neo-colonial North America.

This desire to assimilate with cultural prestige and without critical interrogation is especially exposed with regard to Africa. Through the same rhetoric of exclusion which reserves the right to emulate white bourgeois culture while protesting any related scrutiny as a lack of inclusion, the film later asks, "Who's African?" and "Who Isn't?" Black identity is supposed to be reclaimed quite liberally by the close of *Black Is . . . Black Ain't*. Yet no one can unabashedly affirm *African* identity in the film except designated objects of scorn. Viewers are encouraged to mock Molefi Asante's "Afrocentricity" and the Oyotunji's "African village" in South Carolina, but not the university-trained critics who profess no interest in Pan-African life or struggle whatsoever. Eurocentricity and its white world order are never mocked or made objects of scorn. When Riggs recalls his own linguistic shift from "Negro" to "Black," he recounts his efforts to convince someone else to make the change, joking, "Now, to be real, Edward Lee was *so* dark, he could have passed as ONE OF THE ORIGINAL AFRICANS!" An old *National Geographic* image is flashed before other voices are allowed to corroborate. No sanctioned voices are allowed to identify with an Africa beyond this ancient Africa of Europe. Nor is any space allowed for African Diaspora, conceptually. There is no more of a contemporary African world in Riggs (and his commentators) than in Asante, for example. "Black" in *Black Is . . . Black Ain't* is defined wholly in terms of U.S. geopolitics and its white settler colonization. No one envisions a Caribbean or South American component that could in principle help give anti-imperialist meaning to the name "African American." How ironic that the "gumbo" rhetoric claiming to rewrite Black culture in Riggs manages to repress its past and present Pan-African basis.[8]

The notion of nationalism that is vilified intellectually is so makeshift and misconceived that bell hooks, who was indicted by Clarke for her "unbearable" homophobia in "The Failure to Transform" (Clarke 1983, 205), groups together George Jackson, Eldridge Cleaver, and Eddie Murphy in the same "antinationalist" breath. Neither of the three actually subscribed to Black nationalist ideology. Nor can their relationships to sexism be accurately described as identical. To be sure, hooks would have been a dangerous presence in *The Darker Side of Black*. Her position in "Gangsta Culture—Sexism and Misogyny: Who Will Take the Rap?" (in hooks 1994) could have sabotaged Julien's efforts:

> A central motivation for highlighting gangsta rap continues to be the sensationalist drama of demonizing black youth culture in general and the contributions of young black men in particular. It is a contemporary remake of *Birth of a Nation*, only this time we are encouraged to believe it is not just vulnerable white womanhood that risks destruction by black hands but everyone. (hooks 1994, 115)

"Everyone" here includes the colonized middle class, gay and straight. Unfortunately, no comparable take on the vilification of Black "nationalism" comes from hooks in Riggs's film (or elsewhere).

Black Is . . . Black Ain't paradoxically begins and ends in a language of national identity that is much more white than Black. "When I was a boy," asserts Riggs in his patriotic opening, "our nation was in turmoil." When the film comes to a close, and mere symbols of an ill-defined nationalism (such as Minister Louis Farrakhan) have been condemned, Black politics are confined to a need for jobs and education. How can nationalism be to blame, then, for all the sexual ills elaborated throughout *Black Is . . . Black Ain't*? Why is the ruling nation or nationality never condemned by this narrow ideological approach? It is important to recognize, therefore, that the narrative voice in Riggs is not anti-nationalist, in truth. It is fundamentally nationalist vis-à-vis the U.S. state; and this *anti–Black nationalism* is brandished like a flag.

Angela Davis in "Black Nationalism: The Sixties and the Nineties" (1992) invokes an editorial statement issued by Huey P. Newton in the newspaper *The Black Panther* on the relevance of movements for women's liberation and gay liberation for Black liberation struggle. Davis upholds this equally anti-sexist and anti-homophobic polemic as an example for young people of today who, she believes, lack models of Black nationalism that are neither sexist nor homophobic in character. Davis disavows all nationalism herself, positing the phenomenon as a sort of necessary evil for this latest generation, who will not do without it. Still, she says nothing of the sweeping condemnation of "nationalism," whether sexist or anti-sexist, homophobic or anti-homophobic, by the academic establishment in neo-colonial times. She does not see the Black intellectual elite itself as in need of reeducation on the history and politics of nationalism, only misguided Black youth who insist on militancy of some kind.

The chronic misattribution of the name or term "nationalist" is overlooked as well. It was Newton (1972, 1973) who made popular a distinction between "revolutionary nationalism" and "reactionary nationalism," the brand routinely espoused by the Black "bourgeoisie." The fashionable, academic vilification of "Black nationalism" as nationalism pure and simple cannot recognize this distinction. It would require that sexism and homophobia be addressed as such, in every situation; and it might restrain the exploitation of the matter for non-revolutionary or counter-revolutionary, reactionary agendas. As a matter of fact, Newton and the Panthers came to promote "internationalism," until he proposed his notion of "intercommunalism," having realized that contemporary empire had made national boundaries virtually insignificant. Without the neo-liberal, neo-colonial celebration of "globalization" now in vogue, this was precisely the position put forth by C. L. R. James in "Towards the Seventh." So how can the Panthers and other Black world militants be pigeonholed as "nationalists" when anti-imperialist activism is at stake?

Newton's sexual intervention is not mentioned in *Black Is . . . Black Ain't*.[9] Evidently, some people are supposed to represent sexism and homophobia in easily predictable ways, with Black radical politics being a perverse ideological prerequisite. Another connection between Julien and Riggs can be seen in Julien's "Black Is, Black Ain't: Notes on De-essentializing Black Identities" (1992). The same sermon by Ellison that Riggs uses for the title of his film provides the title of this Julien piece, which employs the rhetoric of essentialism in the same counter-insurgent fashion in which the rhetoric of nationalism is regularly employed. No white racial identity is "de-essentialized" in Julien. Its essence is always preserved wholly intact for the practice of "inter-racial desire." It is telling that this very partial reading of Ellison, promoted by both Riggs and Julien, evades the novelist's renowned love for Black folk culture and, indeed, the rest of *Invisible Man*. What's more, Riggs and Julien never think to interrogate Ellison's own sexual politics. He was a conservative individualist who feared Black militancy every bit as much as these filmmakers.

Riggs separates himself from Davis and hooks, for instance, insofar as he advocates "androgyny" over "masculinity" as a social ideal for Black men. It "is not manhood that we're trying to reach," he concludes, in opposition to "nationalists," "but being human." It is by being "both masculine and feminine" that "you can be what it means to be a man, which I think is to be human." Notice that what Toni Cade Bambara called the "madness of 'masculinity' and 'femininity'" is not rejected by this position at all. The argument for a kinder, gentler masculinity in no way dismantles the dichotomy between manhood and womanhood as construed in the West. The basic categories of sex or gender are not only preserved as useful social divisions, they are again naturalized and universalized as static categories of cultural historical life. These conventionally racist constructions are in no way renounced by the intellectual voices of *Black Is . . . Black Ain't*. They are no less colonized by these norms than are those they confidently scorn. Many of these figures played a similar role in *The Darker Side of Black*. Both films suggest that a "good" education in white bourgeois society somehow makes respectable Black academics anti-homophobic and anti-sexist. The Clarke who criticized hooks and Wallace in *Home Girls* must find this assumption hugely ironic, as Riggs fails to interrogate them about Black female intellectuals and homophobia because of his narrow focus on Black male "nationalists" or militants.

Interestingly, John Champagne scolds Riggs for a certain middle-class sensibility in *The Ethics of Marginality: A New Approach to Gay Studies* (1995). But his selective reading of *Tongues Untied* does not uncover the bourgeois Occidentalism at play. Such a critique is certainly rare, if resistance to Black sexual criticism is not. Champagne uses his rather weak class analysis to ward off charges of racism on behalf of gay white men. Otherwise, his theorizing provides no critique of middle-class culture or politics, not to mention economics; and his anti-humanism ("post-structuralism") makes no issue of Western domination, as does Sylvia Wynter (1979, 1987, 1990, 1992, 2000, 2003) and her radical demystification of humanist imperialism. There is no categorical inspection of masculinity and femininity, or heterosexuality and homosexuality, which the humanity of Occidentalism disseminates with such racist historical violence. The middle-class androgynous human being idealized by Riggs still demands critical analysis after *The Ethics of Marginality*, almost half of which revolves around anxieties of race and racism.

Gordon wrote in his review of Julien's *Frantz Fanon* that the criticism of homophobia in Black communities presented in *Tongues Untied* is "inspired by a profound love for those communities" (Gordon 1996, 152). He implies that the cinematic politics of Riggs and Julien are not exactly one and the same. Be that as it may, it might also be acknowledged that the voices heard on camera in *Tongues Untied* are not the voice of the filmmaker. In the film's final scene, the audience sees and hears Black men chanting, "Black men loving black men is *the* revolutionary act." Their statement reiterates the unabashed militancy of many of the speakers who make themselves known throughout *Tongues Untied*. This is similar to what happens in *The Darker Side of Black*. There are barely any militant voices to be found in *Black Is . . . Black Ain't*, which identifies militancy rigidly with heterosexuality. Moreover, in "*Tongues Untied:* An Interview with Marlon Riggs" (1991), conducted by Ron Simmons, Riggs was wary of the testimony that climaxed in that final chant (Riggs 1991, 194). He does so for the same reason that Julien rejected such an idea in "Confessions of a Snow Queen" (Julien 1994a, 126). A sexual priority is placed on the non-Black body of "interracial desire." While in gay and lesbian politics the gender of one's object of desire is highly politicized, the race of one's object of desire is immediately and crudely depoliticized as socially insignificant—for whiteness. Neither Riggs nor Julien shows interest in any brand of actual revolution, anti-colonial or Black revolution least of all. And the neo-colonial climate at the close of the white Western millennium, as Gordon wrote, seemed to ensure that they could be canonized as Black gay men (or "Black queers") in ruling-class North America.

Categorical Decolonization

It was in Beam's *In the Life* that we saw a veritable decolonization of sexual classification very much akin to Lorde's *Zami: A New Spelling of My Name*. Like hip-hop and dancehall, *Zami* and *In the Life* are sibling signs.[10] They resist and refuse the reduction of African Diasporic eroticism to Black imitations of white cultural identities. As we have seen, Beam stressed the problem with considering "Black gay men" as a category of struggle when he noted that "gay male" means "white, middle-class, youthful, nautilized, and probably butch" (Beam 1986, 14–15). "Black" is appended as a modifier, a belated qualifier, a sign of sexual assimilation for a select class. This is irrefutably the case for heterosexuality, as homosexuality and heterosexuality both have very specific histories in Europe and North America. Yet when sexuality is said to be a social construction in academia, the social constructions of Western empire are sanctified above all. The gender and sexuality of Occidentalism are reified rather than challenged. Its erotic schemes are naturalized by theories of denaturalization. African peoples have no history in this history of sex and sexuality; no culture to make history in such neo-colonial conceptions.

Zami and *In the Life* stand as instructive rather than normative categories of identity which avoid many problems associated with Western sex ideology. Neither privileges a class in bourgeois or pseudo-bourgeois terms. Neither enforces a strict erotic division between heteroerotic and homoerotic sexual desire. No absolute exclusivity of desire is ever dictated or implied. Neither would fix sex or sexuality as "gay," "lesbian," "bisexual," or "transgender." Both focus less on identity as something static, universally given and unchanging, and more on living, working, and loving—in motion. *In the Life* and *Zami* advance an unabashed sex radicalism that recognizes neo-colonialism and resists it in the Pan-African name of Black folk.

One could hear in Julien the special Queer Theory issue of the journal *differences*, even though its white female editor apologizes for the absence of "Black gay men" among its contributors: Teresa de Lauretis (1991) proposed that "they" might be preoccupied with less "theoretical" things. She could not imagine that these terms and concepts, or institutional power politics, might be the problem. An academic division between sexual theory and practice was firmly in place, along with a division of intellectual labor defined by race and class. Black critics and critics of color may be given some space to criticize, and denounce, their own communities in white publications. But publication of Black and other non-white criticism of white Queer Theory is something else; and perhaps the price of inclusion is best seen in what was published in that issue of *differences*: Tomás Almaguer's "Chicano Men: A Cartography of Homosexual Identity and Behavior" (1991).

Almaguer outlines a typology of sex identity containing five personas. The first two are (1) "working class Latino men" who are "effeminate" or erotically "passive" and (2) "primarily working class Latino men" who may be "heterosexual or bisexual," but have "furtive" sex with other men in Latino gay bars. These working-class personas are firmly grounded in Chicano/Latino community space (88). The next three personas are "more likely" to "come from middle class backgrounds." They are (3) those who "participate in the emergent gay Latino subculture in the Mission District" of San Francisco, (4) "Latino men" who "maintain a primary identity as Latino and only secondarily a gay one," and (5) those who "fully assimilate" into the "white gay male community in the Castro District" (Almaguer 1991, 89). The accuracy or inaccuracy of this taxonomy aside, Almaguer takes for granted the rhetoric of gay and homosexual identity and concludes with a call to "unmask" the "Chicano gay man." The two working-class personas of his typology, who are firmly grounded in Chicano community space, are completely deleted from consideration. It is far from clear that all of the other three personas are retained, either. Colonial assimilation is mandated for inclusion into the category of gay identity, which, Almaguer writes, it took white middle-class "skills and talents" to create (87).

That he uses Cherríe Moraga and Gloria Anzaldúa to arrive at this conclusion is alarming. Also in 1991, Anzaldúa wrote in "To(o) Queer the Writer—*Loca, Escritora y Chicana*," "As a working-class Chicana, *mestiza*—a composite being, *amalgama de culturas y de lenguas*—a woman who loves women, 'lesbian' is a cerebral word, white and middle class, representing an English-only dominant culture, derived from the Greek word *lesbos*" (Anzaldúa 1991, 249). She confronts, head-on, even the elite appropriation of "queer" by white academics (251). Anzaldúa also attacks rather than advocates Almaguer's assimilation: "When a lesbian names me the same as her she subsumes me under her category. . . . Call me *de las otras*. Call me *loquita, jotita, marimacha, pajuelona, lambiscona, culera*—these are words I grew up hearing. I can identify with being '*una de las otras*' or a '*marimacha*,' or even *jota* or a *loca porque*—these are the terms my home community uses" (249-50). Moraga's *Atzlán* politics are no different in *The Last Generation* (1993). Maria Lugones may help get at the root of things ethnocidal, regarding white lesbian feminism, with her contention: "heterosexualism is not a cross-cultural or international system but a series of systems some of which dominate over others and threaten their extinction" (Lugones 1990, 143). What happens when the *blanqueamiento* politics of *mestizaje* and Spanish imperialism are challenged with "Afro-Latin" peoples in mind? This would bring us back to the spirit of *Zami* and *In the Life*—in the vernacular of another colonized tongue—well beyond Queer Theory and the like.

COINTELPRO Canons

When the counter-revolutionary character of neo-colonialism is understood, we can see why contemporary, canonical gender and sexuality studies
could essentially negate Black "nationalism" or militancy and Black popular culture, which constitute a socio-political complex of which Beam and Lorde are
very much a part. On the domestic front of U.S. national empire, neo-colonial
reaction must be thought in terms of COINTELPRO (an acronym for "counter-
intelligence program"). As ex–Black Panther Party activist and Black Liberation
Army soldier Assata Shakur attests in "Assata Shakur Speaks: Letter to the Pope"
(1998a), this program "was set up by the Federal Bureau of Investigation (FBI)
to eliminate all political opposition . . . and destroy the Black Liberation Movement" (44). She would never appear in a film by Isaac Julien or Marlon Riggs,
not because she lives in Cuba as a revolutionary in exile, but because she remains a committed Black revolutionary woman, who writes, "A revolutionary
woman can't have no reactionary man" (Shakur 1998b). Riggs and others masculinize the category of revolutionaries as much as Julien and others masculinize the category of rappers and deejays, erasing Black female revolutionaries
and Black female rappers and deejays who function as radical agents and symbols of Black resistance to white and male domination. Shakur in particular
does not present African revolutionism as atavistic or anachronistic. Nor would
she present anti–Black nationalism as progressive. She gives the lie to a million
statements on gender and sexuality, nationalism and militancy, and she en-
hances Rodney's understanding of neo-colonialism with her own Black Power,
"New Afrikan" understanding of "neo-*slavery*" (1987, 1998c).

There is an amazing analysis of COINTELPRO outside academia in texts
such as *Still Black, Still Strong: Survivors of the War against Black Revolutionaries,*
by Dhoruba Bin Wahad, Mumia Abu-Jamal, and Assata Shakur. None of them
fit the pejorative profile of nationalist militants proffered by works like *Black
Is . . . Black Ain't.* Abu-Jamal is celebrated and condemned as an ex-Panther political prisoner on death row. Bin Wahad is a former political prisoner of nineteen years himself, who is now living another brand of exile in Ghana. He is
director of the Institute for the Development of Pan-African Policy, which performs liaison work for Africa's Diaspora. He is also director of BlackStar Con-
sults, Ltd., a musical production company that promotes artists in the genre
known as hip-life (a continental mix of hip-hop and high-life music). Notwithstanding Abu-Jamal's many publications, Shakur's *Assata: An Autobiography*
(1987), and her many communiqués posted on the Internet, it is Bin Wahad who
most thoroughly dissects COINTELPRO in *Still Black, Still Strong.*[11]

Bin Wahad's "War Within" in *Still Black, Still Strong* is an extended essay
transcribed from *Framing the Panthers . . . in Black and White,* a 1990 documen-

tary filmed by Chris Bratton and Annie Goldson at Eastern Prison in Napanock, New York. In it he classifies COINTELPRO as a "domestic war program . . . aimed at countering the rise of Black militancy, Black independent thought, and at repressing the freedoms of Black people in the United States" (Bin Wahad 1993b, 18). He identifies Operation Chaos as an equivalent program of the Central Intelligence Agency (CIA): "It dealt with domestic surveillance and international surveillance of domestic activists, and to this very day no one knows the depths of that program" (22). He mentions the Law Enforcement Assistance Act (LEAA) as part of "the militarization of police in the Black community" and "the militarization of police in America" overall, because it supplied local police with military technology, assault rifles, and army personnel carriers (19).

> Concepts like block watches, and community patrols, and community outreach programs, were all further developments of the ideas and concepts that were outlined to destroy the Vietcong—the village watcher, the spy who could inform the police as to who was an NLF cadre and who wasn't. These techniques, the techniques of disinformation, of counterinsurgency—they were brought home. (39)

COINTELPRO calls to mind a vast network of national and international repression for super-colonial imperialist ends. "War Within" combines with Bin Wahad's "The Cutting Edge of Prison Technology" (1993a), also in *Still Black, Still Strong,* to document COINTELPRO, Operation Chaos and NEWKILL ("New York Killings") and Operation PRISAC ("Prison Activists") and Operation Mirage ("Arab Americans") and FEMA (the Federal Emergency Management Act) and JATTF (the Joint Anti-Terrorist Task Force) and SWAT/BUT (Special Weapons and Tactics/Basic Unit Tactics), etc., etc., etc. This was all before "Patriot Acts" and "Homeland Security," scripted around much later actions in Iraq and Afghanistan: Bin Wahad's work on counter-insurgency, surveillance, and counter-intelligence was surreally prophetic.

While some anti–Black nationalist critics have made clichéd references to gender or sexuality and COINTELPRO, they do so in a campaign against militants which condemns militants more than it does J. Edgar Hoover, his FBI, and the U.S. imperialist state. It is as if Black militants are to blame for sexual ideologies embedded in the history of colonial empire and employed to ravage Black people in and outside revolt. Rarely are Black militants imagined to reflect on this process themselves, in the spirit of a continuing Black militant praxis. Yet those who do have advanced powerful reflections that are completely absent among academics, who assume a monopoly over the power to think, especially when it comes to gender and sexuality, nationalism, and COINTELPRO.

For one, Bin Wahad reflects in "War Within" on how COINTELPRO's divide-and-conquer scheme would capitalize on sexism in addition to regionalism and individual differences (Bin Wahad 1993, 11). He goes on to argue that the FBI/state obsession with the Black Panthers was "psycho-sexual" in nature (24).

He examines the threat that Black male assertion poses to white male suprem-acy, together with white society's sexist underestimation of Black females as potential and actual revolutionaries: "Women tend not to be perceived as great a threat, and often for this reason when they become revolutionaries they break the sexist mold. Historically, Black women were always at the forefront of the struggle. Certainly Harriet Tubman, Sojourner Truth and Assata Shakur, among others, inspired fear in the white man's heart" (25). The "sexual flavor" of anti-Black violence is discussed vis-à-vis current events in Bensonhurst and Howard Beach (26) as well as Judge Lynch: "Lynchings invariably involved the dismem-berment of sexual organs (breasts, penises, testicles)" (25). This destruction of the genitals (38) is treated repeatedly as a sort of rite of slave and neo-slave so-cieties, for these societies license destruction and sexual racism. The FBI's Hoover could say, accordingly, "the three things a 'Negro' wants most are money, a white woman, and a Cadillac" (42), without anti-nationalist interrogation by those who share his aversion to Black militants. The former Panther can see Hoover and company for what they are, however: "If I was to value Black womanhood to the same degree as white males claim to value white womanhood and virtue, I would be considered a Black nationalist extremist" (37). He exposes the white nationalist extremism of Hoover, his FBI, and the U.S. imperial state, and the way in which the "prison-industrial complex" functions as a "trade in Black flesh for white rural employment" (93), with the common prison strip search functioning as a form of sexual abuse: "Probing into their body cavities is an act of rape, an act of complete dehumanization" (96).

Many have heard him speak out for years against homophobia and sexism in public lectures on both Black Panther revolt and neo-colonial empire. Recently, for Black Solidarity Day on college campuses in upstate New York (with its whole network of political prisons), he spoke eloquently on what others call nationalism.[12] He rejects the European nation-state as the "foremost enemy of people of color" worldwide. He speaks of "democratic fascism," "modern-day Babylon," and "new-age imperialism." The neo-liberal globalization of new millennial capitalism is not celebrated as "transnationalism." It proves the Black popular-culture statement "the whole world's a ghetto," in effect. Bin Wahad treats the European nation-state in North America as the "European settler state," now a "national security state," a police state, representing racist Occi-dentalism with a supra-national, still super-national vengeance. How bizarre that such ideas could be stigmatized as the ideas of a sexually backward Black "nationalist," when they are so timely and correct.

If "COINTELPRO" should be read as shorthand for a whole counter-revolutionary network of repression, national and international, it is past time for it to be seen as a historical phenomenon as consequential as McCarthyism's "Red Scare." Making this connection is key—socially, politically, and sexually.

Unlike the craze of overt criminal prosecution under McCarthyism, COIN-TELPRO was a covert operation, shrouded in secrecy, to effect state repression after overt measures of a certain stripe had fallen out of favor (if only temporarily). McCarthyism is known to have entailed intellectual persecution, creating an atmosphere of academic censorship thanks to the prospect of the prosecution and even execution of anyone demonized as dangerous and unpatriotic. COINTELPRO entails the close association of diverse media and government agencies, making diverse media into state media even though state ownership of media is stigmatized as "Soviet" or "Communist" in Cold War propaganda. It is all too easy for academics to exclude academic media from this damning analysis. Bin Wahad and others do not. When COINTELPRO is critically connected to McCarthyism, its political and intellectual effects can be envisioned. McCarthyism is officially regretted since it is supposed to be over, exposed: CO-INTELPRO is underexposed, and it continues on with the revival of overt repression in the name of "anti-terrorism." It continues under a neo-colonialism dominated by the security apparatus of a super-colonial empire; and this counter-revolution resounds in the canons of academia where hostility to Black militant radicalism abounds, as in the rest of this society, as canonical intellectual discourse on gender and sexuality amply demonstrates.[13]

Conclusion

Black "nationalist" militancy, however internationalist, Pan-African, and anti-nationalist, and despite anti-sexist, anti-homophobic, and gender-revolutionary embodiments, is presented in essentially negative terms by hegemonic gender and sexuality discourses which turn out to have a great deal in common with J. Edgar Hoover, the FBI, and the U.S. imperialist state. They leave the white power of the West unchallenged as they vilify Black Power wholesale. Black popular culture is equally negated, by extension. Neither sexism nor homophobia (nor nationalism) is criticized as a result so much as Black people's cultural and political insurgence, real or imagined. The sexism and homophobia of colonialism and neo-colonialism have yet to be dealt with in a truly anti-racist, anti-imperialist manner.

The colonial politics of sex, gender, and sexuality could not possibly be confronted by critiques that presume U.S. (or British) nationality at the same time that they condemn what they presume to be Black nationalism. This is counter-insurgency, simply put. Blackness is presented as the problem, at bottom, not whiteness, colonial nationalism, or imperialism and its colonizing sexism, misogyny, heterosexism, and homophobia. The dominant or hegemonic geopolitics are upheld, locally and globally, most of all when Black culture and politics resist or rebel against them and the counter-insurgency—with whatever degree of success. No anti-colonial theory or practice of erotic embodiment can be imagined or endorsed, as a result, by the neo-colonial articulation of sex, gender, and sexuality critiques, despite the fact that they have been commercially enshrined as "radical" (as well as "chic") in the West.

When Frances M. Beale critiqued the sexist Black male politico in "Double Jeopardy: To Be Black and Female" (1970), she wrote that "he sees the system for what it really is for the most part." "When it comes to women," nevertheless, he sounds like he's been reading *Ladies' Home Journal* (92). Her point was that he should radicalize his militancy with anti-sexism. He should liberate it from the sex of his colonizer. Beale prefigured Cheryl Clarke's *Home Girls* essay on homophobia by declaring that "Black women must closely examine the class aspirations of those blacks who promote backward ideas vis-à-vis black women and continue to distort our historical and economic realities" (Beale 1975, 23): "If we want to understand revolution, we have to take part in revolution" (22). Clarke and Joseph Beam are supported by Charles I. Nero's contribution to *Brother to Brother* (1991). Writing on Toni Morrison, Nero argued that the author's "homophobia, as that of so many other black intellectuals, is perhaps more closely related to Judeo-Christian beliefs than to the beliefs of her ancestors." It helps uphold "an oppressive Eurocentric view of reality" (Nero 1991, 235). This anti-colonial inscription was echoed by Beam when he named the sources that sustained him outside white gay literature and politics: the journal *Habari-Daftari, Moja, Yemonja,* and a book by Yulisa Amadu Maddy. It is also echoed in Audre Lorde's ill-acknowledged adoption of Gamba Adisa, meaning "warrior: she who makes her meaning known," as a new and proper name.[14] The repression of their Pan-African insurgence by academic rhetorics of gender and sexuality speaks volumes.

Before his brutal assassination in Guyana on June 13, 1980, Walter Rodney decoded the "neo" of neo-colonialism to describe the creation or consolidation of a "petty-bourgeois" elite meant to perpetuate empire in the face of people's struggle. This current phase of colonialism is counter-revolutionary through and through. The recent canonization of sexual discourse in the West is a political and intellectual sign of these times. As a rule, this commerce is both bourgeois and counter-revolutionary. It does not sanction the struggle of Assata Shakur as she lays bare, from her Cuban exile, the vicious forces of COINTELPRO and U.S. domination. She denounces racism and sexism as a self-identified "Maroon woman" in a long tradition of African resistance. Her struggle was heard in Claudia Jones's "An End to the Neglect of the Problems of Negro Women!" and Toni Cade Bambara's "On the Issue of Roles," not to mention Ama Ata Aidoo's "The African Woman Today" (1992) and Ifi Amadiume's *Daughters of the Goddess, Daughters of Imperialism* (2000). Conversely, counter-insurgent critiques of sexism and homophobia which naturalize Western middle-class categories of gender and sexuality "masculinize" and "heterosexualize" Black militancy and attempt to make any revolutionary praxis appear "primitive" or "pathological." Still, Africa and its Diaspora must battle continual colonization by "masculinity" and "femininity," "manhood" and "womanhood," as well as the "heterosexuality" and "homosexuality" commanding them. Then and only then, without neo-colonial delusions, we will subvert the sexual demon of white power in "America" and beyond.

Conclusion

I got the 5 hundred year black hostage
             colonialism never never stops blue-ooze
I got the francophone anglophone   alementiphone
                 lusophone   telephone   blue-ooze
I got this terminology is not my terminology
                 these low standards are not my standards
                 this religion is not my religion and
                 that justice has no justice for me blue-ooze
I got the blue-ooze
I got the gangbanging police brutality blue-ooze
I got the domestic abuse battered body blue-ooze . . .
I got the television collective life is no life to live
             and this world is really becoming
             a fucked up crowded place to be blue-ooze
    I got to find a way out this blue-ooze

From Jayne Cortez, "I Got the Blue-Ooze 93"[1]

The world put in place by colonialists is not the only world that has ever been. It is not even necessarily the only world that is. It is most assuredly not the only world that can be. To contest this world, it is nonetheless necessary to criticize and contextualize it in ways which it could or would never envision. To replace it also requires collective work in theory and practice that recognizes the extent to which this world has colonized us and continues to colonize us mentally and physically, in so many dimensions. No doubt, such a revolution would require resistance, inspiration, memory, imagination, more resistance, and then some. The movement from one world order to another, more desirable one must involve a spirited movement of bodies and minds. These movements must move against an order of knowledge that articulates and organizes minds and bodies in a fundamentally colonialist fashion. This is a conclusion not to be ignored. We need to plot a way out of the world of social ideas and structures analyzed here, to replace the world put in place by colonialism.

This project has been about body politics, but not in the fashion that has become typical over the last several decades. The now institutionalized form of raising questions about gender and sexuality fails to question how such issues might be raised without reinscribing well-established institutions of domination. It avoids facing the very same questions it poses to others, never able to ask why it could not or would not think to interrogate its own basic approach to the world. When questions of gender and sexuality are on the table for discussion, even if sex and eroticism or embodiment in general are not, who asks how they get there? What form should they take or not take? Why do they communicate explicit and/or implicit scenarios of race, class, and empire? Which specific order of knowledge dictates the limited shape and purpose of such inquiries, artificially separating race, gender, class, and sexuality, without recognizing this as a very specific kind of intellectual operation rooted in a very specific intellectual culture and history? It is as if it were enough to raise the subject, and magically some moral superiority of politics ensues. Since gender and sexuality criticism is not exempt from radical criticism itself, simply because it is about gender and sexuality, it remains necessary to determine what is just, progressive, or radical about any instance of this criticism, particularly if it cannot analyze its complicity with the sexual politics of white Western imperialism—past, present, and, unfortunately, future. This project has been about body politics, but in a mode that aims to retain nothing of that system of domination taken for granted today in the contemporary context of neo-colonialism.

It means to disturb the form and content of a series of dichotomies, and it has no desire to leave them intact. This goes for masculinity and femininity, heterosexuality and homosexuality, masculinism and feminism, not to mention manhood and womanhood, bisexuality, transgenderism, etc. The same must be said analytically for sexism, misogyny, homophobia, and heterosexism, as well as their alleged opposites or antitheses. It strives to dismantle all of the above because conventional work on these subjects may problematize sexual oppression, when it fits an established paradigm, but it also preserves the conceptual framework of this oppression. This work moves toward an understanding of the politics of intellectual work on gender and sexuality: how it continues to contribute to oppression, sexual and otherwise, and how it is grounded in historical and contemporary situations of empire.

What is necessary, therefore, is a fresh approach to all matters at hand. This approach would not assume that currently dominant concepts and politics are trans-cultural or trans-historical. As a consequence, it could detect and discuss the relationship between sexuality and geopolitical hegemony, gender and slavery, eroticism and comprador class elitism, mis-education and sex identification, racist sexual repression and racist state repression. While gender and sexuality studies traditionally assume they are radical by virtue of being gender and sexuality studies, they traditionally reinforce these relationships rather then subvert them; and, what's more, they are routinely counter-revolutionary with regard to traditions deemed radical by the state or government, the ruling political order of the globe. It is this order of culture and politics that generates the concepts and categories assumed by scholars and non-scholars alike. Thinking otherwise is imperative; and it could be no more urgent for Black folk, for Pan-Africanism, here and there.

* * *

My engagement with the historic writings of Cheikh Anta Diop and the reading of them advanced by Ifi Amadiume means to encourage a radical new interpretation of what is hailed as the history of sexuality in Europe and North America. In Western scholarship, this history of the West is misunderstood as the history of the *world,* or historicity proper. From this cultural historical imperialism comes the conventional system of classification which views heterosexuality and homosexuality as the ultimate categories of human sexuality in modern social life. When the logic of European empire is undermined, an entirely different picture emerges. Exposed then is how the West mobilizes the concepts of human sexuality and sexual historicity in its mission to present itself as the epitome of culture and civilization, the brutalities of colonization aside. Diop and Amadiume help unseat this politics of sex by recasting the history of Africa and the globe. They attack the white racist appropriation of history and its patriarchal demonization of matriarchy outside Europe. The anti-matriarchalism of imperialism reveals a metaphysics of sexuality beyond the narrow, nineteenth-century, racially-exclusive binary between bourgeois heterosexuality and bourgeois homosexuality. The hegemonic conception of culture and history places Europe and North America on the side of human civilization (or the human sexualities of heterosexuality and homosexuality), while Africa (or the non-West) is placed in the realm of sexual savagery and barbarism. This greater sexual division between the colonizer and the colonized is uncritically presupposed by the history of sexuality imagined by gender and sexuality studies which never dismantle Occidentalism, or Aryanism, not in the least. Hence, the provincial sexual dichotomies of the West must be discerned and debunked in order to recognize Pan-African cultural historicity, white racist sexual violence under empire, and Black radical traditions of resistance writ large in Diop and Amadiume, even as I extended their writings to combat all sexualities of colonization.

Amadiume's emphasis on flexible gender systems and traditions of female empowerment on the continent supplies a distinct point of contrast for the treatment of concepts and categories of gender in the context of chattel slavery in the Americas, North America in particular. The essential racialization of manhood and womanhood as white manhood and white womanhood is underscored with regard to plantation societies that make this fact abundantly clear. It is exceptionally difficult for academic studies of the matter to accept that this is the case in the present as it has been in the past. No question, Toni Cade Bambara is the antidote in her polemical declaration of the madness of masculinity and femininity, the insanity of accepting or internalizing this gender or any gender, at any time or in any place, especially in the international struggle for Black liberation. Oyèrónké Oyêwùmí and Sylvia Wynter bolster this perception in myriad ways. But official histories of gender and slavery have become increasingly conservative since Angela Davis published her potent prison writing on the topic in the 1970s. Neither they nor she interrogates the ideological essence of manhood and womanhood, even though the social construction of gender has become a cliché in U.S. intellectual circles; and even though slaveocratic imperialism so violently established the white racist character of these identities. I remarked this as the greatest of ironies, since Black communities throughout the Americas and the world remain assailed by a colonial madness that connects this history of gender to the history of sexuality, not to mention slavery and neo-slavery in what George L. Jackson called "the greatest slave state in history" (Jackson 1972, 10).

In this setting, the history of African peoples is too often told from the perspective of Black pseudo-bourgeois elites, which is why I paired Frantz Fanon and E. Franklin Frazier to examine the central role of these elites in the cultural reproduction of racist gender and sexual norms or ideologies. The empirical, historical sociology and class analysis of Frazier verifies the radical psychosexual and political economic analysis of Fanon, over and over again. It barely matters that Frazier was always a pro-Western assimilationist, and that this actually motivated his class critique, for his body of work exposes a range of erotic conflicts that expose the extreme limitations of conventional frameworks of gender and sexuality. If in those frameworks there are merely two possible genders and two possible sexualities, so to speak—a universal man and woman who may engage in a universal heterosexuality or homosexuality—there lies in Frazier a wide range of sexual identities riven by basic race and class realities. The genders and sexualities of the white aristocracy, bourgeoisie, and proletariat are rigidly opposed not only to each other but also to the genders and sexualities of the colored elite and the Black lumpen-bourgeoisie, all of which are most rigidly opposed to the erotic persons of the Black folk majority or masses. Reading Frazier against the grain with the revolutionized Fanon highlights rather than hides these social divisions and can demystify heterosexuality and homosexuality as well as manhood and womanhood as the racist ruling-class conceits of Western empire. The socio-economic collaboration of the colonized elite in this politics of sex was no less corroborated by Fanon as he moved from Martinique and France to continental Africa.

There is a relatively more conservative version of Fanon who could speak to Frazier as much as the revolutionary version of Fanon would speak to him and surpass him, politically; and it is the later Fanon whom I revisited to think further about the body politics of this "greedy little caste" under European colonization and imperialism in Africa and the Americas. When considered in light of the bulk of Fanon's work, his early discussion of Negrophobia has incredibly radical implications for sexual thought of all kinds. As it wreaks havoc on the heterosexual and homosexual self-descriptions of the white West by demonstrating how racism consumes all colonial sexual desires and identities. The homosexuality and heterosexuality of Occidentalism are revealed to be Negrophobic sexualities which defy strictly gender-based distinctions. This psychopathology of white racist sexuality is diagnosed next from the battles of the Algerian revolution. One of the most important lessons learned there may be that revolutionary sexual change is possible across the board, even if it requires revolutionary vigilance to sustain it against sabotage and recolonization. Fanon's insistence on the veritable ecstasy of Pan-African revolt takes this discussion beyond gender and sexuality, per se, toward embodiment as a whole; and this is vital given the conceptual limitations of established gender and sexuality studies for the study of empire and anti-imperialist studies of humanity (or humanism). Like Frazier, nonetheless, Fanon was analyzed to deploy these various insights against the social and sexual conservatism of the "greedy little caste," its colonized intellectuals, and, of course, their colonial masters and mistresses.

Perhaps the protagonist of Jamaica Kincaid's literature does not fit this profile of the colonized pseudo-bourgeois elite at the outset, yet we saw that the impact of colonial mis-education on her status and psyche was consequential for her formation as a subject of British Empire in the Caribbean. This process is eminently erotic, and emblematic enough to function as an object lesson and a case study. The girl child in Kincaid begins by narrating an idyllic homoerotic paradise identified with her mother or her maternal body. When her mother enforces a distance between them at adolescence in accordance with certain social customs, the daughter is devastated. She displaces this eroticism onto her schoolgirl acquaintances for a while, in hopes of making her mother jealous, but to no avail. Pivotally, she retreats into her colonial schooling to compensate herself for the crushing loss of this special, specific kind of love. As a result, any culturally induced shame in having too close a relationship with her mother is tragically transformed into a colonially induced shame in being Black or African and having any homoerotic desire at all. The child's aesthetic, intellectual socialization through an Anglophile literature of imperialism is what drives Kincaid's complete corpus. This vain individual struggle for a normative Western heterosexuality is somehow ignored by critics. I maintained that the clash between an indigenous homoeroticism and an invasive, invading heterosexualism illustrates the sexual politics of white racist empire quite plainly, as Kincaid relocates from a previous center of British colonialism to the present center of colonial imperialism in North America.

The wonderful, revolutionary work of Cheryl Clarke and Joseph Beam was recalled in the end to mark a time when Black revolutionary work was not widely construed as incompatible with critical work on sex, gender, and sexuality, especially in U.S. academia. Their articulations of sexism and homophobia commit them to grassroots Black radicalism as they combat ruling-class politics, gay and lesbian white racism, state repression, and, in fact, all manner of oppressions. As Clarke upholds Black poor and working-class culture and its potential for political transformation, Beam upholds a culture of Pan-Africanism in the vein of Audre Lorde. Her *Zami* formulation is supplemented with *In the Life* as an anti-colonial alternative to sexual classification and identification in the African Diaspora. None of this is conceivable in the sexual intellectual commerce currently canonized. It reinscribes Occidentalism as a rule. It is predominantly white and economically privileged, but not exclusively so. It has championed select figurations of "Black gay men" that are themselves antithetical to the radicalism represented by Beam, Clarke, Lorde, and others. Routinely in this environment, critiques of sexism and homophobia see Black "nationalist" militancy as synonymous with sexism and homophobia or sexual pathology, period, as if Black radical traditions of sexual politics could not possibly exist. This is a white, anti–Black nationalist ideology itself. It is perfectly continuous with the erotics of Aryanism that have historically depicted the West as sexually civilized and Africa or the non-West as sexually savage. In closing, I confirmed the existence of another Western bourgeois school of criticism that dovetails with what Walter Rodney and other Black revolutionaries would call neo-colonial counter-revolution, which flourishes in spite of the urgent need for sex-radical Pan-African traditions, old and new.

* * *

The presence of demons is undeniable and profound in the social and political commentary of Black populations dispersed across the Western hemisphere. The testimony may be secular, sacred, or profane, so to speak, all the more so when devils allegorically count as demons, too. The African Diaspora in North America has addressed devils and demons in a number of domains. There are the poetic sermons by preachers who may cast out demons, in churches or on streetcorners, often accompanied by a soundtrack of ever-changing chords of Black music. There is Black folklore, with its tales of the Devil outwitting God— and Black trickster-heroes consistently outwitting both. Some of these are collected in Zora Neale Hurston's *Mules and Men* (1935), and she reflects upon them nicely in *Dust Tracks on a Road* (1942). The demon of racism or white power is denounced most powerfully, of course, by Malcolm X and the Black Power movement he inspired in words and deeds. He managed to place this language on Black tongues as a lingua franca—a common speech, a speech in common—so effectively that it might parallel in significance, paradoxically, the Christian substitution of "Esu-Elegbara" for "Satan" (or "Devil") by European colonizers in Yoruba translations of their Bible.

A consummate trickster if not a divine figure himself, Malcolm Little was nicknamed Satan before he became Malcolm X and El-Hajj Malik El-Shabazz and Omowale, or "the [child] who has come home," according to *The Auto-biography of Malcolm X: As Told to Alex Haley* (1965, 403). This means that the Pan-Africanist militant would reverse a white-supremacist society's demonization of his Black self and community when he chanted down the white man as devil. With Elijah Muhammad and without him, he translated this demon or devilry as the historical creation of white racist imperialism; the hell-on-earth effects of its cruelty, evil, and greed; the collective act of oppression and repression of Africa and Africans, at home and abroad. This was what he came to identify as a demonology common to all Western religions as he resignified it for a praxis of worldwide Black revolution. His nephew Rodnell P. Collins, son of his eldest sister and mentor, Ella Little Collins, traces in *Seventh Child: A Family Memoir of Malcolm X* (1998) his uncle's internationally renowned interpretation of spirits back to the comparable interpretation of bad spirits recounted in the 1789 *Interesting Narrative of the Life of Olaudah Equiano or Gustavus Vassa, the African,* interestingly enough; and a wide range of these concerns, including his pre-assassination revolution in thinking on gender and revolution, may come full circle in Laini Mataka's poem "Were U There When They Crucified My Lord?" which is included in her *Bein a Strong Black Woman Can Get U Killed!!* (2000).

This book critically regards the past five-hundred-plus years as a paradigm, as it resists entrapment by the paradigm of Western bourgeois domination. The sexual logic or illogic of this domination has proved most difficult to shake. Neither the colonizer, for certain, nor the colonized has crafted a satisfactory opposition to this erotics of racism and empire. Cultural institutions, academic scholarship, and political organizations tend to reinforce it, when they might otherwise struggle toward anti-racism, anti-colonialism, and anti-imperialism. But none of this is really possible without systematic opposition to sexual racism, sexual colonialism, and sexual imperialism, epistemically as well as culturally, politically, and economically. There can be no independence of persons in the colonization of territories, bodies, and minds: this revelation by the revolutionary Fanon is sorely underappreciated. The relation of the bodily to the mental and the spiritual demands non-Western attention, given the Western hierarchical schism of mind, body, and spirit. Such a revolution in ideas and embodiment would not leave us possessed by the erotic schemes of empire—a possession which is by no means the benevolent African mounting or riding of spirit which has led to revolutionary resistance in Africa and the Americas. The logic or illogic that depicts Africans as property for slavery and colonialism must be undermined by attacking the whole complex of white racist imperialism, including its many sexual demons. They have vexed and shackled us for more than five centuries too long.

Notes

1. Pan-Africanism or Sexual Imperialism

1. While Coronil (1996) offers one definition of "Occidentalism," Sylvia Wynter, in "Beyond Liberal and Marxist Leninist Feminisms," an unfortunately unpublished conference paper, has defined it as "Western chauvinism" which reenacts "gender, class and race chauvinism at the level of culture" (1982, 39n7). Even so, since Africa is traditionally defined as neither East nor West, our use of these terms remains strategic.

2. Still, I must articulate these insights against the grain of Amin's Marxist historical universalism (which is, at bottom, nonetheless Western itself).

3. Very important here is Karen M. Gagne's treatment of Indian loving/Indian hating in "Falling in Love with Indians: The Metaphysics of Becoming America" (2003). Roscoe's discussion of berdaches in Native America (1992) (not to mention India's subcontinent) takes the loving half of this dialectic quite literally. Anti-imperialism or decolonization is never the issue, simply the sexual concerns of a gay ruling class of settlers. Why should genocided and ethnocided peoples produce erotic alternatives for the West, especially when such narrow social reform would serve to solidify colonial populations and, in the absence of an anti-colonial agenda, like all cultural imperialism, strengthen colonial domination? Indian loving facilitates Indian hating once again. The colonized are to provide salvation, sexual and otherwise, for colonizers and for colonial society at large.

4. Were we to define racialization, analytically, as the cultural-historical process by which race is conferred or assumed, at both individual and collective levels, then we would define sexualization as the cultural-historical process by which sex or sexuality is conferred or assumed, both individually and collectively, as if this social identification is natural and not in fact normative; as if, furthermore, social processes of racialization and sexualization are not in fact one and the same in their constitution of embodiment. There could be no sex on the one hand, and race on the other—as understood in the racist epistemology of a single, hegemonic group, no less. Although normally described as dimorphic or dichotomous (that is, composed of exactly two), sexual identities can instead be seen as multiple (or multitudinous) once this racializing component is identified. There must be many more than a couple of sexes and sexualities, in other words, outside European idealizations of its colonial imperialist manhood and womanhood as well as of its heterosexuality and homosexuality.

5. This phrase was coined by my friend and colleague Janis A. Mayes. Her "Mercer Cook, Hearing Things Unspoken: The Politics and Problematics of

TransAtlantic Literary Translation" is currently in process. See, meanwhile, "'Her Turn, My Turn': Notes on TransAtlantic Translation of African Francophone Women's Poetry" (Mayes 2001).

6. The Dakar honor was shared with W. E. B. Du Bois. Amadiume (1989) brings into sharp rhetorical focus Diop's predictable and widespread erasure by Western academe. There is precious little left of the West to fetishize (*as* Western) in his wake. The repression of his work is therefore required by empire. The same is obviously not the case with Du Bois. Thanks to Janis A. Mayes, again, for her help with this Les Nubians transcription, and for her original, innovative take on intonation.

7. The theory and practice of "Ethiopianism" is creatively guided by a Biblical expression: "Princes shall come out of Egypt and Ethiopia shall soon stretch forth her hand unto God" (Psalms 68:31). See Erna Brodber's "Re-engineering Blackspace" (1997) for a striking review of Ethiopianism as a basis for continued social struggle in the age of neo-colonial domination.

8. This piece was been republished as "Towards an African Political Ideology" in a collection of Diop's essays from his years in Paris as a student and militant (C. Diop 1996).

9. This point is crisply rearticulated by Nkiru Nzegwu (1996). She blasts Kwame Anthony Appiah's blind naturalization of patriarchy or "patrilineal*ization*" in Africa, as he assumes "the inevitability of a linear trajectory of cultural development with technologized Europe in the lead" (184–85). When Appiah himself briefly references Diop in one chapter of *In My Father's House*, which is subtitled "Africa in the Philosophy of Culture," he reduces the debate to the practice of academic philosophy in modern Europe (Appiah 1992, 101–102). Not only is the subject of cultural conflict rhetorically effaced, but the centrality of matriarchy (or matriliny) to this entire discussion is simply disregarded. Appiah avoids this sexual political issue; and, as Nzegwu brilliantly illustrates, such maneuvers are a colonialist effect of privileging the "father's house" in the matrikin system of the Akan: "the attempt to overthrow matriliny has nothing to do with the internal inadequacies of the system or the depravity of its social values, but an emotional commitment to a nativist Anglo-Saxon view of social relations" (Nzegwu 1996, 193).

10. Sometimes, Amadiume implies Diop is portraying African societies as culturally and historically static in his writings on matriarchy. But in stressing external factors in the rise of patriarchy on the continent, subsequent to Arab and European invasion, he only argues that what was being called progressive and evolutionary in this case was instead reactionary and imperialist; and this position does not necessarily imply that there cannot be internal transformation within any given society in (or outside) Africa.

11. This is more or less the theme of Amadiume's *Daughters of the Goddess, Daughters of Imperialism: African Women Struggle for Culture, Power, and Democracy* (2000).

12.   See, perhaps especially, "Un-settling the Coloniality of Being/Power/Truth/ Freedom: Towards the Human, after Man, Its Over-representation" (Wynter 2003).

2. The Madness of Gender in Plantation America

1.   As a conceptual tool, "Plantation America" is hemispheric in orientation. Here, its reference to plantation societies throughout the Americas enables a way out of U.S. isolationism, exceptionalism, and imperialism at the level of analysis. I use it to encompass North America as but one instance of a larger unit of historical study and experience, beyond the nationalizing (or regionalizing) interests of any specific state regime, whether that regime represents a past or present organization of geopolitical power and containment.

2.   I focus on these writers specifically because their texts lay the foundation of a wide range of historical and literary-critical studies to come, and because they are of particular interest to Black Studies perspectives. What's more, these texts raise more conceptual, categorical questions than the later texts they would influence, across disciplines, although even more questions need to be raised, as I aim to show.

3.   See Lee Rainwater and William L. Yancey's *The Moynihan Report and the Politics of Controversy* (1967) for more information on the report and its aftermath.

4.   See Carole Boyce Davies, *Left of Marx: The Politics and Poetics of Claudia Jones* (forthcoming). My familiarity with Jones's writing and significance is entirely due to Boyce Davies and her absolutely inspired work to resurrect our consciousness of this figure, politically and intellectually.

5.   "It is impossible within the confines of this article to relate the terrible sufferings and degradation undergone by Negro mothers and Negro women generally under slavery. Subject to legalized rape by the slaveowners, confined to slave pens, forced to march for eight to fourteen hours with loads on their backs and to perform back-breaking work even during pregnancy, Negro women bore a burning hatred for slavery, and undertook a large share of the responsibility for defending and nurturing the Negro family" (C. Jones 1949, 32).

6.   See Walter Rodney's *How Europe Underdeveloped Africa* (1972, 95), in which he argues for this particular phrasing: "the European slave trade."

7.   We get a similar account in Jacquelyn Jones's *Labor of Love, Labor of Sorrow: Black Women, Work, and the Family from Slavery to the Present* (1985), which appeared in the same year as *Ar'n't I a Woman*. In " 'My Mother Was Much of a Woman,' " a previously published chapter cited by White in her introduction, J. Jones writes that "in the fields the notion of a distinctive 'women's' work vanished as slaveholders realized that 'women can do plowing very well and full well with the hoes [are] equal to men at picking' " (16); "according to some estimates, in the 1850's at least 90 percent of all female slaves over sixteen years of age labored more than 261 days per year, eleven to thirteen hours each day" (18). Although Jones never questions the ideology of womanhood

or gender, her sources suggest that pregnancy was met with a new wave of terror at the site of super-exploitation. The Davis of "Legacy" had reminded us already, "Slaveowners naturally sought to ensure that their 'breeders' would bear children as often as biologically possible. But they never went so far as to exempt pregnant women and mothers with infant children from work in the fields" (Davis 1981, 8). Thelma Jennings's "'Us Colored Women Had to Go Through a Plenty': Sexual Exploitation of African-American Slave Women" (1990) notes that new mothers might be given a rest of from two weeks to as little as a single day before returning to their toil. Jennings's article is based mostly on interviews with the formerly enslaved, and as she writes, "In their eagerness for a bumper crop, ['slavemasters'] were determined to discipline pregnant women, as well as other workers, who failed to do the work expected of them. . . . Driven by impulse, masters in a fit of anger also punished pregnant women without ever thinking of the dangerous consequences for them and their unborn children" (55–56). The profit motive is compromised by sadistic impulses, without a doubt, as economism and sadism clash systematically on the plantation. There is a socio-psychological dependency on production *and* punishment, a fact that surely explains the violence which Jones can only describe as inexplicable (J. Jones 1985, 20).

8. This phrase comes from William Grier and Price M. Cobbs's controversial and, indeed, quite problematic *Black Rage*. Although they use it in their "Achieving Womanhood" chapter, they should use it in their "Acquiring Manhood" chapter as well. It should also undermine their unquestioning commitment to Western manhood and womanhood.

9. In *Ar'n't I a Woman?* "The Life Cycle of the Female Slave" imagines a gender-socializing function for the "trash gang," a "low-scale" labor group composed of "pregnant women, women with nursing infants, young teenagers, and old slaves" (White 1985, 94). This trash gang is described as predominantly female in one sentence and overwhelmingly so in the next. Earlier, we were told that differentiation among children ages ten to twelve was, in all likelihood, nil: "If their activities of work and play are any indication of the degree of sex role differentiation . . . then young girls probably grew up minimizing the differences between the sexes while learning far more about the differences between the races" (94). This state of affairs is said to change quite drastically in the "three-generational 'trash-gang'" (95), but how exactly? If the issue is gender, shouldn't we now ask how the trash-gang would socialize, or sexualize, teenage boys and elder males outside their projected prime? They are listed and then quickly forgotten.

10. "Reflections" is cited in a footnote to *Ar'n't I a Woman?*'s introduction (White 1985, 169n9).

11. This position is writ large in Higginbotham's *Righteous Discontent: The Women's Movement in the Black Baptist Church, 1880–1920* (1993).

12. The anti-capitalist Jones was perhaps most remarkable for her radical identification with the Black masses as opposed to the "Negroes who betray their

people and do the bidding of imperialism" (C. Jones 1949, 37). It is the masses of Black women who determine what the problems of Black women are and where the solutions lie. The matter of class or social stratification does not explicitly enter either Davis's or White's commentary on sex, gender, and slavery.

13. Higginbotham should be read in the context of a text like Kevin Gaines's *Uplifting the Race: Black Leadership, Politics, and Culture in the Twentieth Century* (1996), when understood in a global-historical, Pan-African context itself. Interestingly, Higginbotham would adopt a contrary position in "African-American Women's History and the Metalanguage of Race" (1992) just several years later. This article begins by claiming that "feminist scholars, especially those of African-American women's history, must accept the challenge to bring race more prominently into their analysis of power" (252). Higginbotham never looks back to her objections to *Ar'n't I a Woman?*'s alleged overemphasis on "racial difference" or African "cultural difference," as she endorsed the class power of the Black elite. At any rate, proposing a metalanguage of race does little to disrupt the geopolitics of empire, insofar as metalanguages of class, gender, and sexuality can be proposed or privileged in the same mode, without recognizing the white cultural politics of the entire "race, class, gender, and sexuality" refrain as a Western epistemological framework.

14. I thank Jane Iwamura for compelling me to think through this rhetoric of contradiction in Carby's "Slave and Mistress."

15. In Chester Himes's final novel, *Plan B,* one character remarks, "'It is said that black men inspire the baser emotions in white women because they don't consider us as human. Therefore, they can indulge in any depravity at all with us because they believe it doesn't count.' His voice had roughened and it was obvious the memory angered him" (Himes 1993, 161).

16. See, also, Ann Allen Shockley's "The Mistress and the Slave Girl" in her *The Black and the White of It* (1980) and LaMonda Horton-Stallings's reading of it in her doctoral dissertation, "A Revision of the Narrative of the Trickster Trope in Black Culture for Alternative Readings of Gender and Sexuality (Written by Herself)" (2001).

17. Tellingly, there are three listings for Davis in Hine and Thompson's index. She appears twice as a counter-cultural icon (Hine and Thompson 1998, 296, 298), not an author or agent of praxis; and once she is quoted on Billie Holiday (269), even though Davis's *Blues Legacies and Black Feminism* (1998) re-inscribes many an insight from her unacknowledged work in "Reflections" (and "Legacy"): "Women's blues are such an important source of insights about African-American historical consciousness precisely because they do not attempt to eradicate the memory of an era of relatively egalitarian gender relations" (Davis 1998, 121). It may be instructive as well to contrast the interracial sisterhood of Hine and Thompson's text with the radical sisterhood of Angela Davis and Fania Davis's "The Black Family and the Crisis of Capitalism" (1986), a more recent publication in *The Black Scholar.*

18. Characteristically, Wynter's "1492: A New World View" (1995) insists that

from "this ultimate mode of otherness based on 'race,' other subtypes of otherness are then generated—the lower classes as the lack of the normal class, that is, the *middle class;* all other cultures as the lack of the normal culture, that is, *Western culture;* the non-heterosexual as the lack of *heterosexuality,* represented as a biologically selected mode of erotic preference; women as the lack of the normal sex, *the male*" (42). Wynter's writings systematically undermine the naturalization of heterosexuality by Western humanism.

3. Sexual Imitation and the Lumpen-Bourgeoisie

1. This reduction and distortion of Fanon's corpus is writ large in Alan Read's collection *The Fact of Blackness* (1996) as well as filmmaker Isaac Julien's *Frantz Fanon: Black Skin, White Mask* (1995).

2. See also "The 'Funny' Mental Facts of Race Prejudice" in Frazier's papers at the Moorland-Spingarn Research Center at Howard University, in which he writes (like Fanon), "Race prejudice does not grow up in a social vacuum, so to speak; for it is related to the existing economic organization and the social or moral order" (5).

3. See Platt (1990, 1991) for details of Frazier's intellectual biography recounted here and elsewhere.

4. Herein lies a statement about Black possibilities under white territorial rule. The logic of "Edward F. Frazier" justifies the fugitive emigrationist repatriationism of Martin Delaney and many others, for Black Studies fixed more on Frederick Douglass, even if "E. Franklin Frazier" could never concede this point. And in "The So-Called Dependency Complex of Colonized Peoples," Fanon would declare, "As a psychoanalyst, I should help my patient to become conscious of his unconscious and abandon his attempts at a hallucinatory whitening, but also to act in the direction of a change in the social structure. . . . [T]he black man should no longer turn white or disappear; but should be able to take cognizance of a possibility of existence" (F. Fanon 1967a, 100). He went even further with "The Racist Fury in France" (written in 1959), when he was no longer a civil servant of colonial empire: "Yes, when racism in France reaches such dimensions, it is time for Negroes to leave the ship" (F. Fanon 1967b, 166). Dramatically parting ways with this later Fanon, Frazier's *The Negro in the United States* drew the following spurious conclusion about the post-bellum period in North America: "The American Negro slave was a broken man and the only alternative left to him was to acquire a motive for living under American culture or die" (Frazier 1957b, 93).

5. Dale Vlasek (1982) considers this theme in Frazier. But he celebrates the doctrine of assimilation scripted for white nationalism in the West.

6. My illustration of the oneness of Frazier's "anti-bourgeois" and "pro-assimilationist" intellectual politics confirms this remark by Harold Cruse in *Rebellion or Revolution?* "despite all the furor made over party labels, Negro integrationism is the same thing, whether it emanates from the NAACP, the Urban League,

SNCC, CORE, SCLC, the Communist Party, Howard University, or the American Society of African Culture" (Cruse 1969, 22).

7. Amilcar Cabral's *Revolution in Guinea* (1971) described such a "class" as the *declassés,* since in the absence of a true proletariat there can be no "lumpenproletariat" proper. Our usage of class categories derived from the specific class structure of Europe must be metaphorical, at best.

8. Decades later George Jackson would come to similar consciousness in *Soledad Brother:* "I know now that the most damaging thing a people in a colonial situation can do is to allow their children to attend any educational facility organized by the dominant enemy culture" (Jackson 1970, 7).

9. Woodson reiterates throughout that the "chief difficulty with the education of the Negro is that it has been largely imitation resulting in the enslavement of his mind" (Woodson 1933, 134).

10. Reviewing a "new" Du Bois for the journal *Race* in "Dubois' Program for the Negro in the Present Crisis" (1935–36), Frazier insisted that the subject of *The Souls of Black Folk* was by no means the masses of "folk," but the "marginal man" prototypically embodied by Du Bois: "He has only an occasional romantic interest in the Negro as a distinct race. Nothing would be more unendurable for him than to live within a Black Ghetto or within a black nation unless, perhaps, he were king, and then he would probably attempt to unite the whites and the blacks through marriage of the royal families. When Garvey attempted his genuine racial movement, no one was more critical and contemptuous than Dubois of the fantastic glorification of the black race and all things black. Garvey's movement was too close to the black ignorant masses" (E. Franklin Frazier Papers at Howard University's Moorland-Spingarn Research Center, 5). Similarly, Daryl Michael Scott's *Contempt and Pity* (1997) argues convincingly that the famous sociological concept of the "marginal man" was even modeled on Du Bois himself. The contemporary idolization of Du Bois and *The Souls of Black Folk* is, without a doubt, very telling.

11. Tuskegee's training for outmoded peonage was more than anything a formula for social control, socio-sexual control, and so was its supposed ideological opposite. The "man-training" desired by Du Bois and Frazier relays the "discourse of Man" sketched by Sylvia Wynter in all her work on the "New World" order of white Western imperialism. This is the global context of gender schooling and sexual repression, erotic assimilation, or the psycho-subjective violence of sex mis-education. For Africa's Diaspora in North America, at the turn of this century, it represents what Donald Spivey terms "schooling for the new slavery" (Spivey 1978).

12. See Malcolm X's comments in *February 1965: The Final Speeches* (1992): "So when America got into the war, immediately she was faced with a manpower shortage. Up until the time of the war, you ["Negroes"] couldn't get inside of a plant. I lived in Lansing, where Oldsmobile's factory was and Reo's. There was about three in the whole plant and each one of them had a broom [Laughter]. They had education. They had gone to school. I think one had

gone to college. But he was a 'broomologist' [Laughter]. . . . And once you properly analyze the ingredients that opened the doors even to the degree that they were cracked open, when you see what it was, you'll better understand your position today. And you'll better understand the strategy you need today. Any kind of movement for freedom of Black people based solely within the confines of America is absolutely doomed to fail [Applause]" (X 1992, 166–67).

13.   The capitalist self-interest behind the "education" promoted by "northern philanthropy" was not lost on Frazier. He notes missionary mis-education designs (Frazier 1957a, 65–68) and the common cause of "classicist" and "industrialist" world-views when it comes to "respectability" (70). Both the "Du Bois" and the "Washington" camps couch their canon in Victorian fashion, and so does Frazier. He considers "pre-marital and unconventional sex relations" along with spiritual "emotionalism" to be the province of "common Negroes," not those studious bodies "uplifted" into a "civilized class" via "moral" discipline: "Was this not the best proof of respectability in the eyes of the white man, who had constantly argued that the Negro's savage instincts prevented him from conforming to puritanical standards of sex behavior?" (71). A "conventional family" does not shout in church. Its members "avoid the more extravagant forms of religious ecstasy" (Frazier 1963, 302). They embody respectability over and against the sexuality of the masses; and therein lies the reasoning behind Frazier's statement in "The Negro Middle Class and Desegregation" that his study of the "black bourgeoisie" was a "logical outgrowth" of his history of "the Negro family" (Frazier 1957c, 291).

14.   See William G. Martin and Michael O. West's "Future with a Past: Resurrecting the Study of Africa in the Post-Africanist Era" (1997), as well as their edited volume *Out of One, Many Africas: Reconstructing the Study and Meaning of Africa* (1999), for more on Herskovits, race, and U.S. imperialism.

15.   Not only would the "American Negro" delegation become embroiled in a controversy surrounding CIA funding, but a message from a radicalized Du Bois was also read at Diop's conference: "I am not present at your meeting today because the United States government will not grant me a passport for travel abroad. Any Negro-American who travels abroad today must either not discuss race conditions in the United States or say the sort of thing which our State Department wishes the world to believe" (Présence Africaine Conference Committee 1956, 383). A conference report is supplied by a young James Baldwin in *Nobody Knows My Name* (1961), expressing serious dismay, interestingly, at Du Bois's trans-Atlantic intervention.

16.   Robert L. Allen wrote in *Black Awakening in Capitalist America* (1969) that while white and "Negro" critics balked at Frazier's critique of the Black "bourgeoisie," they were compelled to concede its accuracy with the advent of more "respectable" academic studies (Allen 1969, 28). William B. Gatewood's *Aristocrats of Color: The Black Elite, 1880–1920* (1993) supplies a perfect example. Barely mentioning Frazier at all, the white scholar is nonetheless apprehensive about the "controversial" *Black Bourgeoisie* (Gatewood 1993, 335), even as his

own book replicates almost every detail of the Black scholar's work, often in precisely the same language. For instance, having dealt with rampant depictions of "pampered house slaves" (17), Gatewood concludes, "The class and color divisions and caste distinctions that developed within the black population before the Civil War did not suddenly disappear with Emancipation: rather they gave rise to a complex class structure topped by those who prided themselves on being 'colored aristocrats'" (27). Repressing Frazier, *Aristocrats of Color* is frankly euphemistic: "admission to the upper reaches of society required a combination of respectability, moral rectitude, social grace, education, and proper ancestry, as well as wealth and color" (15). We get no mention of "raw sexual impulses" or raw sexual racism, the ideology of race, class, and sex that underpins what are otherwise termed "credentials." This description of the older caste undeniably paves the way for the new elite captured by Frazier. Gatewood confirms the anterior history of *Black Bourgeoisie,* without "controversy," for where Frazier condemned its comprador's elitism, Gatewood consistently defends it: "Critics of educated, upper-class blacks sometimes accused them of being 'lamp black whites' or of aping the ways of middle- and upper-class whites. While there was obviously some truth to the accusation, it is difficult to see how it could have been otherwise" (270). This apology is the difference between Frazier and other, more "respectable" academic studies. The Black masses be damned; Frazier's book can be politically contained and devalued as "polemic" by the same critics who will opportunistically claim him as the father of Black sociology.

17.   Remarkably exceptional, Cruse carried the torch in his use of this term in an interview conducted by Van Gosse and published in *Radical History Review* 71: "Nothing's changed. That basically is correct. They are a lumpen bourgeoisie. They were from the beginning a lumpen bourgeoisie. But this lumpen character has been, in recent years, augmented or influenced by the fact that it's grown larger, because of or in spite of the welfare state, in spite of what the Civil Rights Movement has accomplished, they've grown larger, but that does not mean that they are any less a lumpen bourgeoisie: 'We just some other black people out here suffering from racism. . . . ' So that complicates the matter for us blacks who are trying to concoct theories about this stuff, about American realities" (Cruse 1998, 115).

18.   The phrase is translated as "a sort of little, greedy caste, avid and avaricious" in the first English edition of *The Wretched of the Earth* (F. Fanon 1963, 175). The original French text reads, rather literally in certain respects, "une sorte de petite caste, aux dents longues, avide et vorace" (F. Fanon 1961, 168). I am slightly retranslating the first part of this phrase, then, when I write of the "greedy little caste" here in Fanon.

4. Sexual Imitation and the "Greedy Little Caste"

1.   For instance, Hodge points out "peasant" class-based Black pride in Joseph Zobel's work versus more alienated texts by French-colonized Caribbean intel-

lectuals in France: "To the Frenchman on board ship who mistakes him for a Guadeloupean because of his deep black complexion: 'That is true,' said the Negro. 'In Martinique, one is more likely to be mulatto. . . . But I, you see, have not been watered down.' He was laughing heartily" (quoted in Hodge 1972, 223).

2.   In "Racism and Culture," Fanon comes back to this former self: "His knowledge, the appropriation of precise and complicated techniques, sometimes his intellectual superiority as compared to a great number of racists, lead him to qualify the racist world as passion-charged" (F. Fanon 1967b, 40).

3.   This reading totally recasts Kobena Mercer's "Decolonisation and Disappointment: Reading Fanon's Sexual Politics" in Alan Read's *The Fact of Blackness* (1996). Mercer does not so much "read" Fanon's corpus as cite a couple of passages from *Black Skin, White Masks,* without context, while always assuming a "homophobic" impulse along with all the orthodoxies of sexual imperialism in the West. He can himself be read in his "reading" of the "Fanon" he only partially imagines.

4.   Recalling Frazier yet again, Fanon elaborates a very complex framework to analyze the racist sexual violence endemic to colonial situations: "At the level of the psychological strata of the occupier, the evocation of this freedom given to the sadism of the conqueror, to his eroticism, creates faults, fertile gaps through which both dreamlike forms of behavior and, on certain occasions, criminal acts can emerge" (F. Fanon 1965, 45).

5.   There is the idealized notion of "Universal Man" and "Universal Woman" out of Europe, on the one hand, and the antithetical notion of the "Fatmas" (F. Fanon 1965, 52), for example, on the other hand. Every one of these categories must be distinguished and violently undone, according to Fanon in *A Dying Colonialism.* He is compelled to rebuff facile comparisons of Algerian female militants to white female "secret service" agents: "She does not have the sensation of playing a role she has read about ever so many times in novels, or seen in motion pictures. There is not that coefficient of play, of imitation, always present in this form of action when we are dealing with a Western woman" (50). He also differentiates the male anti-colonial militant, "the Algerian *fidai,*" from another Western cipher, "the unbalanced anarchists made famous in literature" (59). Tellingly, the "Universal Love" treated by Hodge is nowhere to be found in this Fanon.

6.   In a footnote to her chapter in Gibson's *Rethinking Fanon,* Sharpley-Whiting powerfully addresses some of the serious distortions that precede her. She locates Diana Fuss in Capécia's colonialist school. Fuss confuses psychiatry and psychoanalysis as well as "blacks" with "Algerians" in "Interior Colonies" (Sharpley-Whiting 1999, 351n5). She pauses in the end to ask a question that should begin her inquiry and interrogate feminist as well as gay and lesbian discourses at least as much as they interrogate Fanon: "Is it really possible to speak of 'homosexuality,' or for that matter 'heterosexuality' or 'bisexuality,' as universal, global formations?" (Fuss 1999, 315). The same question is not then

asked about "homophobia," nor are such questions asked of white Western academics in the way criticisms are aimed at "Fanon." Fuss easily reproduces what Sharpley-Whiting, in *Frantz Fanon: Conflicts and Feminisms,* called "a recurring antiblack male bias," a recurring anti-Black revolutionary bias that casts revolutionary activity, especially by Blacks, as "essentially" and negatively masculist and male.

Sharpley-Whiting also reads the "selective" citation of Fanon in Anne McClintock, who virtually rewrites "Algeria Unveiled" in her "Fanon and Gender Agency" (Sharpley-Whiting 1999, 352n5). It is not surprising that the consumption of *Black Skin, White Masks* would begin to expand itself, like imperialism, and spread to works by Fanon previously untapped by Western academia. Sharpley-Whiting reiterates *A Dying Colonialism* as originally written by Fanon himself. Yet several sexual paradoxes are still noteworthy in McClintock's short and more than sketchy essay. For instance, she suggests that Fanon preserves "the heterosexual family" in "Algeria Unveiled" (McClintock 1999, 293). Fuss would do well to criticize McClintock, were critiques of "homophobia" and "misogyny" not now routinely riveted to Black bodies, insurgent Black bodies most of all. What is "the heterosexual family"? This particular formation of family, along with particular formations of sexuality and nationalism, is categorically naturalized and universalized from the bourgeois West by McClintock. By contrast, in *A Dying Colonialism* Fanon questions and specifies most of what she takes for granted. Nothing "old" is to remain intact, of course, in his ecstatic advocacy of the "new." A fundamental heterosexualism is quite visible in McClintock herself when she faults Fanon for valorizing Algerian women who "penetrate the flesh" of the revolution: "A curious instability of gender power is here effected as the women are figured as masculinized and the male revolution is penetrated" (McClintock 1999, 292). It is therefore McClintock who seeks to stabilize the colonial categories of "masculinity" and "femininity," "male" and "female," "manhood" and "womanhood," to preserve "the heterosexual family" whose preservation she then projects onto Fanon. Where she presumes revolutions and roles should always, metaphysically, have gender, Fanon and the revolution he upholds argue strenuously against such gendering. They aggressively unsettle such assumptions. Critically, penetrating or "phallic women" are only cast as pejorative monstrosities here by McClintock. Fanon actually rejects the representation of women as "only penetrated," showing how colonialism strives to rape and penetrate Algerian women as well as how Algerian women counter-penetrate in revolt; and, beyond heterosexuality, they penetrate the flesh of a people's revolution ("revolution is not a war of men"), not a "male revolution," which McClintock can only impose here. This is what is so profoundly revolutionary about Fanon's conversion in *A Dying Colonialism,* and so profoundly reactionary about so much Fanon criticism in neo-colonial times.

7. Alioune Diop voiced his position in "Colonialisme et nationalisme culturel" (1955) even before he delivered his opening address to the 1956 conference in Paris. He sharpens his analysis of what Fanon came to call "cultural racism,"

speaking of cultural, political, and economic independence as specific yet interdependent aspects of Black liberation, in his "Remarks on African Personality and Negritude" (1962).

8. Cheikh Anta Diop's writings collected in *Alerte sous les tropiques* (1990; as *Towards the African Renaissance,* 1996) reveal his advanced articulation of some of the most radical ideas of *The Wretched of the Earth.* His *African Origin of Civilization* (1974) effects a double demystification, "ancient" and "modern." Diop was "among the first" to call for Pan-African decolonization (C. A. Diop 1996, 143), militating for transnational federations in Africa and the Caribbean, at the Paris conference of 1956. He defined "culture" as an instrument of popular liberation struggle, promoted continental coalition to battle U.S. neo-colonialism, and proposed the exacerbation of "metropolitan" class conflict as a means of destabilizing the power of empire. He challenges the sexuality of humanist imperialism, too, as he champions "African matriarchy" against the European patriarchy upheld by colonial anthropology, history, etc. This Diop could further criticize Senghor, some parts of Césaire, and all neo-colonial parliamentarians, without ever denying Black world culture in the least. What's more, his Pan-Africanism had no problem including Africans colonized in North America under U.S. settler imperialism.

9. Much as "The Fact of Blackness" has come to stand for *Black Skin, White Masks* and all of Fanon himself, "Concerning Violence" can be read as shorthand for *The Wretched of the Earth*—in a shortcutting criticism. Accordingly, a few critics have excerpted this one line, as translated by Constance Farrington, for an all-too-quick sexual analysis: "The look that the native [*sic*] turns on the settler's town is a look of lust, a look of envy; it expresses his dreams of possession—all manner of possession: to sit at the settler's table, to sleep in the settler's bed, with his wife if possible. The colonized man is an envious man" (F. Fanon 1963, 39). A standard critique may then charge that Fanon standardizes a "masculine" perspective in his narrative of colonialism and anti-colonialism. Yet, thus interpreted, this sentence would hardly be standard in *The Wretched of the Earth.* Nor is its meaning self-evident in the vein of certain chapters of *Black Skin, White Masks.* Some particular example of this "lust," this "envy," and these "dreams of possession" presented by Fanon could or could not be more or less gendered without any particular example's being presented as representative of the whole experience of colonization; it is far from clear that among the masses of "colonized women" there is a desire to "sleep" with the colonizing man in a comparable fashion, given the male colonizer's rapist access to colonized female bodies under colonialism, a historical situation which contrasts significantly with the eroticizing taboo enveloping white female persons physically idolized by empire. In any event, Fanon cannot standardize masculinity in *The Wretched of the Earth* when he actually and frequently disrupts the French language's standardization of masculinity by emphatically writing "men and women" (instead of simply "men"). This is in addition to his insistence on egalitarian ideology, as scrupulously expressed in his statement on "sexual feudalism," and his sexually inclusive definition of

"lumpen-proletariat" as well as "peasant" participation in anti-colonialist revolution. It is surely interesting that writers such as Ifi Amadiume and Oyèrónké Oyěwùmí have consistently criticized masculine standardization as a hallmark or inescapable feature of European languages in the colonization of African peoples. For this criticism extends to masculinist as well as feminist schools of thought in the West, certain feminist criticisms of Fanon (and others) notwithstanding, as anti-colonialist writing struggles to write its way out of colonialist patriarchy when writing within the constraints of French, English, etc.

5. Colonialism and Erotic Desire—in English

1. See, for more on her "tragedy of color" formulation, Robert Hemenway's *Zora Neale Hurston: A Literary Biography* (1977, 332–36).

2. Standard critiques of Chodorow can be found in texts by Pauline Bart (1981), Adrienne Rich (1980), Elizabeth Spelman (1988), and Iris Marion Young (1983); and a more anti-racist, anti-imperialist criticism of this motherhood can be found in the work of Gloria Joseph and Jill Lewis (1981) and Audre Lorde (1986).

3. Carole Boyce Davies is rather exceptional in this respect. In *Out of the Kumbla*'s "Writing Home: Gender and Heritage in the Works of Afro-Caribbean/American Women" (1990) and *Black Women Writing and Identity: Migrations of the Subject* (1994), she makes reference to sexual "allusions" in Kincaid which, I argue, centrally define her writing as a whole.

4. So when Lucy does have sex with Hugh, a man who impresses her at a party by asking, "Where in the West Indies are you from?" (Kincaid 1990b, 65), the act only brings the beloved mother to mind (67). Peggy herself fades from the romantic picture, just like Gwen and the Red Girl did in another life, as the maternal figure reappears to make all disavowal impossible. Every sexual escapade or erotic entanglement in *Lucy* is all about "Miss Annie." It may be indulged in to trigger her anger or jealousy; it may be engaged in with hopes of repressing her memory; or it may be initiated in an attempt to recapture the pleasure of her affection. In the end, Lucy suspects that Paul and Peggy have begun a secret liaison of their own. She hopes that they won't get angry when they realize she really doesn't care (163). Her life remains preoccupied with the very thing she sought to escape before her arrival in a strange land. She speaks of her mother as an ancient (150) and god-like (153) presence, conjuring up "the face she used to have when she loved me without reservation" (155). The erotic tragedy of *Annie John* is reiterated, palpably: "One day I was living silently in a personal hell, without anyone to tell what I felt, without knowing that the feelings I had were possible to have" (136).

5. It can be argued that a key difference between Freud and Chodorow is that she simply assumes "penis envy" with his legitimating authority, while Freud himself worked hard to establish this "idea" as a desperate last resort. In any

event, what could be more foreign to Kincaid? In *Annie John*, as elsewhere, it is always and forever a mother's form that physically mesmerizes the primary character. It is not the lack of a penis that she can never forgive; it is its conventional intrusion. She resents her mother for ending their erotic relation and imposing "young ladyhood" (after "puberty" rather than before). The writings of Chodorow and her school of thought take Freud's "Oedipal" fiasco for granted, despite all the many frustrations of its first theoretician, insofar as "normal feminine heterosexuality" is not much of a rhetorical crisis for "the daughter" of *The Reproduction of Mothering*. The "homoerotic," "primitivized" girl-child in Kincaid can then be effaced by the psychoanalytic arm of what Wynter called "universal feminism."

6. This line of resistance can be seen elsewhere. "Hiccups" recalls an earlier manifesto from the Harlem Renaissance which was a major source of inspiration for the trans-Atlantic Negritude of Damas, Césaire, and Léopold Senghor. Langston Hughes, in "The Negro Artist and the Racial Mountain," scorned the pretensions of a young male poet and a Philadelphia clubwoman who lived by the "Don't be like niggers" motto of the "smug Negro middle class" home (Hughes 1926, 302). In Schwarz-Bart's *The Bridge of Beyond*, Télumée makes this point anew as the narrator hears

> the latest news about my sister, Regina, who was now living with her real father in Basse-Terre, sleeping in a bed, eating apples from France, wearing a dress with puff sleeves, and going to school. . . . A few years later I saw my sister in a procession of married couples outside the church in La Ramée. Regina had become an elegant city lady. I took advantage of the crowd to go up to her unobtrusively, and as I bent forward to kiss her she held out a gloved hand and said awkwardly, "Why, you must be Télumée!" (Schwarz-Bart 1974, 41)

7. Interestingly, when Annie John falls prey to what we can call her "love sickness" in the chapter "The Long Rain," her parents believe that the trials of colonial schooling are to blame: "Most likely, my father said that it was all the studying I had been doing at school, that I had moved along from form to form too fast and it had taken a heavy toll. Most likely, my mother agreed" (Kincaid 1985, 109).

8. This reading applies no less to Kincaid's essay in *Transition* 51, "On Seeing England for the First Time" (1991), in which resentment (or "tragic" sentiments) should not be confused with rebellion.

9. See, for a summation of these ties between Kincaid's "fiction" and autobiography, "Through West Indian Eyes" by Leslie Garis (1990), in which *Lucy* is explicitly categorized as "non-fictional." Also documented here is the public controversy regarding concrete correlations between its characters and the white upper-class family who had been Kincaid's employers. (For this citation I can thank Catherine John, with whom I've had countless conversations about Kincaid and criticism in the past.)

10. A completely different politics of "brotherhood" in the context of "AIDS" is certainly inscribed by the anthology conceived by Joseph Beam and edited by

Essex Hemphill, *Brother to Brother: New Writings by Black Gay Men* (1991), not that Kincaid desires kinship of any kind. In a presentation at the 1998 Caribbean Women Writers Conference in Grenada, Meredith Gadsby reported that Kincaid asked the audience at the Miami Book Fair of 1997 to buy her new book to help cover the costs of "my brother's" medical bills. This line is legible in the "memoir" text itself. She presents herself as a financial savior of sorts thanks to her easy access to the drug AZT. But not only does Kincaid fail to mention the potentially horrifying side effects of this medication, about which many patients have testified, she also omits that the average annual cost of AZT or AZT "cocktail" treatments at that time might run from $3,000 to $10,000. Her readers are not likely to ask how this amount could "almost break" someone of her stature over the course of three or so years. (The figures cited here were obtained from Pauline Jolly of the University of Alabama–Birmingham during a panel she chaired entitled "Sexually Transmitted Diseases and HIV in the Caribbean" at the Twenty-third Annual Conference of the Caribbean Studies Association in St. John's, Antigua, in 1998.)

11.   Evelyn O'Callaghan is scarcely an exception in her "Compulsory Heterosexuality and Textual/Sexual Alternatives in Selected Texts by West Indian Women Writers" (1998). She asks, "*Are* West Indian women writers party to an unthinking naturalization of 'compulsory heterosexuality'? *Do* they partake in the silencing of lesbian existence or are there texts which demonstrate such existence as resistance to male supremacy?" (Callaghan 1998, 298). As she struggles to answer in the negative, partly as a result of her acceptance of Western bourgeois categories of sex and sexual analysis, she includes Kincaid in a survey of purportedly anti-heterosexualist authors. She is given a central place despite a serious concession: "While Kincaid's characters move from female bonding to 'compulsory heterosexuality,' there is still an openness in the evocation of physical affection between women" (299). If this "openness" is closed down in the move toward "compulsory heterosexuality," which still in fact naturalizes it, what sense does it make to say there is "openness" or an "alternative" to be found in Kincaid? The mere presence of "female bonding" in a narrative does not entail anti-heterosexualism in its author or in the narrative, especially if author and critics fail to recognize this "bonding" in sexual terms—as such an asexual description ("female bonding") itself suggests. Freudian psychoanalysis recognizes such sex before pathologizing it with Victorian social norms. The critic assigns intentions to the author imagined from interpretations of text, a fundamental exegetical mistake, much as most critics make no differentiation between Kincaid's statements in interviews, the narrative voice of her main characters, and the "truth" or significance of the texts. O'Callaghan misses the politics of sexuality in *Annie John* and *Lucy* so much that she writes, "mother/motherland is rejected in *Annie John* for 'her' indoctrination in colonial discourse" (318), and "only in the wider and more sexually tolerant world of the metropole [can] such frank, erotic language be spoken" (300). On the contrary, mother, daughter, and "motherland" are colonized with puritanical mores which are, like coloniality in general, the antithe-

sis of freedom. The "metropolis" is in actuality the center or capital of this unfreedom, not freedom's paradise as colonialism would have it.

12.   Toni Cade Bambara's "A Sort of Preface" in *Gorilla, My Love* (1972) problematizes "autobiographical fiction" in the vernacular. She says it does no good, "cause the minute the book hits the stands here comes your mama screamin how could you." And your best friend "says that seeing as how you have plundered her soul and walked off with a piece of her flesh, the least you can do is spin off half the royalties her way" (Bambara 1972, n.p.). But whereas Bambara spurns this genre for its social politics of narcissism, Kincaid *works* it; and her critics overwhelmingly indulge her.

13.   It is no surprise then that Lorde is included in Catherine Reid and Holly Iglesias's collection *Every Woman I've Ever Loved: Lesbian Writers on Their Mothers* (1997).

6. Neo-colonial Canons of Gender and Sexuality, after COINTELPRO

1.   See ZAMI, "Atlanta's Premiere Organization for Lesbians of African Descent," whose "primary mission is to empower and affirm the lives of lesbians of Africain descent through scholarships, leadership development, support/discussion groups, social activities, drum performances, outreach and education," at http://www.zami.org.

2.   This is not to overlook the Black leftist revisitation of Clarke by Cathy J. Cohen and Tamara Jones in Eric Brandt's *Dangerous Liaisons: Blacks, Gays, and the Struggle for Equality* (1999), an anthology in which another important essay by Clarke appears. I offer a very different reading of "The Failure to Transform" inasmuch as I endorse and emphasize Clarke's rejection of petty-bourgeois classism vis-à-vis Black working- and non-working-class culture; and I do not assume that the passage of time has entailed progress, ideologically, in intellectual production.

3.   Boyce Davies makes a similar point about Black feminisms in *Left of Marx: The Politics and Poetics of Claudia Jones* (forthcoming). She persuasively argues that earlier anti-imperialist/anti-capitalist models of Black feminism have been supplanted intellectually by academic versions which fail to challenge U.S. world hegemony. These older models provide the inspiration for Beam, who credits them for his own sexual political consciousness.

4.   The racist media construct of "Black-on-Black violence" is also disrupted when Cube casts "Bosnia and Herzegovina" as "white-on-white violence" in an international context.

5.   Blackman's sexual radicalism is trumped by the cinematic space and sympathy given to Suggs. He boasts of the campaign by GLAAD, the Gay and Lesbian Alliance against Defamation, to block Shabba Ranks's appearance on the country's most "successful" talk show, *The Tonight Show,* hosted by Jay Leno: "We didn't want him to get this kind of mainstream exposure without him having to take some responsibility for his homophobic comments."

Significantly, it is not a "homophobic" song that GLAAD wants him to repudiate, but homophobic "comments," for which the music of the Black popular masses must be attacked as a whole. Suggs maintains that the talk show's staff was "horrified" when some of these comments were relayed; and they "immediately decided that they didn't want him to go on." He expresses pride in a "public service" well done, for having issued a "societal advisory" against "homophobic lyrics." But this campaign presumes that this society itself is not homophobic, that homophobia is not mainstream, and that Jay Leno does not make a song out of homophobic comments himself on a nightly basis. His sex jokes are not the target of campaign tirades against all white middle-class humor, for instance. So what can Leno and GLAAD's Suggs "protect" their country from in the form of Ranks? Ranks was invited to appear only because he had recently won a Grammy award. In general, the "genteel" audience of this show is "protected" from the "rude" displays of Black popular culture without the aid of any sexual alibi. It continues to bond with the host and his homophobic racism rather than with hip-hop and dancehall, which do not write Leno's opening monologues. The "public service" done by Suggs and company is thus to absolve a more powerful white audience of its institutionalized homophobia with a myopic focus on deejays and rappers. It absolves a colonial republic of its standing as a homophobic public; and it absolves it of its standing colonization of Black communities through a homophobic heterosexualism which is notoriously racist. It is through these strange yet standard strategies that someone could say, "Homophobia in hip hop is more powerful than the New Right." It would be necessary to "forget" that the "New" in "New Right" is like the "Neo" in "Neo-Colonialism," a counter-insurgent world order in which "Left" and "Right," "gay" and "straight" do participate.

6.   In 2004, Cooper published *Sound Clash: Jamaican Dancehall Culture at Large*.

7.   Note Julien's relative neglect of sexual politics in *BaadAsssss Cinema: A Bold Look at 70's Blaxploitation Films* (2002). Where is the wholesale dismissal of this art form on the basis of "sexism" and "homophobia," so to speak? "Cinema," normally coded as elitist, is uncritically endorsed, while hip-hop and dancehall are maligned as if hip-hop in particular were not in large part a massive reinscription (or reincarnation) of this Black culture of the 1970s.

8.   In hindsight, it is surprising that Riggs states, early on, his desire to deal with identity "in the global perspective," given the provincial critique of sex and sexuality found in *Black Is . . . Black Ain't*.

9.   The "Nineties" reconstruction of "Sixties nationalism" by Davis should be contrasted with Assata Shakur's "Thoughts on Cuba, Black Liberation, and Hip Hop Today: As Told to Cristina Veran" (1998).

10.   We see both terms come together in Lorde's *Zami*: "I told her that Muriel and I weren't together any more. 'Yeah? That's too bad. You-all were kinda cute together. But that's the way it goes. How long you been in the "life"?'" (Lorde 1982, 244).

11. At the time of this writing these websites were http://www.AssataShakur.org and http://www.AfroCubaWeb.com/assata.htm. No less important in the following respect are all of Shakur's writings and Abu-Jamal's *We Want Freedom: A Life in the Black Panther Party* (2004), especially its seventh chapter, "A Woman's Party," with its substantial discussion of the late Safiya Bukhari.

12. During the week of November 3, 2004, Dhoruba Bin Wahad delivered lectures at Syracuse University and the State University of New York at Binghamton. See *Pipe Dream: The Free Word on Campus* (SUNY-Binghamton) 65 (November 7, 2003), 16, and *The Black Voice: Syracuse University's Black Student Publication* 34 (November 5–19, 2003), 5.

13. Bin Wahad insists that COINTELPRO has its basic origins on the plantations of chattel slavery (Bin Wahad 2003, 97, 99). More narrow histories of the FBI program focus on its anti–Communist Party beginnings, perhaps with a detour to accommodate Puerto Rican *independentistas*. This ignores a number of things. Reading texts like Theodore Kornweibel's *"Seeing Red": Federal Campaigns against Black Militancy, 1919–1925* (1999) will confirm that "Red Scares" are often, and perhaps even always, "Black Scares" in the U.S. Activists from the Universal Negro Improvement Association, the African Blood Brotherhood, and the NAACP, as well as Black socialists, were heavily targeted by 1920s counter-intelligence, whether they espoused a Marxist ideology or not. By the 1950s, Robert F. Williams would take serious offense at the red herring of "red-baiting" Black radicals who promoted Black self-determination against Cold War politics of any sort. The presence of Black people in a white racist society completely transforms the picture of political antagonism in anti-communist capitalist contexts. So when the FBI declares Black Panthers "Public Enemy #1," we are definitely in the midst of a "Black Scare." COINTELPRO may confirm this even more crudely than McCarthyism. Yet McCarthyism and COINTELPRO are both Negrophobic to the core.

14. This naming is mentioned in the very final pages of *Warrior Poet: A Biography of Audre Lorde* by Alexis De Veaux (2004, 365). She notes that it was adopted as part of a "communal naming ceremony" in St. Croix, Virgin Islands, in 1991 (423n6).

Conclusion

1. Jayne Cortez, *Somewhere in Advance of Nowhere* (New York: High Risk Books, 1996), 65.

References

Abu-Jamal, Mumia. 2004. *We Want Freedom: A Life in the Black Panther Party*. Boston: South End Press.

Adisa, Opal Palmer. 1991. "Island Daughter." *Women's Review of Books* 9:5 (February): 56–58.

Aidoo, Ama Ata. 1992. "The African Woman Today." *Dissent* 39 (Summer): 319–25.

Allen, Paula Gunn. 1986. *The Sacred Hoop: Recovering the Feminine in American Indian Traditions*. Boston: Beacon Press.

Allen, Robert L. 1969. *Black Awakening in Capitalist America: An Analytic History*. New York: Anchor Books, 1970.

Almaguer, Tomás. 1991. "Chicano Men: A Cartography of Homosexual Identity and Behavior." *differences: A Journal of Feminist Cultural Studies* 3:2 (Summer): 75–100.

Amadiume, Ifi. 1987a. *African Matriarchal Foundations: The Case of Igbo Societies*. London: Karnak House.

———. 1987b. *Male Daughters, Female Husbands: Gender and Sex in an African Society*. London: Zed Books.

———. 1989. "Cheikh Anta Diop's Theory of Matriarchal Values as the Basis for African Cultural Unity." Introduction to Cheikh Anta Diop, *The Cultural Unity of Black Africa: The Domains of Matriarchy and Patriarchy in Classical Antiquity* (London: Karnak House), ix–xix.

———. 1995. *Ecstacy*. Lagos, Nigeria: Longman.

———. 1997. *Re-inventing Africa: Matriarchy, Religion, and Culture*. London: Zed Books.

———. 2000. *Daughters of the Goddess, Daughters of Imperialism: African Women Struggle for Culture, Power, and Democracy*. London: Zed Books.

Amin, Samir. 1989. *Eurocentrism*. Trans. Russell Moore. New York: Monthly Review Press.

Ani, Marimba. 1994. *Yurugu: An African-Centered Critique of European Cultural Thought and Behavior*. Trenton, N.J.: Africa World Press.

Anzaldúa, Gloria. 1991. "To(o) Queer the Writer—*Loca, Escritora y Chicana*." In *InVersions: Writings by Dykes, Queers, and Lesbians*, ed. Betsy Warland, 249–63. Vancouver, B.C.: Press Gang Publishers.

Appiah, Kwame Anthony. 1992. *In My Father's House: Africa in the Philosophy of Culture*. New York: Oxford University Press.

Aptheker, Bettina. 1975. *The Morning Breaks: The Trial of Angela Davis*. Ithaca, N.Y.: Cornell University Press, 1999.

Armah, Ayi Kwei. 1969. "Fanon: The Awakener." *Negro Digest* 18 (October): 4–9, 29–43.

Baldwin, James. 1961. *Nobody Knows My Name: More Notes of a Native Son*. New York: Dial Press.

Bambara, Toni Cade. 1970a. "On the Issue of Roles." In *The Black Woman: An Anthology,* ed. Toni Cade Bambara, 101–10. New York: Mentor.

———. 1970b. Preface to *The Black Woman: An Anthology,* ed. Toni Cade Bambara, 7–12. New York: Mentor.

———. 1972. *Gorilla, My Love.* New York: Vintage Books, 1992.

Bart, Pauline. 1981. Review of Nancy Chodorow's *The Reproduction of Mothering.* In *Mothering: Essays in Feminist Theory,* ed. Joyce Trebilcot, 147–52. Totowa, N.J.: Rowman and Allanheld, 1984. Originally published in *off our backs* 11:1.

Beale, Frances M. 1970. "Double Jeopardy: To Be Black and Female." In *The Black Woman: An Anthology,* ed. Toni Cade Bambara, 90–100. New York: Mentor.

———. 1975. "Slave of a Slave No More: Black Women in Struggle." *Black Scholar* 12:6 (November–December 1981): 16–24. Originally published in *Black Scholar* 6:6 (March): 2–10.

Beam, Joseph. 1986. "Leaving the Shadows Behind." Introduction to *In the Life: A Black Gay Anthology,* ed. Joseph Beam, 13–18. Boston: Alyson Publications.

Beauvoir, Simone de. 1992. *Force of Circumstance,* vol. 2, *Hard Times, 1952–1962.* Trans. Richard Howard. New York: Paragon House. Originally published as *La force des choses* (Paris: Gallimard, 1963).

Beckles, Hilary. 1995. "Sex and Gender in the Historiography of Caribbean Slavery." In *Engendering History: Caribbean Women in Historical Perspective,* ed. Verene Shepherd, Bridget Brereton, and Barbara Bailey, 125–40. New York: St. Martin's Press.

Bennett, Lerone, Jr. 1964. *The Negro Mood and Other Essays.* Chicago: Johnson Publishing.

Berlinerblau, Jacques. 1999. *Heresy in the University: The Black Athena Controversy and the Responsibilities of American Intellectuals.* New Brunswick, N.J.: Rutgers University Press.

Bernal, Martin. 1987. *Black Athena: The Afroasiatic Roots of Classical Civilization,* vol. 1, *The Fabrication of Ancient Greece, 1785–1985.* New Brunswick, N.J.: Rutgers University Press.

———. 1989. "*Black Athena* and the APA." *Arethusa* 12:5 (Fall): 17–38.

———. 1991. *Black Athena: The Afroasiatic Roots of Classical Civilization,* vol. 2, *The Archaeological and Documentary Evidence.* New Brunswick, N.J.: Rutgers University Press.

———. 2001. *Black Athena Writes Back: Martin Bernal Responds to His Critics.* Ed. David Chioni Moore. Durham, N.C.: Duke University Press.

Bin Wahad, Dhoruba. 1993a. "The Cutting Edge of Prison Technology." In *Still Black, Still Strong: Survivors of the U.S. War against Black Revolutionaries,* by Dhoruba Bin Wahad, Mumia Abu-Jamal, and Assata Shakur, ed. Jim Fletcher, Tanaquil Jones, and Sylvère Lotringer, 77–102. New York: Semiotext(e).

———. 1993b. "War Within." In *Still Black, Still Strong: Survivors of the U.S. War against Black Revolutionaries,* by Dhoruba Bin Wahad, Mumia Abu-Jamal, and Assata Shakur, ed. Jim Fletcher, Tanaquil Jones, and Sylvère Lotringer, 9–56. New York: Semiotext(e).

———. 2003. "COINTELPRO and the Destruction of Black Leaders and Organizations (Abridged)." In *Imprisoned Intellectuals: American's Political Prisoners Write on*

Life, Liberation, and Rebellion, ed. Joy James, 97–103. Lanham, Md.: Rowman and Littlefield.

Bin Wahad, Dhoruba, Mumia Abu-Jamal, and Assata Shakur. 1993. *Still Black, Still Strong: Survivors of the U.S. War against Black Revolutionaries.* Ed. Jim Fletcher, Tanaquil Jones, and Sylvère Lotringer. New York: Semiotext(e).

Blackman, Inge, dir. 2003. *Paradise Lost: Journey to Trinidad.* Blackman Vision.

Bleys, Rudi C. 1995. *The Geography of Perversion: Male-to-Male Sexual Behavior outside the West and the Ethnographic Imagination, 1750–1918.* Washington Square, N.Y.: New York University Press.

Bobb, June. 1988. Review of Jamaica Kincaid's *Annie John. Cimarron* 1:3 (Spring): 169–72.

Boswell, John. 1980. *Christianity, Social Tolerance, and Homosexuality.* Chicago: University of Chicago Press.

——. 1989. "Revolutions, Universals, and Sexual Categories." In *Hidden from History: Reclaiming the Gay and Lesbian Past,* ed. Martin Duberman, Martha Vicinus, and George Chauncey, Jr., 17–36. New York: Meridian.

Boyce Davies, Carole. 1990. "Writing Home: Gender and Heritage in the Works of Afro-Caribbean Women Writers." In *Out of the Kumbla: Caribbean Women in Literature,* ed. Carole Boyce Davies and Elaine Savory Fido, 59–73. Trenton, N.J.: Africa World Press.

——. 1994. *Black Women, Writing, and Identity: Migrations of the Subject.* New York: Routledge.

——. Forthcoming. *Left of Marx: The Politics and Poetics of Claudia Jones.* Durham, N.C.: Duke University Press.

Boyce Davies, Carole, and Elaine Savory Fido, eds. 1990. *Out of the Kumbla: Caribbean Women and Literature.* Trenton, N.J.: Africa World Press.

Brand, Dionne. 1989. *Sans Souci and Other Stories.* Ithaca, N.Y.: Firebrand Books.

Brodber, Erna. 1997. "Re-engineering Blackspace." *Caribbean Quarterly* 43:1–2 (March–June): 70–81.

Brown, Elaine. 1992. *A Taste of Power: A Black Woman's Story.* New York: Anchor Books.

——. 2002. *The Condemnation of Little B: New Age Racism in America.* Boston: Beacon Press.

Bulhan, Hussein A. 1980. "Frantz Fanon: The Revolutionary Psychiatrist." *Race & Class* 21:3 (Winter): 251–72.

——. 1985. *Frantz Fanon and the Psychology of Oppression.* New York: Plenum Press.

Bush, Barbara. 1986. " 'The Family Tree Is Not Cut': Women and Cultural Resistance in Slave Family Life in the British Caribbean." In *Resistance: Studies in African, Caribbean, and Afro-American History,* ed. Gary Y. Okihiro, 117–32. Amherst: University of Massachusetts Press.

Butler, Judith P. 1989. *Gender Trouble: Feminism and the Subversion of Identity.* New York: Routledge.

——. 1993. *Bodies That Matter: On the Discursive Limits of "Sex."* New York: Routledge.

Cabral, Amilcar. 1971. *Revolution in Guinea.* New York: Monthly Review Press.

Carby, Hazel V. 1987. *Reconstructing Womanhood: The Emergence of the Afro-American Woman Novelist.* New York: Oxford University Press.

Carmichael, Stokely, with Ekwueme Michael Thelwell. 2003. *Ready for Revolution: The Life and Struggles of Stokely Carmichael (Kwame Ture).* New York: Scribner.

Caute, David. 1970. *Frantz Fanon.* New York: Viking Press.

Césaire, Aimé. 1939. *Notebook of a Return to the Native Land.* Middletown, Conn.: Wesleyan University Press, 2001. Originally published as *Cahier d'un retour au pays natal* in *Volonté* 20 (August).

———. 1956. "Culture and Colonisation." *In Proceedings of the First International Congress of Negro Writers and Artists,* special issue of *Présence africaine* 8-10 (June-November): 193-229.

Champagne, John. 1995. *The Ethics of Marginality: A New Approach to Gay Studies.* Minneapolis: University of Minnesota Press.

Chodorow, Nancy. 1978. *The Reproduction of Mothering: Psychoanalysis and the Sociology of Gender.* Berkeley and Los Angeles: University of California Press.

Clarke, Cheryl. 1983. "The Failure to Transform: Homophobia in the Black Community." In *Home Girls: A Black Feminist Anthology,* ed. Barbara Smith, 197-298. New York: Kitchen Table—Women of Color Press.

Clarke, John Henrik. 1992. *Notes for an African World Revolution: Africans at the Crossroads.* Trenton, N.J.: Africa World Press.

———. 1994. "The Contribution of Nile Valley Civilization to World Civilization." In *Who Betrayed the African World Revolution? and Other Speeches,* 85-95. Chicago: Third World Press.

Cobham, Rhonda. 1991. "Dr. Freud for Visitor?" *Women's Review of Books* 8:5 (February): 17-18.

Cohen, Cathy J., and Tamara Jones. 1999. "Fighting Homophobia versus Challenging Heterosexualism: 'The Failure to Transform,' Revisited." In *Dangerous Liaisons: Blacks, Gays, and the Struggle for Equality,* ed. Eric Brandt, 80-101. New York: New Press.

Cohen, David, and Richard Saller. 1994. "Foucault on Sexuality in Greco-Roman Antiquity." In *Foucault and the Writing of History,* ed. Jan Ellen Goldstein, 35-60. Cambridge: Blackwell Publishers.

Collins, Rodnell P., with A. Peter Bailey. 1998. *Seventh Child: A Family Memoir of Malcolm X.* Secaucus, N.J.: Birch Lane Press.

Cooper, Anna Julia. 1998. *The Voice of Anna Julia Cooper: Including* A Voice from the South *and Other Important Essays, Papers, and Letters.* Ed. Charles Lemert and Esme Bhan. Lanham, Md.: Rowman and Littlefield.

Cooper, Carolyn. 1995. *Noises in the Blood: Orality, Gender, and the "Vulgar" Body of Jamaican Popular Culture.* Durham, N.C.: Duke University Press.

Coronil, Fernando. 1996. "Beyond Occidentalism: Towards Non-imperial Geohistorical Categories." *Cultural Anthropology* 11:1 (February): 51-87.

Cortez, Jayne. 1996. *Somewhere in Advance of Nowhere.* New York: High Risk Books.

Covi, Giovanna. 1990. "Jamaica Kincaid and the Resistance to Canons." In *Out of the Kumbla: Caribbean Women in Literature,* ed. Carole Boyce Davies and Elaine Savory Fido, 345-54. Trenton, N.J.: Africa World Press.

———. 2004. *Jamaica Kincaid's Prismatic Subjects: Making Sense of Being in the World.* London: Mango Publishing.

Crawford, Keith W. 1994. "The Racial Identity of Ancient Egyptian Populations Based on the Analysis of Physical Remains." In *Egypt: Child of Africa,* ed. Ivan Van Sertima, 55–74. New Brunswick, N.J.: Transaction.

Cromwell, Adelaide. 2002. "Frazier's Background and an Overview." In *E. Franklin Frazier and* Black Bourgeoisie, ed. James E. Teele, 30–45. Columbia: University of Missouri Press.

Cruse, Harold. 1969. *Rebellion or Revolution?* New York: William Morrow.

———. 1998. "Locating the Black Intellectual: An Interview with Harold Cruse." Conducted by Van Gosse. *Radical History Review* 71: 96–120.

Cudjoe, Selwyn, ed. 1990. *Caribbean Women Writers: Essays from the First International Conference.* Wellesley, Mass.: Calaloux Publications.

Damas, Léon G. 1972. "Poems from *Pigments.*" Trans. Ellen Conroy Kennedy. *Black World* (January): 13–28.

Davis, Angela Y. 1971. "Reflections on the Black Woman's Role in the Community of Slaves." *Black Scholar* 3:4 (December): 3–15.

———. 1981. "The Legacy of Slavery: Standards for a New Womanhood." In *Women, Race, and Class,* 3–29. New York: Vintage Books.

———. 1992. "Black Nationalism: The Sixties and the Nineties." In *Black Popular Culture: A Project,* by Michelle Wallace, ed. Gina Dent, 317–24. Seattle, Wash.: Bay Press.

———. 1998. *Blues Legacies and Black Feminism: Gertrude "Ma" Rainey, Bessie Smith, and Billie Holliday.* New York: Pantheon Books.

Davis, Angela Y., and Fania Davis. 1986. "The Black Family and the Crisis of Capitalism." *Black Scholar* 17:5 (September–October): 33–40.

de Lauretis, Teresa. 1991. "Queer Theory: Lesbian and Gay Sexualities." *differences: A Journal of Feminist Cultural Studies* 3:2 (Summer): iii–xviii.

De Veaux, Alexis. 2004. *Warrior Poet: A Biography of Audre Lorde.* New York: W. W. Norton.

Diop, Alioune. 1955. "Colonialisme et nationalisme culturel." *Présence africaine* 4 (October–November): 5–15.

———. 1956. "Opening Address to the First International Congress of Negro Writers and Artists." *Presence Africaine* 8:10 (June–November): 9–18.

———. 1962. "Remarks on African Personality and Negritude." In *Pan-Africanism Reconsidered,* ed. American Society of African Culture. Berkeley and Los Angeles: University of California Press.

Diop, Boubacar Boris, Odile Tobner, and François-Xavier Verschave. 2005. *Negrophobie.* Paris: Les Arenes.

Diop, Cheikh Anta. 1974. *The African Origin of Civilization: Myth or Reality.* Ed. and trans. Mercer Cook. Chicago: Lawrence Hill Books. Contains selections from *Nations nègres et culture* (Paris: Présence Africaine, 1955) and *Antériorité des civilizations nègres: Mythe ou vérité historique?* (Paris: Présence Africaine, 1967).

———. 1987a. *Black Africa: The Economic and Cultural Basis for a Federated State.* Revised edition. Trans. Harold J. Salemson. Chicago: Lawrence Hill Books. First English edition published 1974; originally published as *Les fondements économiques et culturels d'un état fédéral d'Afrique noire* (Paris: Présence Africaine, 1974).

———. 1987b. *Precolonial Black Africa: A Comparative Study of the Political and Social Systems of Europe and Black Africa, from Antiquity to the Formation of Modern States.* Trans. Harold J. Salemson. Chicago: Lawrence Hill Books. Originally published as *L'Afrique noire précolonial* (Paris: Presses universitaires de France, 1960).

———. 1989. *The Cultural Unity of Black Africa: The Domains of Matriarchy and Patriarchy in Classical Antiquity.* London: Karnak House. Originally published as *L'unité culturelle de l'Afrique noire* (Paris: Présence Africaine, 1959).

———. 1991. *Civilization or Barbarism: An Authentic Anthropology.* Ed. Harold J. Salemson and Marjolijn de Jager. Trans. Yaa-Lengi Meema Ngemi. Chicago: Lawrence Hill Books. Originally published as *Civilisation ou barbarie: Anthropologie sans complaisance* (Paris: Présence Africaine, 1981).

———. 1995. "Origin of the Ancient Egyptians." In *Egypt Revisited,* 4th ed., ed. Ivan Van Sertima, 9–37. New Brunswick, N.J.: Transaction. Originally published as "Origines des anciens Egyptiens," in *Ancient Civilizations of Africa,* vol. 2 of *General History of Africa,* ed. G. Mokhtar (Paris: UNESCO; Berkeley and Los Angeles: University of California Press, 1981).

———. 1996. *Towards the African Renaissance: Essays in African Culture and Development, 1946–1960.* Trans. Egbuna P. Modum. London, Karnak House. Originally published as *Alerte sous les tropiques* (Paris: The Estate of Cheikh Anta Diop and Présence Africaine, 1990).

Diop, Cheikh M'Backé. 2003. *Cheikh Anta Diop: L'homme et l'oeuvre.* Paris: Présence Africaine.

Douglas, Mary. 1969. "Is Matriliny Doomed in Africa?" In *Man in Africa,* ed. Mary Douglas and Phyllis M. Kaberry, 121–35. London: Tavistock Publications.

Drake, St. Clair. 1980. "Anthropology and the Black Experience." *Black Scholar* 11:7 (September–October): 2–31.

Duberman, Martin, Martha Vicinus, and George Chauncey, Jr., eds. 1989. *Hidden from History: Reclaiming the Gay and Lesbian Past.* New York: Meridian.

Dutton, Wendy. 1989. "Merge and Separate: Jamaica Kincaid's Fiction." *World Literature Today* 63 (Summer): 406–10.

Ellison, Ralph. 1948. *Invisible Man.* New York: Vintage Books, 1975.

Faderman, Lillian. 1981. *Surpassing the Love of Men: Romantic Love and Friendship between Women from the Renaissance to the Present.* New York: William Morrow.

Fanon, Frantz. 1961. *Les damnés de la terre.* Paris: La Découverte, 2002.

———. 1963. *The Wretched of the Earth.* Trans. Constance Farrington. New York: Grove Press. Originally published as *Les damnés de la terre* (Paris: François Maspero, 1961).

———. 1964. "Aux Antilles, naissance d'une nation?" In *Pour la révolution africaine: Écrits politiques,* 101–108. Paris: François Maspero.

———. 1965. *A Dying Colonialism.* Trans. Haakon Chevalier. New York: Monthly Review Press. Originally published as *L'an V de la révolution algérienne* (Paris: François Maspero, 1959).

———. 1967a. *Black Skin, White Masks.* Trans. Charles Lam Markmann. New York: Grove Press. Originally published as *Peau noire, masques blancs* (Paris: Éditions du Seuil, 1952).

———. 1967b. *Toward the African Revolution: Political Essays.* Trans. Haakon Chevalier. New York: Grove Press. Originally published as *Pour la révolution africaine: Écrits politiques* (Paris: François Maspero, 1964).

Fanon, Joby. 2004. *Frantz Fanon: De la Martinique à l'Algerie et à l'Afrique.* Paris: L'Harmattan.

Ferguson, Moira. 1993. *Colonialism and Gender Relations from Mary Wollstonecraft to Jamaica Kincaid: East Caribbean Connections.* New York: Columbia University Press.

Foucault, Michel. 1978. *The History of Sexuality,* vol. 1, *An Introduction.* Trans. Robert Hurley. New York: Vintage Books, 1990. Originally published as *La volonté de savoir* (Paris: Gallimard, 1976).

———. 1985. *The History of Sexuality,* vol. 2, *The Use of Pleasure.* Trans. Robert Hurley. New York: Vintage Books, 1990. Originally published as *L'usage des plaisirs* (Paris: Gallimard, 1984).

Frazier, E. Franklin. 1925. "Durham: Capital of the Black Middle Class." In *The New Negro,* ed. Alain Locke, 333–40. New York: Albert and Charles Boni.

———. 1927. "The Pathology of Race Prejudice." In *The Negro Caravan: Writings by American Negroes,* ed. Sterling A. Brown, Arthur P. Davis, and Ulysses Lee, 904–909. New York: Arno Press, 1969.

———. 1928–30. "La bourgeoisie noire." In *An Anthology of American Negro Literature,* ed. V. F. Calverton, 379–88. New York: Modern Library, 1929. Originally published in *Modern Quarterly* 5: 78–84.

———. 1935–36. "Dubois' Program for the Negro in the Present Crisis." *Race* 1 (Winter): 1–6.

———. 1948. *The Negro Family in the United States.* Revised and abridged edition. Chicago: University of Chicago Press, 1966. Originally published 1939.

———. 1955. "The New Negro Middle Class." In *The New Negro Thirty Years Afterward,* ed. Rayford W. Logan, Eugene C. Holmes, and G. Franklin Edwards, Howard University Graduate School, Division of the Social Sciences, 26–33. Washington, D.C.: Howard University Press.

———. 1957a. *Black Bourgeoisie: The Rise of a New Middle Class.* New York: Collier Books, 1962. Originally published as *Bourgeoisie noire* (Paris: Librairie Plon, 1955).

———. 1957b. *The Negro in the United States.* Revised edition. New York: Macmillan. Originally published 1949.

———. 1957c. "The Negro Middle Class and Desegregation." *Social Problems* 4: 291–301.

———. 1957d. *Race and Culture Contacts in the Modern World.* New York: Alfred A. Knopf.

———. 1958. "What Can the American Negro Contribute to the Social Development of Africa?" In *Africa Seen by American Negroes,* ed. John A. Davis, 263–78. Paris: Présence Africaine.

———. 1961. "Negro, Sex Life of the African and American." In *Encyclopedia of Sexual Behavior,* ed. Albert Ellis and Albert Abarbanel, 769–75. New York: Hawthorn Books, 1973.

———. 1962. "The Failure of the Negro Intellectual." *Negro Digest* 7 (February): 56–66.

In *The Death of White Sociology,* ed. Joyce Ladner, 52–66. New York: Vintage Books, 1973.

——. 1963. *The Negro Church in America.* New York: Schocken Books, 1974.

Freud, Sigmund. 1933. "Femininity." In *Issues in Feminism,* ed. Sheila Ruth, 97–114. Mountain View, Calif.: Mayfield Publishing, 1994.

Fuss, Diana. 1999. "Interior Colonies: Frantz Fanon and the Politics of Identification." In *Rethinking Fanon: The Continuing Dialogue,* ed. Nigel C. Gibson, 294–328. Amherst, N.Y.: Humanity Books.

Gagne, Karen M. 2003. "Falling in Love with Indians: The Metaphysics of Becoming America." In "Coloniality's Persistence," ed. Greg Thomas, special issue of *CR: The New Centennial Review* 3:3 (Fall): 205–34.

Gaines, Kevin. 1996. *Uplifting the Race: Black Leadership, Politics, and Culture in the Twentieth Century.* Chapel Hill: University of North Carolina Press.

Garis, Leslie. 1990. "Through West Indian Eyes." *New York Times Magazine* (October 7): 42–44, 70, 78, 80, 91.

Gatewood, William B. 1993. *Aristocrats of Color: The Black Elite, 1880–1920.* Bloomington: Indiana University Press.

Gates, Henry Louis, Jr. 1998. *The Two Nations of Black America.* Originally broadcast as an episode of *Frontline.* Melbourne, Fla.: PBS Video.

Gayle, Addison, Jr. 1970. "Cultural Hegemony: The Southern White Writer and American Letters." In *Amistad 1,* ed. John A. Williams and Charles F. Harris, 1–24. New York: Vintage Books.

Gibson, Nigel C., ed. 1999. *Rethinking Fanon: The Continuing Dialogue.* Amherst, N.Y.: Humanity Books.

——. 2003. *Fanon: The Postcolonial Imagination.* Cambridge: Polity.

Glissant, Edouard. 1989. *Caribbean Discourse: Selected Essays.* Trans. with an introduction by J. Michael Dash. Charlottesville: University Press of Virginia. Originally published as *Discours antillais* (Paris: Éditions du Seuil, 1981).

Goggin, Jacqueline. 1993. *Carter G. Woodson: A Life in Black History.* Baton Rouge: Louisiana State University Press.

Gordon, Lewis R. 1996. "Black Skins Masked: Finding Fanon in Isaac Julien's *Frantz Fanon: 'Black Skin, White Mask.'*" *differences: A Journal of Feminist Cultural Studies* 8:5 (Spring): 148–62.

Grier, William H., and Price M. Cobbs. 1968. *Black Rage.* New York: Bantam Books.

Halperin, David M. 1989a. *One Hundred Years of Homosexuality and Other Essays on Greek Love.* New York: Routledge.

——. 1989b. "Sex before Sexuality: Pederasty, Politics, and Power in Classical Athens." In *Hidden from History: Reclaiming the Gay and Lesbian Past,* ed. Martin Duberman, Martha Vicinus, and George Chauncey, Jr., 37–53. New York: Meridian.

Halperin, David M., John J. Winkler, and Froma I. Zeitlin, eds. 1990. *Before Sexuality: The Construction of Erotic Experience in the Ancient Greek World.* Princeton, N.J.: Princeton University Press.

Hemenway, Robert E. 1977. *Zora Neale Hurston: A Literary Biography.* Urbana: University of Illinois Press.

Hemphill, Essex, ed. 1991. *Brother to Brother: New Writings by Black Gay Men.* Conceived by Joseph Beam. Boston: Alyson Publications.

———. 1992. *Ceremonies: Prose and Poetry.* New York: Plume.

Herdt, Gilbert H. 1984. *Ritualized Homosexuality in Melanesia.* Berkeley and Los Angeles: University of California Press.

Herskovits, Melville J. 1941. *The Myth of the Negro Past.* Boston: Beacon Press.

Higginbotham, Evelyn Brooks. 1989. "The Problem of Race in Women's History." In *Coming to Terms: Feminism, Theory, Politics,* ed. Elizabeth Weed, 122–33. New York: Routledge.

———. 1992. "African-American Women's History and the Metalanguage of Race." *Signs: Journal of Women in Culture and Society* 17:2 (Winter): 251–73.

———. 1993. *Righteous Discontent: The Women's Movement in the Black Baptist Church, 1880–1920.* Cambridge, Mass.: Harvard University Press.

Hilliard, Asa, III. 1994. "Bringing Maat, Destroying Isfet: The African and African Diasporan Presence in the Study of Ancient Kmt." In *Egypt: Child of Africa,* ed. Ivan Van Sertima, 127–47. New Brunswick, N.J.: Transaction.

Himes, Chester. 1993. *Plan B.* Jackson: University Press of Mississippi. Originally published in French translation as *Plan B* (Paris: Éditions Lieu Commun, 1983).

Hine, Darlene Clark, and Kathleen Thompson. 1998. *A Shining Thread of Hope: The History of Black Women in America.* New York: Broadway Books.

Hodge, Merle. 1972. "Novels on the French Caribbean Intellectual in France." *Revista/ Review Interamericana* 4:3 (Fall): 211–31.

———. 1974. "The Shadow of the Whip: A Comment on Male-Female Relations in the Caribbean." In *Is Massa Day Dead? Black Moods in the Caribbean,* ed. Orde Coombs, 111–18. Garden City, N.J.: Anchor Books.

Holloway, Joseph E., ed. 1994. *Africanisms in American Culture.* Bloomington: Indiana University Press.

hooks, bell. 1992. *Black Looks: Race and Representation.* New York: Routledge.

———. 1994. *Outlaw Culture: Resisting Representations.* Boston: South End Press.

Horton-Stallings, LaMonda. 2001. "A Revision of the Narrative of the Trickster Trope in Black Culture for Alternative Readings of Gender and Sexuality (Written by Herself)." Ph.D. diss., Michigan State University.

Hughes, Langston. 1926. "The Negro Artist and the Racial Mountain." In *Amistad 1,* ed. John A. Williams and Charles F. Harris, 301–305. New York: Vintage Books, 1970.

Hull, Gloria T., Patricia Bell Scott, and Barbara Smith, eds. 1982. *All the Women Are White, All the Blacks Are Men, But Some of Us Are Brave: Black Women's Studies.* New York: Feminist Press.

Hurston, Zora Neale. 1928. "How It Feels to Be Colored Me." In *I Love Myself When I Am Laughing . . . and Then Again When I Am Looking Mean and Impressive: A Zora Neale Hurston Reader,* ed. Alice Walker, 152–55. New York: Feminist Press, 1979.

———. 1934. "Characteristics of Negro Expression." In *The Sanctified Church,* 49–68. Berkeley, Calif.: Turtle Island Foundation, 1981.

———. 1935. *Mules and Men.* New York: Harper Perennial, 1990.

——. 1938. *Tell My Horse: Voodoo and Life in Haiti and Jamaica.* New York: Harper and Row, 1990.

——. 1942. *Dust Tracks on a Road.* New York: Harper Perennial, 1996.

——. 1955. "Court Order Can't Make the Races Mix," letter to the *Orlando Sentinel.* In *Zora Neale Hurston: A Life in Letters,* ed. Carla Kaplan, 738–40. New York: Anchor, 2003.

Jackson, George. 1970. *Soledad Brother: The Prison Letters of George Jackson.* Chicago: Lawrence Hill Books.

——. 1972. *Blood in My Eye.* Baltimore, Md.: Black Classic Press, 1990.

James, C. L. R. 1938. *The Black Jacobins.* New York: Vintage Books, 1989.

——. 1969. "Black Studies and the Contemporary Student." In *The C. L. R. James Reader,* ed. Anna Grimshaw, 390–404. Oxford: Blackwell Publishers, 1992.

——. 1970. "*The Black Scholar* Interviews C. L. R. James." *Black Scholar* 2:1 (September): 35–43.

——. 1976. "Towards the Seventh: The Pan-African Congress—Past, Present and Future." In *At the Rendez-Vous of Victory,* 236–50. London: Allison and Busby, 1984.

JanMohamed, Abdul R. 1992. "Sexuality on/of the Racial Border: Foucault, Wright, and the Articulation of 'Racialized Sexuality.'" In *Discourses of Sexuality: From Aristotle to AIDS,* ed. Domna C. Stanton, 94–116. Ann Arbor: University of Michigan Press.

Jennings, Thelma. 1990. "'Us Colored Women Had to Go through a Plenty': Sexual Exploitation of African-American Slave Women." *Journal of Women's History* 1:3 (Winter): 45–74.

Johnson, Michael P. 1981. "Smothered Slave Infants: Were Slave Mothers at Fault?" *Journal of Southern History* 47:4 (November): 493–520.

Jones, Claudia. 1948. "I Was Deported Because I Fought the Colour Bar." In *"I Think of My Mother": Notes on the Life and Times of Claudia Jones,* ed. Buzz Johnson, 129–32. London: Karia Press, 1985.

——. 1949. "An End to the Neglect of the Problems of Negro Women!" *Political Affairs* 53 (March 1974): 28–42.

Jones, Gayl. 1975. *Corregidora.* Boston: Beacon Press.

Jones, Jacqueline. 1985. *Labor of Love, Labor of Sorrow: Black Women, Work, and the Family from Slavery to the Present.* New York: Vintage Books.

Jones, John Henry. 1968. "On the Influence of Fanon." *Freedomways* 8:3 (Summer): 209–14.

Joseph, Gloria, and Jill Lewis. 1981. *Common Differences: Conflicts in Black and White Feminist Perspectives.* Garden City, N.J.: Anchor Books.

Julien, Isaac, dir. 1989. *Looking for Langston.* Water Bearer Films.

——. 1992. "Black Is, Black Ain't: Notes on De-essentializing Black Identities." In *Black Popular Culture: A Project,* by Michelle Wallace, ed. Gina Dent, 255–63. Seattle, Wash.: Bay Press.

——, dir. 1993. *The Attendant.* San Francisco: Frameline Distribution.

——. 1994a. "Confessions of a Snow Queen: Notes on the Making of *The Attendant.*" *Critical Quarterly: Critically Queer* 36:1 (Spring): 120–26.

——. 1994b. *The Darker Side of Black.*

———. 1994c. "Queering the Pitch: A Conversation." Interview conducted by Jon Savage. *Critical Quarterly: Critically Queer* 36:1 (Spring): 1–12.

———, dir. 1995. *Frantz Fanon: Black Skin, White Mask.* California Newsreel.

———, dir. 2002. *BaadAsssss Cinema: A Bold Look at 70's Blaxploitation Films.* New Video Group.

Kilson, Martin. 2002. "E. Franklin Frazier's *Black Bourgeoisie* Revisited." In *E. Franklin Frazier and* Black Bourgeoisie, ed. James E. Teele, 118–36. Columbia: University of Missouri Press.

Kincaid, Jamaica. 1983. *At the Bottom of the River.* New York: Plume, 1992.

———. 1985. *Annie John.* New York: Plume, 1986.

———. 1988. *A Small Place.* New York: Plume.

———. 1990a. "Jamaica Kincaid and the Modernist Project: An Interview." In *Caribbean Women Writers: Essays from the First International Conference,* ed. Selwyn Cudjoe, 215–32. Wellesley, Mass.: Calaloux Publications.

———. 1990b. *Lucy.* New York: Farrar, Straus and Giroux.

———. 1991. "On Seeing England for the First Time." *Transition* 51: 32–40.

———, ed. 1995. *The Best American Essays.* Boston: Houghton Mifflin.

———. 1996. *The Autobiography of My Mother.* New York: Farrar, Straus and Giroux.

———. 1997. *My Brother.* New York: Farrar, Straus and Giroux.

———, ed. 1998. *My Favorite Plant: Writers and Gardeners on the Plants They Love.* New York: Farrar, Straus and Giroux.

———. 1999. *My Garden (Book).* New York: Farrar, Straus and Giroux.

———. 2001. *Talk Stories.* New York: Farrar, Straus and Giroux.

———. 2002. *Mr. Potter.* New York: Farrar, Straus and Giroux.

———. 2005a. *Among Flowers: A Walk in the Himalaya.* Washington, D.C.: National Geographic.

———, ed. 2005b. *The Best American Travel Writing.* Boston: Houghton Mifflin.

Kornweibel, Theodore, Jr. 1999. *"Seeing Red": Federal Campaigns against Black Militancy, 1919–1925.* Bloomington: Indiana University Press.

Lefkowitz, Mary. 1996. *Not Out of Africa: How Afrocentrism Became an Excuse to Teach Myth as History.* New York: Basic Books.

Les Nubians. 2003. *One Step Forward.* Malibu, Calif.: Higher Octave/Virgin France.

Lil' Kim. 1996. *Hard Core.* Atlantic Records/Undeas/Big Beat Records, Inc.

Lorde, Audre. 1982. *Zami: A New Spelling of My Name.* Freedom, Calif.: Crossing Press.

———. 1984. "Uses of the Erotic: The Erotic as Power." In *Sister Outsider: Essays and Speeches,* 53–59. New York: Crossing Press.

———. 1986. *A Burst of Light.* Ithaca, N.Y.: Firebrand Books.

Lugones, Maria. 1990. "Hispaneando y Lesbiando: On Sarah Hoagland's *Lesbian Ethics.*" *Hypatia* 5:3 (Fall): 138–47.

Magubane, Bernard Makhosezwe. 1987. *The Ties That Bind: African-American Consciousness of Africa.* Trenton, N.J.: Africa World Press.

Martin, Tony. 1970. "Rescuing Fanon from the Critics." *African Studies Review* 13 (December): 381–99.

Martin, William G., and Michael O. West. 1997. "Future with a Past: Resurrecting the

Study of Africa in the Post-Africanist Era." *Africa Today* 44:3 (June–September): 309–26.

———, eds. 1999. *Out of One, Many Africas: Reconstructing the Study and Meaning of Africa.* Urbana: University of Illinois Press.

Mataka, Laini. 2000. *Bein a Strong Black Woman Can Get U Killed!!* Baltimore, Md.: Black Classic Press.

Mayes, Janis A. 1998. "Mercer Cook, Hearing Things Unspoken: The Politics and Problematics of TransAtlantic Literary Translation." Unpublished manuscript.

———. 2001. " 'Her Turn, My Turn': Notes on TransAtlantic Translation of African Francophone Women's Poetry." In *Femmes africaines en poesie,* special issue of *Palabres: Revue d'études africaines:* 87–106.

McClintock, Anne. 1999. "Fanon and Gender Agency." In *Rethinking Fanon: The Continuing Dialogue,* ed. Nigel C. Gibson, 283–93. Amherst, N.Y.: Humanities Books.

Mercer, Kobena. 1996. "Decolonisation and Disappointment: Reading Fanon's Sexual Politics." In *The Fact of Blackness: Frantz Fanon and Visual Representation,* ed. Alan Read, 114–31. Seattle, Wash.: Bay Press.

Mondimore, Francis Mark. 1996. *A Natural History of Homosexuality.* Baltimore, Md.: Johns Hopkins University Press.

Montejo, Esteban. 1968. *The Autobiography of a Runaway Slave.* Ed. Miguel Barnet. Trans. Jocasta Innes. New York: Pantheon.

Moraga, Cherrie. 1993. *The Last Generation: Prose and Poetry.* Boston: Beacon Press.

Morrison, Toni. 1987. *Beloved.* New York: Random House.

Mosse, George L. 1985. *Nationalism and Sexuality: Respectability and Abnormal Sexuality in Modern Europe* (also published with the subtitle *Middle-Class Morality and Sexual Norms in Modern Europe*). New York: Howard Fertig.

Mudimbe, V. Y. 1994. "The Power of the Greek Paradigm." In *The Idea of Africa,* 71–104. Bloomington: Indiana University Press.

Natov, Roni. 1990. "Mothers and Daughters: Jamaica Kincaid's Pre-Oedipal Narrative." *Children's Literature* 18: 1–16.

Nero, Charles I. 1991. "Towards a Black Gay Aesthetic: Signifying in Black Gay Literature." In *Brother to Brother: New Writings by Black Gay Men,* ed. Essex Hempill, conceived by Joseph Beam, 229–52. Boston: Alyson Publications.

Newton, Huey P. 1972. *To Die for the People: The Writings of Huey P. Newton.* New York: Writers and Readers, 1995.

———. 1973. *Revolutionary Suicide.* New York: Harcourt Brace Jovanovich.

Nzegwu, Nkiru. 1996. "Questions of Identity and Inheritance: A Critical Review of Kwame Anthony Appiah's *In My Father's House.*" *Hypatia* 11:1 (Winter): 176–99.

Obenga, Théophile. 1970. "Méthode et conception historiques de Cheikh Anta Diop." *Présence africaine* 74:2 (June–November): 3–28.

O'Callaghan, Evelyn. 1998. "Compulsory Heterosexuality and Textual/Sexual Alternatives in Selected Texts by West Indian Women Writers." In *Caribbean Portraits: Essays on Gender Ideologies and Identities,* ed. Christine Barrow, 294–319. Kingston, Jamaica: Ian Randle Publications, in association with the Centre for Gender and Development Studies, University of the West Indies.

Omolade, Barbara. 1994. *The Rising Song of African American Women.* New York: Routledge.

Oyêwùmí, Oyèrónké. 1997. *The Invention of Women: Making an African Sense of Western
Gender Discourses.* Minneapolis: University of Minnesota Press.

Padmore, George. 1956. *Pan-Africanism or Communism? The Coming Struggle for Africa.*
New York: Roy Publishers.

Paravisini-Gebert, Lizabeth. 1999. *Jamaica Kincaid: A Critical Companion.* Westport,
Conn.: Greenwood Press.

Perry, Donna. 1990. "Initiation in Jamaica Kincaid's *Annie John.*" In *Caribbean Women
Writers: Essays from the First International Conference,* ed. Selwyn Cudjoe, 245–
53. Wellesley, Mass.: Calaloux Publications.

Platt, Anthony M. 1990. "Racism in Academia: Lessons from the Life of E. Franklin Frazier." *Monthly Review* (September): 29–45.

———. 1991. *E. Franklin Frazier Reconsidered.* New Brunswick, N.J.: Rutgers University
Press.

———. 2002. "Between Scorn and Longing: Frazier's *Black Bourgeoisie.*" In *E. Franklin
Frazier and* Black Bourgeoisie, ed. James E. Teele, 71–84. Columbia: University
of Missouri Press.

Présence Africaine Conference Committee. 1956. *Proceedings of the First International
Conference of Negro Writers and Artists.* Special issue of *Présence africaine* 8–10
(June–November).

Rainwater, Lee, and William L. Yancey. 1967. *The Moynihan Report and the Politics of
Controversy.* Cambridge, Mass.: MIT Press.

Read, Alan, ed. 1996. *The Fact of Blackness.* Seattle, Wash.: Bay Press.

Reddick, L. D. 1976. "Black History as a Corporate Colony." *Social Policy* 7:1 (May–June):
36–40.

Reid, Catherine, and Holly Iglesias. 1997. *Every Woman I've Ever Loved: Lesbian Writers
on Their Mothers.* San Francisco, Calif.: Cleis Press.

Rich, Adrienne. 1980. "Compulsory Heterosexuality and Lesbian Existence." *Signs: Journal of Women in Culture and Society* 5:4 (Summer): 128–37.

Riggs, Marlon, dir. 1989. *Tongues Untied: Black Men Loving Black Men.* Strand Home
Video.

———. 1991. "Tongues Untied: An Interview with Marlon Riggs." In *Brother to Brother:
New Writings by Black Gay Men,* ed. Essex Hempill, conceived by Joseph Beam,
189–99. Boston: Alyson Publications.

———, dir. 1995. *Black Is . . . Black Ain't.* California Newsreel.

Robinson, Cedric J. 1980. "Domination and Imitation: *Xala* and the Emergence of the
Black Bourgeoisie." *Race & Class* 22:2 (Autumn): 147–57.

———. 1983. *Black Marxism: The Making of the Black Radical Tradition.* London: Zed
Press.

———. 1993. "The Appropriation of Fanon." *Race & Class* 35:1 (July–September): 79–89.

Rodney, Walter. 1969. *The Groundings with My Brothers.* London: Bogle-L'Ouverture
Publications, 1996.

———. 1970. *A History of the Upper Guinea Coast, 1545–1800.* New York: Monthly Review Press.

———. 1972a. *How Europe Underdeveloped Africa*. Washington, D.C.: Howard University Press, 1982.

———. 1972b. "Problems of Third World Development." *Ufahamu* 3 (Fall): 27–47.

———. 1981a. *A History of the Guyanese Working People, 1881–1905*. Baltimore, Md.: Johns Hopkins University Press.

———. 1981b. *People's Power, No Dictator and The Struggle Goes On: Two Moving Speeches by Dr. Walter Rodney*. London: WPA Support Group; Harlem, N.Y.: Black Liberation Press.

———. 1990. *Walter Rodney Speaks: The Making of an African Intellectual*. Trenton, N.J.: Africa World Press.

Roscoe, Will. 1992. *The Zuni Man-Woman*. Albuquerque: University of New Mexico Press.

Roumain, Jacques. 1995. *When the Tom Tom Beats: Selected Prose and Poetry*. Trans. Joanne Fungaroli and Ronald Sauer. Washington D.C.: Azul Editions.

Schomburg, Arthur A. 1925. "The Negro Digs Up His Past." In *The New Negro*, ed. Alain Locke, 231–44. New York: Albert and Charles Boni.

Schwarz-Bart, Simone. 1974. *The Bridge of Beyond*. Trans. Barbara Bray. Portsmouth, N.H.: Heinemann, 1982. Originally published as *Pluie et vent sur Télumée Miracle* (Paris: Éditions du Seuil, 1972).

Schwarz-Bart, Simone, with André Schwarz-Bart. 2001. *In Praise of Black Women*. 3 vols. to date. Trans. Rose-Myriam Réjouis and Val Vinokurov. Madison: University of Wisconsin Press. Originally published as *Hommage à la femme noire* (Paris: Éditions Consulaires, 1988).

Scott, Daryl Michael. 1997. *Contempt and Pity: Social Policy and the Image of the Damaged Black Psyche, 1880–1996*. Chapel Hill: University of North Carolina Press.

Sedgwick, Eve Kosofsky. 1990. *Epistemology of the Closet*. Berkeley and Los Angeles: University of California Press.

Shakur, Assata. 1987. *Assata: An Autobiography*. Chicago: Lawrence Hill Books.

———. 1998a. "Assata Shakur Speaks: Letter to the Pope." *Rap Pages* 7:5 (May): 44.

———. 1998b. "A Message to My Sistas." *U.F.S. Black P.O.W. Report* (March). http://www.mumia.org/wwwboard/messages/430.html.

———. 1998c. "Thoughts on Cuba, Black Liberation, and Hip Hop Today: As Told to Cristina Veran." *The Source: The Magazine of Hip Hop Music, Culture & Politics* (January): 136.

Sharpley-Whiting, T. Denean. 1998. *Frantz Fanon: Conflicts and Feminisms*. Lanham, Md.: Rowman and Littlefield.

———. 1999. "Fanon's Feminist Consciousness and Algerian Women's Liberation: Colonialism, Nationalism and Fundamentalism." In *Rethinking Fanon: The Continuing Dialogue*, ed. Nigel C. Gibson, 329–53. Amherst, N.Y.: Humanity Books.

Shockley, Ann Allen. 1980. *The Black and the White of It*. Tallahassee, Fla.: Naiad Press.

Simmons, Diane. 1994. *Jamaica Kincaid*. New York: Twayne Publishers.

Smith, Barbara. 1990. "Homophobia: Why Bring It Up?" In *The Lesbian and Gay Studies Reader*, ed. Henry Abelove, Michèle Aina Barale, and David M. Halperin, 99–102. New York: Routledge, 1993.

Spelman, Elizabeth V. 1988. *Inessential Woman: Problems of Exclusion in Feminist Thought.* Boston: Beacon Press.

Spivak, Gayatri Chakravorty. 1988. "Can the Subaltern Speak?" In *Marxism and the Interpretation of Culture,* ed. Cary Nelson and Lawrence Grossberg, 271–313. Urbana: University of Illinois Press.

Spivey, Donald. 1978. *Schooling for the New Slavery: Black Industrial Education, 1868–1915.* Westport, Conn.: Greenwood Press.

Stuckey, Sterling. 1971. "Twilight of Our Past: Reflections on the Origins of Black History." In *Amistad 2,* ed. John A. Williams and Charles F. Harris, 261–95. New York: Random House.

———. 1987. *Slave Culture: Nationalist Theory and the Foundations of Black America.* New York: Oxford University Press.

Teele, James, ed. 2002. *E. Franklin Frazier and* Black Bourgeoisie. Columbia: University of Missouri Press.

Timothy, Helen Pyne. 1990. "Adolescent Rebellion and Gender Relations in *At the Bottom of the River* and *Annie John.*" In *Caribbean Women Writers: Essays from the First International Conference,* ed. Selwyn Cudjoe, 233–42. Wellesley, Mass.: Calaloux Publications.

Turner, James, and W. Eric Perkins. 1976. "Towards a Critique of Social Science." *Black Scholar* 7:7 (April): 2–11.

U.S. Department of Labor. Office of Policy Planning and Research. 1965. *The Negro Family: The Case for National Action.* Washington, D.C.: Government Printing Office.

Van Sertima, Ivan. 1994. "Egypt Is in Africa, but Was Ancient Egypt African?" In *Egypt: Child of Africa,* ed. Ivan Van Sertima, 75–80. New Brunswick, N.J.: Transaction.

Vincent, Theodore G. 1973. *Voices of a Black Nation: Political Journalism of the Harlem Renaissance.* Trenton, N.J.: Africa World Press, 1991.

Vlasek, Dale. 1982. "E. Franklin Frazier and the Problem of Assimilation." In *Ideas in American Cultures,* ed. Hamilton Cravens, 141–79. Ames: Iowa State University Press.

Warner, Keith. 1973. "New Perspectives on Léon Damas." *Black Images* 2:1 (Spring): 3–6.

Washington, Mary Helen. 1991. "Commentary on Jamaica Kincaid." In *Memory of Kin: Stories about Family by Black Writers,* ed, Mary Helen Washington, 125–29. New York: Anchor Books.

Wells, Ida B. 1972. *Crusade for Justice: The Autobiography of Ida B. Wells.* Ed. Alfreda M. Duster. Chicago: University of Chicago Press.

White, Deborah Gray. 1983. "Female Slaves: Sex Roles and Status in the Antebellum Plantation South." In *Unequal Sisters: A Multicultural Reader in U.S. Women's History.* ed. Vicki L. Ruiz and Ellen Carol DuBois, 22–33. New York: Routledge, 1994.

———. 1985. *Ar'n't I a Woman? Female Slaves in the Plantation South.* New York: W. W. Norton.

———. 1999. "Revisiting *Ar'n't I a Woman?*" In *Ar'n't I a Woman? Female Slaves in the Plantation South.* Revised edition. New York: W. W. Norton.

Williams, Eric. 1944. *Capitalism and Slavery.* Chapel Hill: University of North Carolina Press.

———. 1970. *From Columbus to Castro: The History of the Caribbean, 1492–1969.* New York: Vintage Books, 1984.

Williams, Larry. 1989. "Black Women in Search of Kemet: A Bibliography." In *Egypt Revisited,* ed. Ivan Van Sertima, 413–15. New Brunswick, N.J.: Transaction, 1995.

Woodson, Carter G. 1933. *The Mis-education of the Negro.* Trenton, N.J.: Africa World Press, 1990.

Wynter, Sylvia. 1979. "Sambos and Minstrels." *Social Text* 1 (Winter): 149–56.

———. 1982. "Beyond Liberal and Marxist Leninist Feminisms: Toward an Autonomous Frame of Reference." Unpublished paper presented at the annual conference of the American Sociological Association, San Francisco (September).

———. 1987. "Beyond the Word of Man: Glissant and the New Discourse of the Antilles." *World Literature Today* (Winter): 637–47.

———. 1990. "After/Word. Beyond Miranda's Meanings: Un/Silencing the 'Demonic Ground' of Caliban's 'Woman.'" In *Out of the Kumbla: Caribbean Women and Literature,* ed. Carole Boyce Davies and Elaine Savory Fido, 355–72. Trenton, N.J.: Africa World Press.

———. 1992. "Beyond the Categories of the Master Conception: The Counterdoctrine of the Jamesian Poiesis." In *C. L. R. James's Caribbean,* ed. Paget Henry and Paul Buhle, 63–91. Durham, N.C.: Duke University Press.

———. 1995. "1492: A New World View." In *Race, Discourse, and the Origin of the Americas: A New World View,* ed. Vera Lawrence Hyatt and Rex Nettleford, 5–57. Washington, D.C.: Smithsonian Institution Press.

———. 2000. "The Re-enchantment of Humanism: An Interview with Sylvia Wynter." *Small Axe* 8 (September): 119–207.

———. 2003. "Un-settling the Coloniality of Being/Power/Truth/Freedom: Towards the Human, after Man, Its Overrepresentation." In "Coloniality's Persistence," ed. Greg Thomas, special issue of *CR: The New Centennial Review* 3:3 (Fall): 257–338.

X, Malcolm. 1965. *The Autobiography of Malcolm X: As Told to Alex Haley.* New York: Ballantine Books, 1992.

———. 1991. *Malcolm X: Speeches at Harvard.* Ed. Archie Epps. New York: Paragon House.

———. 1992. *February 1965: The Final Speeches.* Ed. Steve Clark. New York: Pathfinder.

Yee, Shirley J. 1992. *Black Women Abolitionists: A Study in Activism, 1828–1860.* Knoxville: University of Tennessee Press.

Young, Iris Marion. 1983. "Is Male Gender Identity the Cause of Male Domination?" In *Mothering: Essays in Feminist Theory,* ed. Joyce Trebilcot, 129–46. Totowa, N.J.: Rowman and Allanheld.

Index

FBI (Federal Bureau of Investigation), 55, 72, 148–51, 177n13

femininity, 27–28, 36, 38, 42, 44, 45–46, 50, 90, 93, 102, 115–16, 128, 139, 153, 170n6. *See also* madness (of masculinity and femininity)

feminism, 19, 20–21, 24, 29, 41, 50, 90, 95–96, 107–108, 111, 116, 133, 145, 147, 155, 170n6, 172n9, 173n5, 176n3

Ferguson, Moira, 118, 119

First International Congress of Black Writers and Artists (Paris, 1956), 3, 55, 57, 71–72, 78, 80, 172n8

First World Festival of Black Arts (Dakar, 1966), 10

FLN (Front de liberation nationale in Algeria), 55, 81, 82, 92, 93

Fogel, Robert, and Stanley Engerman, 34, 39

Foucault, Michel, 2–7, 9, 24, 49, 96, 107

Frazier, E. Franklin, 34, 40, 41, 51–75, 141, 166n2

  Black Bourgeoisie, 56, 57, 58, 63, 65, 69, 71, 75, 81, 102, 141, 168n16

  Bourgeoisie noire, 57, 63, 71, 97

  "La bourgeoisie noire," 58, 61–62

  de-Africanization debate, 69–71

  "Durham: Capital of the Black Middle Class," 58–60

  on education (of class elites), 63–66, 67, 168n13

  "Edward F. Frazier" (former signature), 54

  Fanon and, 51–56, 59, 71, 74–75, 76, 80–81, 96–97, 102–103, 157–58, 166n4, 170n4

  "The Failure of the Negro Intellectual," 72

  genders and sexualities in, 67–68

  The Negro Church in America, 67

  The Negro Family in the United States, 68, 73, 141

  The Negro in the United States, 65, 166n4

  "The Negro Middle Class and Desegregation," 57, 60, 68, 167n13

  "The New Negro Middle Class," 66

  "Negro, Sex Life of the African and the American," 67–71

  on old vs. new elite, 60, 62–68, 70

  "The Pathology of Race Prejudice" (and "the Negro-complex"), 52–55, 71, 81

  Race and Culture Contacts in the Modern World, 69

  "What Can the American Negro Contribute to the Social Development of Africa," 56, 70

Freedomways, 76, 96

Freud, Sigmund, 76, 83, 86, 87, 111, 115–16, 117, 173n5, 175n11

Fuss, Diana, 170n6

Gagne, Karen, 161n3

Gaines, Kevin, 164n13

Garvey, Marcus, 70, 71, 167n10

Gates, Henry Louis, Jr. ("The Two Nations of Black America"), 74

Gatewood, William, 168n16

gay. *See* Gay and Lesbian Studies; homosexuality; lesbian; Queer Theory

Gay and Lesbian Studies, 4, 108, 134, 170n6

Gayle, Addison, Jr., 21

Genovese, Eugene, 28, 34, 39

Gibson, Nigel, 94–95

Gilroy, Paul, 136, 137

Glissant, Edouard, 8, 107

Gordon, Lewis, 135, 145–46

Great Chain of Being, 7, 21

Greece, 2, 5–8, 11, 15, 16, 18–19, 20, 21–22, 107, 147

Gutman, Herbert, 28, 31, 34

Halperin, David, 2, 9. *See also Before Sexuality* (Halperin, Winkler, and Zeitlin)

Hegel, G. W. F., 3, 84

Hellenomania, 2, 7, 9, 10, 15, 19

Hemphill, Essex, 141–42

Herdt, Gilbert, 5

Herskovits, Melville J., 69–70, 167n14

heterosexualism, 31, 34, 43, 46, 50, 84, 105, 108, 114, 122, 127, 136, 138, 147, 152, 170n6, 175n11, 176n3

heterosexuality, 2, 5, 9, 10, 21, 22–23, 30, 43, 46, 49, 68, 86–89, 91, 101, 104, 107, 115, 124, 126–28, 145, 146, 152, 153, 155, 157, 158, 161n4, 170n6

Hidden from History (Duberman, Vicinus, and Chauncey), 2, 4, 7

Higginbotham, Evelyn Brooks, 39–40, 41, 164n11,13

Hilliard, Asa, 13

Himes, Chester, 164n15

Hine, Darlene Clark, and Kathleen Thompson (*A Shining Thread of Hope*), 49–50, 164n17

hip-hop, 135–40, 143, 146, 148, 177n7

historicity, 2–6, 8, 23, 111, 155, 156

historiography, 2, 7, 14–15, 23, 33, 34, 38, 44, 46, 48

HIV, 121, 122, 174n10

Hodge, Merle, 48, 78, 84, 85, 169n1

Holloway, Joseph E. (*Africanisms in American Culture*), 69

homophobia, 21, 47, 96, 127, 130–46, 150, 151–53, 155, 158, 159, 170nn3,6, 176n5, 177n7

homosexuality, 2, 5, 9, 10, 21, 22–23, 30, 46, 49, 68, 86–89, 90, 101, 104, 122, 124–25, 127–28, 131, 133–34, 138, 146–47, 153, 155, 157, 158, 161n4

hooks, bell, 18, 77, 131, 143–45

Hoover, J. Edgar, 149, 150

"Hottentot Venus." *See* Baartman, Saartjie

humanism, 23, 49, 83, 84, 94, 98–101, 107–108, 119, 145, 158

human sexuality, 2–3, 5–6, 22–23, 74, 88, 89, 156

Hughes, Langston, 174n6

Hurston, Zora Neale, 52, 74, 126, 173n1
  "Characteristics of Negro Expression," 73, 105–106
  Dust Tracks on a Road, 159
  "How It Feels to Be Colored Me," 72, 105–106
  Mules and Men, 159

"In the Life," 133–35, 146–47, 159, 177n10. *See also* Beam, Joseph

individualism, 78, 88, 120

Jackson, George, 34, 77, 143, 157, 167n8. *See also* neo-slavery

James, C. L. R., 8, 130, 144

JanMohamed, Abdul, 3–4

Jennings, Thelma, 47, 163n7

Johnson, Michael P. ("Smothered Slave Infants"), 36

Jones, Claudia, 31–33, 34, 39, 40, 44, 50, 74, 130, 152, 163nn4,5, 164n12, 176n3

Jones, Gayl (*Corregidora*), 46–47

Jones, Jacquelyn, 163n7

Jones, John Henry, 76

Julien, Isaac, 135–40, 143, 144, 145, 148, 166n1, 177n7

Kilson, Martin, 73

Kincaid, Jamaica, 105–128, 158, 174n8
  Among Flowers, 121
  Annie John, 105, 108–113, 118, 119, 120, 121, 122, 124–25, 173n5
  At the Bottom of the River, 105, 110, 111, 114, 117, 121, 124–25
  The Autobiography of My Mother, 121
  The Best of American Travel Writing, 121

"Girl," 117
  Lucy, 105, 108, 110, 111, 113–118, 121, 122, 123, 124–25, 127, 174n9
  Mr. Potter, 121
  My Brother, 105, 121–25, 174n6
  My Favorite Plant, 121
  My Garden (Book), 121
  A Small Place, 105, 106, 118–21
  Talk Stories, 121

Lacan, Jacques, 76, 86, 87, 96

Lady Saw, 139

Lamming, George, 107

La Rue, Linda, 77

lesbian, 5, 20, 21, 96, 125, 132, 133, 139, 140, 145, 146–47, 159, 176n13

Les Nubians, 10, 162n6

liberalism, 84, 107, 139, 140

Lil' Kim, 139

Little (Collins), Ella (elder sister and mentor of Malcolm X), 160

Locke, Alain (*The New Negro*), 59, 61, 70

Lorde, Audre, 72, 127–28, 133, 152, 159, 173n2, 176n13, 178n14

Lugones, Maria, 147

madness (of masculinity and femininity), 25–26, 27, 45, 46, 49, 50, 130, 144, 156–57. *See also* Bambara, Toni Cade

Magubane, Bernard Makhosezwe, 64

Malinowski, Bronislaw, 86

Mannoni, Octave, 52

Maran, René, 85, 87

Martin, Tony, 77, 82

Marxism, 32, 33, 77, 82, 108, 161n2, 176n2

masculinity, 38, 45–46, 93, 102, 115, 128, 139, 140, 144, 145, 152, 153, 155, 170n6, 172n9. *See also* madness (of masculinity and femininity)

Maspero, François, 81, 82

Mataka, Laini, 160

matriarchy, 13, 15–16, 18–20, 22, 27, 30, 31, 34, 37, 48, 86, 90, 124, 156, 162nn9,10, 172n8. *See also* Amadiume, Ifi; Diop, Cheikh Anta

matrifocality, 34, 35, 37–38

matriliny, 19, 115, 162n9

Mayes, Janis A., 10, 161n5, 162n6

McCarthyism, 150–51, 177n13

McClintock, Anne, 170n6

McLennan, J. M., 33

Mercer, Kobena, 170n3

Montejo, Estaban, 47

GREG THOMAS is Assistant Professor of English at Syracuse University, where his teaching and research focus on the literature and culture of Africa and African Diaspora. He is a champion of Black Studies, in general, and his specific interests include Pan-Africanism, hip-hop, and Black radical traditions. Born and raised in Washington, D.C., he is the founder and editor of *Proud Flesh: New Afrikan Journal of Culture, Politics & Consciousness.*